RED MASQUERADE

RED MASQUERADE
Undercover for the F.B.I.

47751

by
ANGELA CALOMIRIS

J. B. LIPPINCOTT COMPANY
Philadelphia   New York

To

Kenneth M. Bierly

CONTENTS

RED MASQUERADE

1. WHO—ME?

I WAS FINANCIAL SECRETARY of the West Midtown Branch of the Communist Party in New York City on April 26, 1949, when I took the stand as a Government witness in the case against the eleven Red leaders. A great many people who didn't read beyond the headlines of the papers assumed that I had been a genuine Communist, one of the many who turned informer. Some thought I sold out to the Government for money.

There's one thing I want to get straight right from the beginning. Never, at any time, have I believed in Communism. I joined the Communist Party because the United States Government asked me to join. My seven years of hard, unpaid labor in the Party really began when two F.B.I. agents called on me early one morning in February, 1942. Their visit was as startling to me then as it would have been to you.

It was back in the dark winter after Pearl Harbor, when everyone was living with one ear glued to the radio. Singapore had fallen a week before and the papers were hinting that it was an inside job, the work of a fantastically clever Asiatic fifth column. That morning the news was closer to home: a Japanese submarine had risen out of the Pacific dusk and shelled the California coast. Betty, the girl who shared the apartment with me, had already left for her job in an advertising agency, and I was going to be late for work if I listened much longer.

I was tuning the radio up so that I could hear it in the kitchen when the doorbell rang.

I opened the door and met the steady eyes of two well-dressed unknown young men. They looked like clean-cut Americans who could have made a living posing for collar ads, and they seemed to be on serious business. One of them was just about the handsomest thing I've ever seen. The other one seemed to be the leader and he did most of the talking.

"Are you Miss Angela Calomiris?" he inquired politely.

"Yes," I said, "and who are you?"

"I'm Kenneth Bierly and this is William South. May we come in for a few minutes?"

"What do you want?" I asked. I certainly wasn't going to let them in before I found out.

"We're from the Federal Bureau of Investigation," Mr. Bierly said crisply. I enjoy a gag when it's a good one.

"Do you really expect me to believe that?" I grinned. For answer, Mr. Bierly produced an F.B.I. card. Solemnly, he vouched for Mr. South, who produced another. Then Mr. South vouched for Mr. Bierly.

I tried to look their credentials over coolly, but I was so excited that I didn't even check the names. My first thought was that I must have done something, but what could it be? I was making twenty-seven dollars a week, but I didn't owe anybody any money. I hadn't lied on any applications for jobs. I owned half a jalopy, but it was in Betty's name, and I hadn't even driven it myself yet.

I invited the two men in. They sat down primly on the studio couch and looked around. The apartment was a lot bleaker than it is now. The place needed paint. I hadn't built in the bookcases, I hadn't whitewashed the old fireplace, and I didn't have a hardwood floor in the living room then. But we did have three rooms, the whole second floor of 9 Jane Street. Our building was one of those narrow four-story Greenwich Village houses that started out about a hundred years ago as family residences, then degenerated into cold water tenements, and are now being either "restored" or "converted into apartments." Our landlord had converted. He simply put in heat and hot water.

My visitors were painfully correct, but they didn't do a thing to put me at my ease. They knew a great deal about me and acted as if they knew more than they were telling. Later, when Ken Bierly and I became good friends, he told me that the F.B.I. always tests potential undercover agents to see how they react in a tight spot. They plied me with questions which would alarm and puzzle anyone. The interrogation was all the more mysterious for the gentle way in which it was administered. In all the years I've worked with F.B.I. agents since, I've never known one to raise his voice above a conversational pitch.

"Now let's see," Mr. South said, as if reviewing a file. "You're working as a playground director on a W.P.A. project, aren't you? How do you like your job?"

"Fine," I said.

"And you've taken some courses in journalism at Brooklyn College?" Mr. Bierly added. "Why did you quit?"

"Financial problems," I said, keeping my temper.

"And you're studying photography at the Photo League?" he pursued. "What kind of photographer do you want to be?"

As long as they knew all the answers, I thought I might as well let them in on the open secret that I was going to be a photo journalist—and a good one. I took them through the kitchen to the bedroom, which I had partitioned off to make a little darkroom and showed them some of my work. I was practising on babies and animals then, and I hadn't sold much beyond a few portraits and a shot of a fire in Haverstraw to the local paper. I didn't even have a good camera.

They said my pictures were good and I think they really meant it. Perhaps they were even a little surprised. Whatever they wanted from me, they were being very smooth about it. They tried to make small talk, but it was obvious that they were gunning for information and I didn't feel like helping them out until I knew what they wanted. The conversation

faltered when they got around to politics, a pretty cold subject
for me.

They asked me what I thought about the non-aggression pact
Germany and Russia had made in 1939. I told them I remembered it vaguely, but I wondered why they were bringing it up
in 1942, after Germany had broken the pact by attacking Russia. I didn't realize that they were giving me an opportunity to
defend Russia. If I had been a Communist I would have had
pat excuses for the strange alliance between Hitler and Stalin
at the tip of my tongue. In 1942, the Communists were still
working overtime to explain the change in their attitude after
the German invasion of Russia. The "imperialist war," which
they did their best to sabotage, had promptly become a "democratic" one, which they were supporting enthusiastically.

The agents went on to ask me if I thought that Russia would
keep her word to us as an ally. I said that many people thought
she wouldn't. They wanted to know if any of my friends were
Communists. I told them that I had met a few but had paid
very little attention to their political beliefs. I told them I was
opposed to Communism but was a confirmed liberal. The conversation made me a little huffy. I didn't think that my politics
—such as they were—were any of their business. Actually, I'd
always voted for Roosevelt and even rung a few doorbells for
him. I didn't see why they cared. Mr. South abandoned the
political line of questioning for an even more offensive one.

"Miss Calomiris," he inquired doggedly, "do you have any
marriage plans?"

That was the last straw.

"No, I'm not interested in anybody at the moment," I replied
as sweetly as I could manage. I tried to speak lightly, but I was
boiling inside. What right had the F.B.I. to inquire into my
personal life? "I'm interested in photography, but I'm planning to join the women Marines or the WAVES, and I've made
several applications for war work as well."

Mr. Bierly ignored the edge in my voice and nodded approvingly. "We've got a war job for you," he announced. "It won't

pay a salary, and it won't bring you any recognition. It's secret work, and not even your closest friends are to know what you are doing. The mission we have in mind will be both dangerous and monotonous. We won't be able to tell you all about it, but we can assure you that it is necessary and important. We're asking you because this job is essential to the internal security of the United States at war and we think you are one of the few people who can do it." He was very solemn now.

"What do you want me to do?" I gasped.

"We would like to have you join the Communist Party and observe it for the F.B.I.," he said gravely.

"But the Russians are our allies!" I objected.

"They are now," Mr. South agreed quietly. "But how long do you think that will last?" They told me that, if Russia's policy should change, leading American Communists would be the first people in the United States to know it. Our Government could learn what was going to happen internationally if it knew exactly what the American Communists were doing and saying. They talked plausibly enough, but it all sounded a little fantastic to me.

"Can't you find that sort of thing out by reading the newspapers?" I asked after a moment's thought. The agents laughed.

"They don't print the kind of information we want even in *The Daily Worker*, the Party's official newspaper," Mr. Bierly said.

The Daily Worker circulates freely in Greenwich Village, sometimes even on newsstands. A comrade usually stands on the corner of Eighth Street and Sixth Avenue every evening hawking copies, but they had always looked dull to me and I had never stopped to buy. Fellow members of the Photo League had brought them into the laboratories, however.

"You'll find that the Communist Party isn't a very typical political party," Mr. Bierly explained. "It keeps the public out of its meetings, instead of trying to get them in. It won't admit anyone to membership unless that person will keep its secrets. That's why we need to get our information from people who are on the inside, active members whom the Party trusts."

"What makes you think I could help?" I asked.

"We've investigated you very thoroughly, Miss Calomiris," he replied, "and we think you are just the kind of person we are looking for."

I tried to find out more, but F.B.I. agents, as I was to learn later, can talk intelligently for hours without saying a thing you want to know. They warned me against mentioning their visit to anyone—and by "anyone" they meant just that. I couldn't tell Betty or my closest friends. I was to think over what they had said and call them at RE 2-3500 in a week.

As they left, I began unconsciously to act like the special agents I had seen in movies. I kept repeating RE 2-3500 to myself in order to memorize it. I was sure they wouldn't want me to write it down and it didn't occur to me that I could find the Federal Bureau of Investigation in the phone book. I was as naive as that.

I got to work late and went through the day in a trance, which is a pretty hard job if you are a playground director handling thirty or more teen-agers. All the time I kept thinking: they want me to be a spy—an American spy right here in America. My idea of a spy came from Grade B movies, and what I had learned from these sources made them seem highly improbable people. I thought of all the stories I had ever heard, and tried to imagine myself racing around in big limousines to meet important people in the dead of night, stealing secret documents, and talking my way out of impossible situations.

A female spy, as far as I could remember, was a sloe-eyed, slim blond beauty who wore black nightgowns, looked divine in sables, and wormed state secrets out of Balkan prime ministers. I looked into my compact mirror to see if I'd suddenly turned into a Mata Hari: I saw a thin face with a little too much nose, a complexion that had become downright sallow in winter, and large dark eyes that dominated otherwise plain features as they searched me. Since this was a frank audit, I decided I could credit my Greek ancestors for a small well-shaped head and dark hair that curled to a good fit. But it didn't add up to movie glamour. A statesman guarding secrets might ask me how the Brooklyn Dodgers had made out. He'd hardly plan to come up and see me some time. The humor of the thing got me and I laughed in my own face. Lady spy indeed!

I tried to see myself as the F.B.I. agents had seen me. How would the bare facts of my biography look on an official report, such as the F.B.I. seemed to have? I reviewed my past life as objectively as possible for incidents which might explain their interest. Nothing I could recall seemed to fit.

I had been what you'd call an underprivileged child. I was born in 1916 on Avenue B on the lower East Side of New York City. Father was a pleasant, kindly man who had had some savings when he and Mother came from Greece in the early 1900s, but he was not a good manager and soon lost the fur business he had established. After that, he got work wherever he could find it—sometimes in restaurants, more often with other furriers.

The fur industry was being unionized in those days, and the constant troubles meant that Father was often out of a job. He was not aggressive, and probably he did not look out for himself very well in the skirmishes that led eventually to racketeering and Communist domination in the furriers' union. At any rate, he blamed the union for his misfortunes. Although he seldom complained, I sensed even as a child that his failure as a provider hurt him all the more deeply because my mother's parents had been against the marriage back in Greece. Constantine was a country boy, born in Sparta, while my mother, Maria, came from an Athenian family with a tradition of Government service. She had been a schoolteacher before her marriage. She had certainly not bettered herself in the New World.

Mother consoled herself in religion. We moved frequently, but never out of walking distance of a Greek church. I was very much awed by the Orthodox priests, swinging their fragrant censers while they chanted in a somber monotone during the colorful services. I was terrified by the painting of a big eye that is hung behind Greek Orthodox altars to symbolize the eye of God watching over the congregation. Unfortunately, most of my early impressions of religion were tinged with fear. I can still remember with horror the paintings of arms and legs hung up in church by communicants who thanked God in this way for healing those members.

Very early I realized that the religious traditions of my mother were not those of the Irish Americans among whom we lived. I was embarrassed that we were the only family on the street who had an altar in the house. Far from feeling proud of my mother's piety, I was ashamed to bring my school friends home for fear that they would hear her praying and laugh. Moreover, Mother's younger brother was an artist who filled the house with pictures of the saints.

Father wasn't devoted to the Orthodox Church. He became an Episcopalian, and I was delighted to go with him and join an Episcopalian Sunday School. I loved to sing in the choir and went regularly until I had acquired twelve beautiful attendance bars.

My mother's mother was as faithful to the Greek Orthodox Church as my mother, but I always imagined that when she prayed she was telling God what to do. She certainly told everybody else. Grandmother dominated the family, partly because we often stayed with her when Father was out of a job, but mainly because she was a natural matriarch. She was the kind of woman who is respectfully referred to as a "pillar of strength," and when I was little I often took the metaphor literally. She weighed over two hundred pounds and we all had to help her dress and get down the stairs when an emergency required her appearance outside the house. The clothes she saved for these rare occasions were very fine. The high shoes we used to lace up on her cost twenty-five dollars.

Grandmother was very proud. She never allowed me or my

sister to do any housework, although she did it herself. She never forgot for a minute that she was the wife of a former captain in the Greek Army. According to her, the Greeks we knew in New York were none of them people she would ever have noticed in Greece. But despite her protests, my companions were the Irish, Italian, Negro and Spanish children I found on the streets.

Grandfather worked for twenty years as a foreman in a butter factory. The pleasantest memories I have of family life are of the occasions on which he put on his red fez and sang for us the stirring songs of the Greek Army. As we listened to the bloodcurdling stories he told of the fierce struggles against the Turks for Greek independence, I wished in my childish way that I too could grow up to be a hero.

My brother and sister were the pride of the family. They had soft brown eyes, luxuriantly wavy hair and the classic features of Mediterranean beauty. By painful contrast, I was a wiry little runt, often sick. On the lower East Side, an undersized child has to depend on his feet and his wits. I worked both overtime to hold my own in that competitive sidewalk society.

I early determined never to let anyone get the better of me. I dramatized my small size and made it an asset. Let the big fellows do the work! If there was a nickel to be had, I cajoled my handsome brother into asking my grandmother for it, knowing that he would succeed better than I would.

I got away with murder at school. I talked back to my teachers, but I was so little and so earnest that they often chuckled instead of punishing me. I found that I could say what I wanted and get what I wanted by making people laugh—a technique that carried me through many an awkward situation in the double life I was to lead for seven years as an adult.

As a child, I got valuable training in the self-reliance which is essential to undercover work. I early learned to take care of myself. I would go to any lengths—even foolish ones—to be independent. No one could teach me to tie a shoelace, and to this day I tie them in the awkward way I worked out for myself. Independence has a price, and I often paid it.

Before I was old enough to go to school I nearly scalded myself to death trying to iron my own dress. Grandmother was heating one of those old-fashioned flatirons on the stove. I picked it up with the removable wooden handle as I had seen her do. When I heard her heavy step returning, I hastily dumped the red hot iron under the cold water faucet with nearly fatal results. I got a good beating for my burns, which somehow proved to me that my grandmother loved me after all.

I was intensely interested in mechanical things, and my curiosity sometimes got me into trouble. When I was thirteen and looked all of nine, the father of a classmate of mine had a huge and very old Graham-Paige that he kept parked on the street in front of our tenement house. I used to eye it enviously. One day Bill told me that his father had gone away and left the ignition key in the lock. "Come on," I said, "let's try it." I was sure I could drive.

We got several pillows and I propped myself up in the driver's seat to the amusement of a gathering crowd of onlookers. My eyes just about cleared the steering wheel, and my legs weren't long enough to reach the pedals, but I found out how to get the car started and was easing along at five miles an hour when a cop called to me. I promptly ran into a pillar.

"Where are your folks?" he asked, not unkindly, as he peered into the car. "You don't look old enough to wash your underwear." The crowd roared.

"You can send me to jail if you want to," I returned with dignity, drawing myself to my full four feet, six inches, "but I'll never tell you my name." They never would have learned it, either, if my sister had not instituted a search and caught up with me at the police station where I was being entertained by several genial officers of the law.

As I learned that my family was different from the people I met at school, at camp, and at Sunday School, I came to rely more and more on myself in dealing with the outside world.

When I was eight, for instance, I had diphtheria and lost all my hair, but I wouldn't wear the lace cap my mother crocheted to cover my head while my hair was growing back. I'd slip it into my pocket every morning as soon as I was out of the door. I didn't mind being called "watermelon head." It was a lot better than being called a "nigger" or a "wop."

The Negro and Italian children had a tough time at school, and by comparison with them, I got off rather easily. The kids could always tell a "wop" to "go home and eat spaghetti." They would have been very glad to taunt me for being a Greek if there had been enough Greeks to make it worth while, and if they had known what to say. Once in a while they called me a "grease-ball."

Whenever there was a choice between the Greek way and the American way, I chose the standards I regarded as American. I'm afraid I was a trial and a disappointment to my grandmother because I wouldn't go to Greek school with my brother and sister. I much preferred to spend my time playing games with the other children. I was always chosen first when the gang on our street divided into teams to play ball. I'm fast and I've always had a good eye for a ball. I was jack champ of the block. I was quick at schoolwork, and the teachers liked me, even the ones who complained that I was fresh. In high school I was head of student council. I took the responsibility so seriously that I once reprimanded my own sister for running in the hall. It took weeks of coaxing before she'd speak to me after that.

I think I got interested in pictures before I could read. When I was in the first grade the bedridden old lady next door to us used to send me to the store for groceries and the old New York *Graphic*. My wages were one penny a trip. The *Graphic* I brought her wasn't a bit like the dull Greek newspapers my grandfather read. It was printed on pretty pink paper, and occasionally it broke out with a section in chartreuse. It wasn't just solid columns of type, but almost all pictures—love nests, gang killings, auto accidents—situations any

East Side kid could understand without reading the captions. I walked as slowly as I could to study the pictures before handing the paper over to my employer.

It was the man at the paper and candy store who first suggested that I could make pictures myself. I had come in with two of my hard-earned pennies to buy a chocolate cherry, but the chocolate cherries were a nickel. An awkward pause ensued. Sometimes the candy store man would let us "owe" for things, sometimes not. It depended on how he felt at the moment. That day he must have been feeling very good indeed.

"How would you like to make pictures of your own?" he asked. He showed me a new gadget on the well-filled counter. It was a metal frame, very tiny, with a dark translucent sheet of film and a dozen little bits of blueprint paper. You laid a sheet of blueprint paper in the frame, put the negative over it, and set it in the sun. After a few minutes, the blueprint paper showed a wobbly but unmistakable portrait of Tom Mix. It cost a whole quarter, but he let me have it anyway. I had the kids in my class begging for a picture of Tom Mix, and I kept the little machine going all day long at school in a ray of sunlight that fell across my desk. Later, when I got a camera of my own, I used to develop my own negatives on the frame.

I got my first camera—a Brownie—as a prize for winning a swimming contest at one of the fresh air camps to which I was sent every summer. I went into business right away. I let it be known that I would take pictures of anyone who would buy films for the camera. My fee was one or two shots in every roll that I could use as I chose.

Counselors helped me in the beginning. Later I discovered that the public library had books on photography that I could borrow and study myself. I don't think I ever consciously made up my mind to be a photographer. I was always going to be one as far back as I can remember.

When I was fifteen my father died and I left home for good. I became a "mother's helper"—you'd call it a baby sitter now—

and I'd go to whatever high school was nearest to the family which was giving me room and board and pocket money in exchange for several hours' work a day. Of course I could never have any dates because I always had to stay in with the children in the evenings. When school was out in June, I was off to camp.

After I was sixteen, I always had a job for the summer as a counselor. I spent one summer working at a small camp for diabetic children run by the New York Diabetic Association. I've worked with overprivileged children at private camps and with underprivileged children from the slums who rushed at food the first day as if they never expected to see another meal. I liked the slum children best because they really appreciated what we did for them. Usually I taught swimming—I had become a Junior Red Cross lifesaver at twelve—and I coached games.

It was a hand-to-mouth existence, all through high school. I lost a lot of time out being sick. I was in and out of St. Luke's Hospital for most of one year with several attacks of pneumonia, but everyone was very good to me and I can't remember worrying much. I finally finished high school in 1934. It wasn't a particularly good year to find a job and photographers were, if anything, a little worse off than other business people. The only ones who managed to make both ends meet were the portrait studios which turned out stiff, formal poses of brides and girl graduates.

Little as I liked this type of photography, I would have been delighted to get any kind of job in a portrait studio if there had been a job to be had. But there was none. A photographer with a going business of any kind could get unlimited free labor from young men willing to work for the experience. Even if I had been in a position to work for nothing, few photographers would have considered a young woman apprentice.

But like most serious photographers, I didn't want to take flattering pictures of people dressed up to sit for a portrait. I wanted to record the things I saw in my everyday life: the expression of an old Italian woman leaning out of a window to watch the life of the street; a tug creeping under Brooklyn Bridge at night; a child sneaking a ride on the roller coaster at Coney Island; the loneliness of a milkman on a deserted city street at daybreak.

I was a city child and I loved New York. Even now my favorite recreation is walking or driving through the side streets of Manhattan. I wanted to be a photographer because I wanted other people to see the many human dramas I saw. I was young and enthusiastic. I could and did talk for hours about documenting scenes exactly as they were with no false props and no sentimental angles.

At eighteen, I had only a very dim idea of how I was going to accomplish all this, but I knew I would need a broad education to interpret what I saw. I also wanted desperately to have a place of my own. Privacy has always been and is now very important to me. I was tired of living in other people's homes and in the regimented atmosphere of even the best run summer camps. The best plan, all considered, was to get a job that would allow me to pay rent and to go to college at night.

Paying work of any kind was scarce in the summer of 1934, but I was one of the lucky ones. I got a job clipping newspapers at ten dollars a week for the Burrelle Press Clipping Bureau. I sat all day at a large tilted table reading and marking out-of-town newspapers. As soon as one stack was marked, a boy would take it away and bring another. It was confining work, but I couldn't help finding out what was going on in the world. In a way, it was an education in itself.

Burrelle's was a small, struggling enterprise then. The young man who owned it was plowing back all the earnings to build it into the great national clip service it is today. He promised us all more money when business got better. Meanwhile, he tried to make it as comfortable as possible for us clippers. One of us was always detailed to clear the big tables and set up ping-pong during the noon recess. In the afternoon, we knocked off for tea on the house.

I thought it was a decent enough place to work, until I got acquainted with one particular girl. She could scarcely conceal a sneer when the boss bought us special posture chairs.

"He acts as if he's doing us a favor, instead of himself," she snorted. "If he has any extra money, why doesn't he put it into a few more bucks for the kids? A backache is the least of my troubles!"

After we had eaten lunch together several times, she confided that she was a Communist. I had never met a Communist before, and I didn't know anything about Communism, but I had to agree with many of the things she said. I knew only too well that most people didn't have enough money to get along. I had only one outfit of clothes myself, and an invitation to dinner was an important event. But I didn't see how anything as abstract as Communism could help make me a good photographer. Instinctively, I felt that was something I would have to do for myself.

I neither liked nor disliked the Communists I met through my discontented friend. To me, they seemed run-of-the-mine people. Like myself, they went to work, and they enjoyed themselves as best they could. They had schemes for getting more money for more people who badly needed it, and they claimed credit for the social gains Roosevelt was promising. This was all fine with me. I was naturally for the working man —the underdog. Like my co-workers, I listened sympathetically to a Communist organizer who came to our shop and told us we ought to form a union.

I had been promoted to reading the metropolitan papers and was making all of fourteen dollars a week, but I went along with the plan. The boss was dead set against it, and our little union died aborning. The ringleaders were fired. I kept my job, but I failed to get the promotion I expected. It didn't matter much because a few months later I got an eighteen dollar a week job as a glorified errand girl for Esther Lape, director of the American Foundation for Social Research.

My new work was broadening. Miss Lape was close to

Eleanor Roosevelt, and the First Lady used to breeze in for surprise visits, Malvina Thompson trailing along with Mrs. Roosevelt's overladen briefcase. Once Miss Thompson sent me out to have a shoemaker sew the briefcase up. I ran all the way for fear Mrs. Roosevelt would be gone before I could get back with it.

I naturally drifted into Greenwich Village. I enjoyed living in an art center, and I met a great many friendly people with whom I found a lot in common. Like myself, all of them aspired to careers in the arts or professions. My first "apartment" was a basement room on Commerce Street that was supposed to have been Aaron Burr's gun room. I paid twenty dollars a month for it, although I had to share a bathroom and had only a hot plate by way of kitchen. I didn't do much cooking, nor, for that matter, much eating. I was always saving up to buy a better camera, and I had a strict budget.

Like all Greenwich Village arrangements, my budget was designed to cover luxuries like a camera instead of necessities like food. Carfare and dinner were interchangeable. If I was more hungry than tired on school nights, I'd walk across the Delancey Street Bridge to Brooklyn College, and spend my nickel on a hamburger. If I was more tired than hungry, I'd ride grandly on the subway instead of eating. One of my friends showed me how to find firewood for the fireplace in my cold water flat. He and I would stay up late and pick up vegetable crates which the pushcart vendors on Bleecker Street threw away.

I had bad luck with my first good cameras. One, a folding Kodak with accessories, was stolen out of my room a few weeks after I got it. I had to save all over again, this time for an Ikoflex that cost over a hundred dollars. I scraped the money together, but very soon had to pawn the camera to meet the rent. I was so green about hockshops that I thought I would have to pay all the money in a lump sum in order to redeem the camera, and I was ashamed I didn't have it the next month. When I came back six months later, money in hand, the pawnbroker had sold my pledge for non-payment of interest. I suppose it wasn't legal for him to do it, but I didn't realize my rights.

These experiences sound more appalling than they were at the time. Everyone around me was hard up, but everyone was putting up a good front. I never believed that the pinch would last—at least not for me. Successes were being made every day, and I never doubted that I could do what anyone else had done.

I had other jobs after the American Foundation, sometimes in offices, sometimes in recreational work. For a short while, I worked in a nursery school in Pennsylvania. I quit to come back to New York, where I felt my real chances lay. Part of the time I was unemployed.

In 1940, I took and passed a civil service examination for playground director in the New York City schools. I liked the work—I've always had more patience with children than with adults—and the job gave me free time at the hours I needed to go to school. When city funds ran out, our unit was taken over by the W.P.A., which hung on with a few programs into the early years of the war.

After I got this job, Betty and I took the apartment at 9 Jane Street. I liked it because I hoped some day to rent the basement of the house behind it for a photographer's studio. In order to reach this second house—9½ Jane Street—you go through a picket fence on the street and down a paved stone alley planted with a central flower bed. I had my eye on the English basement of 9½ Jane, which has a separate entrance several stone steps below the courtyard. In 1944 I was finally able to rent it and it has made an ideal studio for me—informal, small, but as cozy as a home. Little did I realize, when I moved to 9 Jane Street, that the studio I hoped to have would prove a convenient retreat for those sessions of my double life that had to be held in strict privacy.

I was lucky in finding Betty to share the apartment with me. She liked to cook, and I hated to cook. We both liked the country and we shared a cabin near Haverstraw for summer weekends, which meant we had to maintain some kind of car. Betty liked to do the driving and I liked to look out of the window on trips. We both liked gadgets—Betty specialized in toy electric trains—and we both liked animals. Betty shared my respect for privacy. We had an unwritten rule against asking each other personal questions—a tradition that turned out to be very handy when I became involved with the F.B.I. and the Communist Party.

The only disagreement that I can remember was about cats. When I met Betty, she was living with twelve of them. After a few stormy sessions, I separated her from the brood. Later, we both fell in love with Schminck, a tiger-striped gray and white animal which was leading an unhappy life with a cat-hating friend of ours who locked him up in the bathroom all day long and then complained when he chewed up the furniture and ate plants the minute he got out. Schminck was a cat of spirit and I consented to let him come and live with us on condition that he would stay out of my bed. I very soon got interested in taking pictures of him, and owe most of what I know about animal photography to the challenge he presented. A cat won't obey orders like a dog. You have to wait until a cat wants to pose. If Schminck was not in the mood, there was just no use trying to drag him out from behind the couch. After I'd shot several rolls of him he was sleeping in my bed as a matter of course.

I got a lot of pointers on the art of photography from teachers at the Photo League, a group of amateur and professional photographers. Joe ruled us students with an iron hand. We were afraid of his sarcasm but we all respected his ability. I've never known him to hold a job, although he was an excellent photographer. He had the moral drop on us because he wasn't afraid of the things that bothered us. His attitude was: to hell with the world if it "don't realize how good I am." Although I didn't realize it at the time, Joe was a typical Communist. He loved to tell how he allegedly saw his own mother starve to death before his eyes. Joe never gave any details about this family misfortune except to blame it on the "system."

The Photo League was typical of many art organizations. It was informal, friendly, and very badly run. We rented a floor in a dilapidated old town house on East Twenty-first Street. Everyone complained of the dirt, but no one did anything about it. The stairs were grimy. You could always tell a visitor, we used to quip, even if you couldn't see his face. A visitor would be brave enough to grab the bannister. We regulars knew how greasy it was and we didn't touch a thing we didn't have to.

Professional members of the League were supposed to pay for the use of the darkroom. Students were supposed to pay a quarter for lectures. Actually, no one ever paid anything. When the landlord threatened to evict us, we passed the hat among ourselves. We got a little income renting the place out to union meetings and organizations I was to understand better later on.

I soon realized that many members of the Photo League were Communists. Some of them had tried to interest me in joining the Party, but I hadn't listened to them long enough to realize exactly what they wanted to get me into. Nor did I read the Communist literature that was always up on the bulletin board. I signed as few of the petitions the officers of the League were always circulating as I could without offending them personally. I realized that Communism was a going movement, but it seemed to be a minority sect, and from what I could gather, a harmless bore. In any case, there were plenty of eccentric views to be found in Greenwich Village.

I ran into some of the same talk among W.P.A. workers on the recreation project. Clearly, if the F.B.I. agents had come to me because they had heard of me through Communists, the Photo League and the W.P.A. were the only two possible sources.

As I thought over my biography, I could not see myself as a conspicuous citizen. Yet the F.B.I. knew all about me. The agents had even acted as if they knew I had applied for several defense jobs. Somebody must have told them about me, but who could it be?

I reviewed what the agents had told me about Communists. It was hard for me to realize that they were dangerous. But was it up to me to judge? Obviously the Government was in a better position to understand these things than I. Obviously they couldn't tell all they knew in wartime.

I wanted to do my share in the war. I didn't want to profit personally or even professionally by it. If I had been a man, it would have been simple. I would have enlisted without waiting for the draft. Whatever it was that the F.B.I. agents wanted, I was convinced that it must be important. If they thought I could do it, who was I to say I couldn't? It didn't seem the kind of request that anyone could refuse. I decided to accept the work they had offered me.

2. THE F.B.I. AND I

I CALLED RE 2-3500.

"Federal Bureau of Investigation." The anonymous male voice was even, cool, competent—the kind of voice that would direct you to demolish a time bomb without changing pitch. I got Mr. Bierly right away.

There was a little awkwardness about making the appointment. Mr. Bierly didn't want to come to the apartment again, although I explained that Betty was away. "Isn't there some place we can meet convenient to you?" he asked. I thought it strange that he didn't ask me to come to the F.B.I. office at Foley Square.

There are many bars in Greenwich Village where a girl and two young men would attract little attention, but it never occurred to me to suggest one. I knew cops weren't supposed to drink on duty, and I assumed that the same went for F.B.I. agents. Later I learned that this was exactly the case. I thought of a short order restaurant on Greenwich Avenue I passed every day on my way to work. It had comfortable booths, a transient trade, and I had never been in it.

Agents Bierly and South were there when I came in after work. The three of us ordered thick mugs of coffee. I think we all felt a little shy. No one passing by could have possibly taken us for espionage agents keeping a furtive rendezvous.

Mr. Bierly asked me about Greenwich Village. He was as curious, and as ignorant about the Village as any tourist. I told
him about the old gentleman who was writing his oral history
of the world in Washington Square. Mr. Bierly told me that
he had been recently transferred to New York. He referred to
himself as just a country boy. He and his wife hadn't made
many friends in New York yet and they weren't sure they liked
living in the city. Mr. South was pleasant, but he didn't volunteer much conversation. Very soon we were all on a first-name
basis. For me, it was the beginning of a long and happy personal relationship. Ken Bierly and his wife, Billy, are today
among my very best friends.

"We don't want to put any pressure on you to do this thing,"
Ken said, opening the business of our meeting. "If you want to
help, it has to be your own decision. Have you thought it
over?"

"I want to do it," I said. But Ken wanted to point out all the
risks and dangers.

"There's no glory and no dough," he said flatly.

"And you're completely on your own," Bill put in. "If you
get into trouble, the F.B.I. doesn't know you." I was used to
being on my own, but I wanted to know the odds.

"What kind of trouble?" I asked.

"Well, let's take an example," Bill replied. "Suppose you
were arrested for taking part in a Communist demonstration—
a mass rally that turned into a riot, or a picket line incident.
We wouldn't help you. If we did, we would expose you as an
undercover agent. You never know who is in the Party—it
might even be the policeman."

This was a new angle. How could I ever know who was a
Communist and who wasn't if a policeman could be one?
Maybe some of my friends were Communists and I didn't know
it. I tried to figure out what could happen.

"Okay, so I might land in jail," I said. Jail was at least a
tangible danger. "What would happen if the Communists
found out what I was doing?"

"A number of things might happen," Bill continued. "You might be shadowed, watched, expelled. Your character might be attacked."

"And then?"

"We don't want to scare you," Ken said, "but we want you to know that people have disappeared. At the very least, the comrades might break your windows or annoy you in the street. They'd find ways of making life unpleasant for you—they might try to scare you with threatening letters, for instance, or tell lies about you. Lies that would hurt. If you had a good job, they'd try to get you fired. They could always prove that you were a card-carrying member of the Communist Party, and in most business organizations, open Communists don't get very far."

"Yes, but in that case I could prove that I wasn't really a Communist," I pointed out.

Ken smiled gently. "You could try, but we couldn't publicly recognize you."

"Golly—do you mean to say that the Communists would get back at me by telling people that I was a Communist, too?" It dawned on me that I might spend the rest of my life explaining that I was *not* a Communist.

I felt very much alone. So it wasn't going to be enough to keep my contacts with the F.B.I. a secret from the Communists on whom I was spying! I'd have to keep my contacts with the Communists from anyone who might innocently or maliciously label me a Red in circles where the news might get to the advertising agencies and corporations which could give me the kind of photographic assignments I wanted. It certainly wasn't the Mata Hari role I'd dreamed about.

"Okay, I'm in this now." I grinned ruefully. "And heaven help me if I don't do a good job of it. How do I begin?"

"Take it easy," Bill warned. "You can't just walk into the nearest Communist branch and sign up. You have to wait until you're invited to join." They explained that the Party doesn't want everybody. They want people who are willing to work

for the Party day and night, people who are willing and able
to contribute money, do legwork, and become straw bosses in
the Communist machine. I would have to wait until a Communist looked me over, investigated my past life and present
connections, and finally vouched for my sincerity and character.
My sponsor would have to convince himself that I would be
helpful in spreading Communist ideas and above all that I was
not a spy.

Ken told me that the Party had occasionally unmasked and
expelled agents of the New York City police sent into their
ranks to keep the police posted in case the Party plotted a dis-
turbance of the peace, such as a "spontaneous" demonstration
that required extra patrolling. The two agents didn't say so,
but I got the idea that I would be expected to do a better job
of covering myself than the cops had done in the past. It was
very important, they emphasized, to find the right sponsor.

The easiest thing would have been to go back to the people
in the Photo League and on W.P.A. who had tried to interest
me in Communism in the past. But if I didn't want to do it
that way, I could always subscribe to *The Daily Worker* and
wait for a representative of the paper to call at the house and
look me over as a potential recruit. This would be hit or miss,
the agents implied, and not exactly safe.

Years later I found out what happened to one plant who tried
it that way. She wrote an enthusiastic letter to *The Daily
Worker*, praising Communism to the skies. Momentarily off
guard, the Party had admitted her right away. Years later,
when she got into trouble, someone looked up her record
in the Party and found that no one had ever screened her.
"Really, we know nothing about her," her comrades whispered.
As a result, she had to leave the Party, under unpleasant circumstances.

It would be much better, Ken warned, to wait until I was
recruited. "We're not going to tell you how to get in. You'll
have to feel your own way. But keep your tracks covered.
Everyone in the Party spies on everyone else. Take your time.

Don't be too anxious to join. After you're in, don't ask for jobs. Don't ask direct questions. Don't ever ask anyone's full name. The name that they give you is the name that you accept. Above all, be a good Communist. Do as you're told. Don't argue. You are there to observe Communism in the U.S."

We agreed that for the time being it would be better for me to stay on W.P.A. Later, if I found a job in photography, I'd have a plausible excuse for changing.

"No danger of my quitting unless I get something else to do," I reassured them. "I've got to have a job to support myself."

Bill warned me not to change my way of living. For a while, I could probably manage to keep my Party interests a secret from Betty. But, it would be better, of course, if she decided to move away. I told them not to worry about Betty. She was used to my coming in and out without explanations.

"And don't try to change your personality," Ken added. "Be as natural as you can. Most people aren't trained actors and actresses."

"And after I'm in," I said, "what am I going to report to you?"

"Everything," Bill replied simply. "We want you to write us a report on every contact you have with a Communist. Many details will seem unimportant to you. You can't know—we can't know—what will be useful later on. A trivial conversation here may supply the missing link in a case we know nothing about. Names, addresses and descriptions we always want. All reports must be in writing, even if you report orally first. Do you type?"

"A little," I admitted. "But I don't have a typewriter."

"Go out and buy one and we'll reimburse you. We will pay you back for all the expenses you incur in connection with your work. That includes dues to the Party, contributions to Party fund drives, tuition at Party schools, the price of Party literature you have to buy, dues to organizations the Party asks you to join—even telephone calls and gas for your car when on Party or F.B.I. business. Put it all down, exactly as you laid it out, and mail it to us monthly."

They told me to phone if I was ever worried about what to do or if I stumbled on something of unusual interest. The rule about phoning was simple. If in doubt, call, no matter what hour of the day or night. The switchboard at the F.B.I. runs twenty-four hours a day; but if I preferred, I was to feel free to call my agents at their homes at any hour.

I was never to come to the F.B.I. office and they would never come to my house, nor even to my neighborhood or any neighborhood where I might be known. We would arrange meetings as the need arose, by phone. Telephone reports had to be followed up by typewritten reports in triplicate. I was not to sign my name to reports. Henceforth, I would be known to the F.B.I. as ND 107. The initials stood for National Defense. Officially, Angela Calomiris did not exist.

"Any more questions?" Bill asked.

"Yes," I said. "Why did you come to me? Who sent you?"

"We can't tell you that," Ken explained frankly. "Later on you'll understand why." I began to see that a spy has to take his instructions on faith. Okay, I thought to myself, but you can't stop me from trying to find out on my own.

"Will you tell me what kind of person you look for in this work?" I asked.

Ken looked at Bill. "I don't see any objection to telling her the qualifications we look for in a plant, do you? It might help her." It was my first intimation that there were other people already in the adventure I saw before me. Bill nodded his approval. It was apparently a favorite subject for Ken. After we became good friends I found that his job at the time was to find and enlist citizens who would make good plants.

"The ideal plant is a paradox," Ken began. "He should be able to inspire confidence without ever giving any in return. He should be friendly but he should know how to keep his mouth shut. He should be alert and quick-witted, but as stable as the Rock of Gibraltar. He should have a job which allows him to come and go at odd hours without arousing suspicion, but he should have no bad habits, such as a weakness for blondes or three martinis. His morals must be above reproach although he shouldn't, of course, have any family ties."

I told Ken that his description reminded me of a want ad for pony express riders that I had once seen in an old yellowed newspaper. "Boys—16 years of age, preferably orphans."

"Perhaps the crowning paradox of all," Ken went on, warming to the theme, "is that a plant has to be a loyal American with an unshakable faith in our form of government, but he has to seem like a natural recruit to the Communist Party."

"And what kind of people are natural recruits to the Communist Party?"

He didn't change expression when he answered. "People who have had a hard row to hoe and look as if they could be persuaded to stop trying."

I began to see the light. My background of poverty, my foreign-born parents, my depression disappointments—all my liabilities were going to be of use to my country. Ken watched me steadily as I grinned my appreciation of the joke.

"Why don't you boys join the Party yourselves? Fine Communists you would make!" It would be pretty hard to picture Ken or Bill in an underprivileged role.

We all laughed together. The more I thought about it the more reasons I could find why I was a perfect candidate for the Communist Party. I had suffered the kind of deprivation which drives thousands of discouraged Americans into Communism. As a child, I had been discriminated against by virtue of my foreign background. Although I was baptized in the Greek Orthodox Church, and later attended an Episcopalian Sunday School, I was not outwardly religious and was not affiliated with any church. I had seen unions busted by employers and, while I had no well-worked-out political philosophy, my sympathies were with the common people—"the masses" as the

comrades call them—because I felt myself quite naturally one
of them.

I went home that night only half satisfied, however. What
was my status in the F.B.I.? How did the F.B.I. really work?
Why did they need me, or people like me? How long had they
been using plants? What kind of things would I find out, and
what use would they be to the Government?

I was never to get clear answers, although over the years I
got clues, a bit of information here, a guess there. Certainly
the F.B.I. never undertook to explain anything to me. A secret
service operates on the principle that its left hand better not
know what its right hand is doing.

My only contact with the F.B.I. was through the agents
assigned to advise me. Their title, I learned, was "special
agent." All of them worked in the Internal Security Unit of
the F.B.I. Ken and Bill were responsible for me during the
first few years. When they were assigned to other work, I had
a series of new teams. Even when both members of a team were
equal in rank, one always assumed the major responsibility. In
practice, however, there were many emergencies in which I
could reach only one of my agents.

Bill South and Chick Heiner, an agent who worked with me
toward the end of my service, are out of the Internal Security
Unit now. Ken Bierly and Theodore Kirkpatrick, another
former agent who worked with me, are editing *Counterattack*, a
weekly news bulletin exposing Communist activities. I won't
mention the names of others who are still working on Communism in the Bureau, but I will say that there is almost a
family likeness among them all. F.B.I. agents are carefully
selected men who must conform to the very highest standards.

The special agents I knew were all under forty, intelligent,
well-educated, usually in law or accounting, and extremely conscientious—the kind of well-balanced people on whom you feel
you can depend. All were required to dress well but conserva-
tively while on duty. They were all scrupulously courteous and
considerate of me. They never told me what to do; they asked

me if I would be willing to do it. Some of them were punctilious to a fault.

Although Ken had warned me that the Bureau would not
help me if I were arrested, I'm sure that any of the boys at the
"B," as we called the F.B.I. among ourselves, would have moved
heaven and earth to get me out of the pokey—or any lesser
misfortune for that matter. They were careful never to ask me
to do anything that would have exposed me to danger or re-
prisal, even when I was more than willing to take the risk.

Their precautions were founded on experience. Even with
the best will in the world, it was sometimes difficult to protect
plants from exposure or, at least, suspicions that hampered their
work of observation. The only F.B.I. agents who knew I was a
plant were agents working directly with me. Other agents,
investigating other phases of Communism, could have put me
in an embarrassing position by using information that could
have come only from me. Fantastic as it sounds, the Bureau
actually lost a plant that way once.

The story began when one of the secret grand juries investigating espionage activities wanted to question a Communist,
whom we can call John Doe. As is usual in cases of this kind,
the agent detailed to serve the subpoena began his search by
visiting several people who were known to be friends of John
Doe. One of them was a girl by the name of Mary. When the
agent visited Mary, showed his credentials, and asked about
John Doe, Mary simply said she didn't know him. While the
agent was in her apartment, he noticed that she had slipped
some Party literature under her day bed. It had not occurred
to him that Mary might be a Communist too.

Actually, Mary was a Communist. If the agent had thought
to check F.B.I. files, he would have found a complete dossier on
her turned in by Jane, an F.B.I. plant working in the same
branch of the Party. Mary was, of course, very much worried
by the agent's visit, although she had tried to conceal her concern while he was there. Fearing that her own phone was
tapped, Mary rushed out of her apartment to the corner drug-

store to warn John Doe from a public telephone. As luck would have it, she met Jane on the street. In her agitation, she was glad to have a trusted "comrade" in whom to confide.

"Jane, I'm in the worst pickle," she burst out. "The F.B.I. is after a friend of mine. He's lying low and I'm the only one who knows where he is. I've got to reach him immediately. Won't you come with me?" Jane would have preferred to keep out of it, but she did not dare to desert a "comrade" in distress. When the two girls got to the phone, Mary found she had left her glasses behind in her hurry. Would Jane look up the telephone number of a certain firm where John Doe was employed? Jane looked the number up, and of course reported it to her agent at the F.B.I.

The F.B.I. had a delicate problem on their hands. They now knew just where to lay their hands on John Doe, but if they acted on Jane's information, Mary would certainly suspect that the secret had leaked out through Jane.

"Mary is impulsive," Jane pointed out. "In a few days she'll be very sorry that she broke down and told me about John Doe, even if he isn't served. She'll never forgive herself or me if you find him at the address I gave you."

So the agent looking for John Doe agreed to ignore Jane's report, but he kept on the trail and found his man in a very few days through other leads. When he was served, Mary reacted just as Jane predicted she would. She became cool and hostile to Jane. Soon other Party members began avoiding Jane. Once or twice, Jane thought she was being trailed. Finally, her superiors in the Party charged her with reactionary sentiments. She was reprimanded for "anti-Party activities"—although her accusers never spelled out just what activities they meant. No one mentioned the F.B.I. or spying, but Jane and her agent decided it was best for her to quit the Party rather than to undergo a surveillance which might have uncovered her relations with the F.B.I.

From stories like these, and questions referred to me which indicated intimate knowledge of the Communist Party in other

fields than my own, I early concluded that there must be scores
of plants doing the same thing I was doing—an efficient anti-
Red network of volunteer observers.

I also found out that my reports, in which I learned to para-
phrase conversation and describe individuals, were teletyped to
the central F.B.I. office in Washington, where the information
was sifted and checked and "processed" so that it could be made
instantly available to agents working on special cases. I was
always being asked to clarify the description I had given of an
individual, or answer a specific question, such as "Where was
A.B. born?"

I have no inside information on the F.B.I.'s policies or program. Piecing together the information I read in newspapers
and magazines with casual remarks made by Communists and
F.B.I. agents, I've come to realize that the authorities have been
keeping track of the Communist Party ever since the Russian
revolutionists told the world they were going to pull down
every capitalist government by force.

In the beginning both the Communists and the Attorney
General of the United States acted as if the revolution were at
hand. The Bureau of Investigation, as the F.B.I. was called in
the early twenties, had its regular agents join Communist cells
in order to get the blueprint of the uprising. Then, deputizing
hundreds of hysterical citizens, Attorney General Palmer had
everyone in sight herded off to jail.

The revolution didn't come off, and cooler heads began to
feel a little sheepish about the Palmer raids. After all, the
liberals pointed out, ours is a democracy that thrives on the free
exchange of ideas. The Government can't tell citizens which
ideas are good and which are dangerous. All it can do is to
punish overt acts against life and property. The Communists?
Harmless crackpots! Thank God we've got a country where
the police will protect them from rotten tomatoes when they
get up on a soap box and preach violent revolution. Let them
talk!

The Communists took up the weapons left to them. After

1928, they concentrated on "educating" the American people to Communism. They became clever constitutional lawyers. Detectives sent into the Party by big police forces found that the comrades were disciplined to avoid breaches of the peace. But they were always ready to violate Federal laws which would have cut their life line to Russia—our restrictions on passports, naturalization and foreign agents.

The F.B.I. soon found that they had to investigate the whole Communist movement—ideas and all—in order to enforce these Federal laws. They were dealing not with individual criminals, but with a well-drilled organization more effective than any gang of racketeers. Every Communist, if need be, was ready to perjure, to forge, even to murder at the order of the Party. And unlike ordinary criminals, the Communists did not feel that it was wrong to break a law if the Party told them to do it. Their allegiance was to the revolution and to the Soviet Union, the "land of victorious Socialism."

Meanwhile, the Party prepared the revolution by "day-to-day struggles," to use a favorite Communist phrase. The comrades did not get up on the soap boxes and state their ideas so that passers-by could judge them on their merits, according to the theory of democratic freedom. Instead, they "scientifically" exploited actual unrest to lead disgruntled citizens to solutions which only a trained political analyst could see were really designed to help Russia or make the violent overthrow of the Government a little easier.

F.B.I. agents were in a position to see the danger, but they were helpless to combat it. Their job is to enforce laws, and there was as yet no law against so ambitious a threat as the Communists were plotting. The Party was waiting until its propaganda had gained so strong a foothold that ordinary policing would be unable to cope with its bid for power. The depression seemed made to its order. As a precaution, the F.B.I. watched the timetable of the revolution through an occasional Russian-born operative.

Then, after 1938, one country after another in Europe fell

to the Trojan horse methods which the American public regarded as made in Germany, but which the Communists had
been applying all along in the United States. After Hitler and
Stalin came to terms in 1939, the F.B.I. knew that the seventy
thousand American Communists and their friends would bear
more thorough watching.

"The Communist Party is a Fifth Column if there ever was
one," J. Edgar Hoover reported later. "What is important is
the claim of the Communists themselves that for every Party
member there are ten others ready, willing and able to do the
Party's work."

With a world war blowing up, even stout-hearted liberals
reluctantly admitted that ideas, too, were weapons, but they
disagreed on the proper way to defend against them. While the
debate was raging in 1939, J. Edgar Hoover quietly set up a
subversive activities department in the F.B.I. to study the
propaganda of the Nazis, the Fascists, the Japs, the Falange of
Spanish-speaking countries and the Communists, all of whom
were attempting to influence American public opinion without
revealing their real aims.

The F.B.I.'s vigilance over the Communists was as scientific
as the Communist propagandists themselves claimed to be.
Communist "lines"—the causes and concepts the Party uses to
gain its immediate ends—change with every shift in the international balance of power. The techniques by which the comrades promote these "lines," on the other hand, are as constant
as their long-range goal of world revolution. The F.B.I. had
to study the whole pattern.

Scholarly agents in Washington sweated over the writings of
Marx, Lenin, Stalin and the American Communist writers.
They followed political events here and abroad to ferret out
the real purpose behind the hundreds of mass meetings, protests, petitions and strikes the Communists were organizing.
They painstakingly read all the Communist Party publications
from the long-haired philosophical journals to the thousands of
leaflets put out by branches of the Party and Red-inspired or-

ganizations in the furtherance of local "struggles." They analyzed every line in *The Daily Worker* and clipped every
mention of a name, even in the ads, for their biographical files.

In 1940, Congress passed the Smith Act, making it illegal to
advocate or teach the overthrow of the United States Government by force, or to publish written or printed matter for the
purpose of teaching the overthrow of the Government by force
and violence or to organize any society for that purpose. If the
law was constitutional, the Communists surely were guilty.
But the F.B.I. knew from bitter experience that the Communists are experts at covering their tracks. In order to prove
the case, the whole pattern had to be proved in terms that a
jury could see. First-hand witnesses and evidence could only
come from inside the Party itself.

The simplest way to keep the inside dope on the "day-to-day
struggles" flowing into the Washington analysts would probably have been to order a squad of G-men to join the Communist Party. J. Edgar Hoover didn't want to do it that way.
For one thing, it smacked too much of the questionable methods of the Palmer raids. For another, styles in G-men had
changed. Most of them now were hard-headed young lawyers,
accountants and scientists—men who would have had trouble
passing themselves off as plausible Communists. In order to
get past the Party's careful screening, an agent would have had
to provide himself with a watertight false biography that would
have been a nuisance on another assignment. If a regular agent
had been unmasked by the Party, he would, of course, have had
to be transferred to other work. F.B.I. agents are hand-picked,
valuable men. Spies are expendable.

At first, the Bureau tried to use renegades from the Party.
There was no lack of disgruntled Communists, but they didn't
make good witnesses in court. Juries don't trust turncoats, and
it was obvious that many of the renegades had their private axes
to grind.

In 1940, the F.B.I. began to use "plants"—volunteers chosen
for their reliability as reporters. The F.B.I. agents never told

me so, but I can see how the plants were able to do many things that the agents could not have done themselves. It was easy for me to drop into the Worker's Bookshop and ask for an out-of-the-way piece of literature somebody in the Bureau wanted to check. If I had been a Federal agent, I would not have wanted my face to become familiar there. As a Party member, I had access to internal documents that the F.B.I. agents could have secured only by subpoena for a specific purpose. Most important, I was expendable. The Bureau had not spent years training me for my job. If I turned "sour" for any reason, it was easy to drop me from the F.B.I. roles without embarrassment or loss.

I know of several other girl plants, and I think it was very sensible to use us. Girls were draft-proof in the war, and we enjoyed greater freedom inside the Party. Communist officials weren't suspicious of us. I could always ask a dumb question and get away with it. But I'm getting ahead of my story. My first assignment was to wait until I was invited to join the Party.

3. I BECOME A "COMMUNIST"

I COULDN'T FIGURE OUT, afterwards, all that the agents had meant in the coffee shop, but I was jumping to get started. The problem was: what could I do to get recruited? In my previous small experience with organizations and isms, the problem had been exactly the reverse: how to keep from being railroaded into them.

I tried to remember everything I could about the half dozen acquaintances who had, at various times, tried to interest me in Communism. It was hard for me to think of them as sinister, or somehow different from myself, but I had never thought about their arguments seriously. I had listened out of sheer courtesy, because it is hard to work with people without being polite. But I had cut them short so many times that I hesitated to open the subject myself. They might have been delighted by my interest, but they would also say, "What has come over Angela?"

I had another reservation, too. If I went out of my way to get some of the people I knew on W.P.A. to recruit me, they might lose their jobs. When you take a Federal job, you swear to uphold the United States Government. I'd never heard of anyone being fired simply because he was a member of the Communist Party, but I had heard a great deal of talk about it. The W.P.A. in New York City was strongly influenced by Communists. My co-workers often complained that some people were hired on the project for the sole purpose of getting into the confidence of the comrades and reporting their political affiliations. Most of the people left on W.P.A. needed their jobs—for instance, one was a widower trying to support four little children—and I wanted no part of informing on them.

Days went by while I tried to think of a better way. I took long walks in the Village, looking for a typewriter on which to write my reports when and if I should ever have anything to report. I bought an old Royal portable in a hockshop on Perry Street for $23.50 and put it on my first expense account. This was progress of some kind.

Then, before the week was out, Joe, the Photo League officer, asked me to go to a lecture. He said that Joe North was going to talk, that there'd be something to eat, that I'd meet some interesting people, and learn "the real dope" on the war. I didn't know at the time that Joe North was a leading writer for *The New Masses*, but from what the agents had told me, I knew the Communists claimed to have "the real dope" on the war. I let Joe work a little to persuade me, but of course I agreed to go. At the last minute Joe couldn't go himself. He sent Marcia, a girl I knew from the League, to pick me up. I felt it was more than a social invitation, and I was right.

I expected a lecture hall and was surprised to find that the meeting, or "Forum" as Joe had called it, was held in a small apartment in the West Twenties. It was furnished nicely in modern style. There was a big war map over the fireplace which the speaker used to expound Russia's precarious situation—a situation which excited everyone's sympathy at the time.

There were less than a dozen people there all told, but they all seemed to know each other. They were well-educated, professional people and they were talking the same language. Germany's invasion of the Soviet Union in June, 1941, made the "imperialist" war a "people's" war, so it was all right for the Yanks to come after all. I felt as if they had all been reading the same book and were anxious to spout it to each other.

I kept wondering why they were all so nice to me, one running to get me a cup of coffee, another asking me what I thought about the lecture, and all trying politely to find out just who I was, what I thought, and what I did for a living. In the years to come, I was to see these faces again and again at the dreary round of meetings I had to attend.

The most attentive to me was Leona Saron, a tall, thin, humorless girl with glasses. She told me that Earl Browder, the leader of the Communist Party, was in the penitentiary at Atlanta.

"Do you think it's right to jail a man for his political beliefs?" she asked indignantly. I told her that I didn't think it was right at all. Leona laid herself out to make friends with me.

In the weeks that followed, Leona called on me at my apartment and lent me books. One of them was called *They Didn't Ask Utopia*. It was an optimistic account of life in the Soviet Union by a young Quaker couple who had gone to Russia to work in public health there. She treated me to a very dull movie on collective farming in Russia, and took me to dinner in a little restaurant on the second floor of a brownstone house near Irving Place which she described in hushed tones as a favorite eating place of the "top leadership." It was an informal place, like many spots in the Village, and people were always stopping by our table to greet Leona, who seemed well known. She introduced me as "Angie," which seemed to satisfy everybody. First names, she explained, were part of the "comradely atmosphere."

During this courtship, I suddenly became very popular at the Photo League. Joe dropped his surly manner and flattered me with confidences. He told me that the Party had used his house as a secret meeting point for comrades slipping through the blockade in 1938 to fight with the Loyalists in the Spanish Civil War. I remembered that the Loyalists were lavishly praised at meetings of the Photo League I had attended in 1938. For the first time I saw the connection between the Spanish war and Communism. While most Americans sympathized with the Spanish Loyalists, it was the Soviet Union that supplied them with arms and troops—not, one may be sure, out of unselfish devotion to constitutional principles.

Leona told me little about herself, except that she had joined the Party in her teens and had built her whole life around it. To earn a living, she worked in offices, and I imagine she was quite good at it. At all our sessions, she deftly probed my life history, and I answered her questions more or less accurately. The only real lie I told her was that all my family were dead. I told her also that my roommate was too ill to take an interest in outside activities, which happened to be true. Leona was deeply moved by my account of my attempts to get a college education and the low wages I received as a clipper at Burrelle's. "The way it is now you're licked before you start," she commented. "Under Communism, the workers would set their own wages."

She told me that she was a Communist because she believed in the universal brotherhood of man, the abolition of greed, and higher standards of living for everyone. Under Communism, everybody would get a college education for the asking. Everybody would have what he needed. She talked a great deal about the downtrodden "masses," but she spoke about them as if they were an abstract problem instead of human beings like herself.

A great many of the things she told me made sense. As she talked, I wondered what would happen if she succeeded in converting me to Communism. Many of the ideas were new to me, and I had no way of answering them. It all seemed a little too good to be true, though—and I did not see why I should get benefits without earning them, or how they could be provided, for that matter. Cautiously, I asked Leona questions:

How would Communism come? Could I be a photographer under Communism? What would the new Government be like? If I joined the Party now, would it affect my career as a photographer? I tried to see what the abstractions she fed me meant in terms of my own life. Little as I knew about Communism, I

knew that in Russia my success would depend on the whim of
a Government agency and that wasn't the kind of success I was
looking for.

Leona answered in the tone of voice she would have taken
with a bright but ignorant child. "You will understand these
things better when your eyes have been opened. Why don't
you come around to branch headquarters and meet some of the
comrades? We're having a special educational program after
the next regular meeting."

The Tenth Assembly District Branch of the Communist
Party was a bare, rugless room furnished only with folding
chairs and several large tables piled with leaflets urging the
Government to free Earl Browder, national leader of the Party
then serving a term for passport fraud. The floor had obviously not been swept in earnest, and there wasn't anything in
the room that couldn't have been packed up in a few moments
or abandoned without loss. It was like a monastery or a house
after the next to the last load of furniture has been moved out.

I'm told that Party headquarters look that way all over the
world. Certainly all the ones I was to know were drab and
forlorn. I've often wondered how the tradition got started.
Perhaps Party functionaries became used to cutting down to
essentials so that they could clear out one jump ahead of the
police back in the days when Party headquarters were often
raided. However, the real reason, I think, is ideological. An
agency of the working class is supposed to scorn the trappings
of capitalist comfort.

There was not, however, a single pair of overalls among the
comrades at the Tenth A.D. Branch when I slipped in, exactly
at the appointed hour so as not to embarrass Leona by arriving
during the closed part of the meeting. The dozen or so members sitting on folding chairs were well-dressed, obviously successful people who looked out of place in the grim environment.

I learned that Leona was the branch organizer, or leader of
the unit, that the Party was conducting a "selective recruiting
drive," and that the forum at which I had met Leona was one

of a series she had planned to attract "desirable new members."
Apparently I fell into that category.

The "educational" I had been promised turned out to be an
urgent appeal to push the sale of the fifteen dollar edition of
the Little Lenin Library among non-members. It was hard for
me to think why anyone who was not a Communist would buy
fifteen dollars' worth of books by Lenin, and the campaign had,
in fact, been lagging. The Party needed money, Leona pointed
out. And what more appropriate way to raise it than by selling
the Communist classics to people badly in need of education?

After the meeting, Leona asked me if I wanted to join the
Party. I felt as if I were receiving a bid from an exclusive
sorority. Along with other prospects, I was looked over by the
executive board of the branch at a party given in a comrade's
apartment. The conversation was purely social. I passed this
examination and agreed to join.

"You must take another name," Leona said. "What shall we
call you? Most comrades who work for bourgeois employers
find it convenient to use another name in the Party. You'll find
it a protection—to keep your professional life and your Party
life separate." She did not elaborate, since the danger of discovery was obvious to both of us.

"I think I'd like something simple for a change," I replied.
So far, Leona had been careful not to mention my last name to
any of my new friends. Only Joe and Marcia knew me as
Angela Calomiris. We tried various last names beginning with
C. Angela Cole sounded good to both of us, and henceforth to
the Party I was Angela Cole, or more frequently, "Angie."

Leona had planned a special meeting on April 25, 1942, for
the induction of the new members brought in by the recruiting
drive, but when I arrived I found that I was the only new
member to be initiated. The other prospects had either
dropped out or failed to pass the final screening. Leona made
as much of me as she could.

The ceremony was a little like a baptism. Leona made quite
a speech to the effect that a new life was beginning for me.

Looking back on it now, I realize that she was right in more ways than she knew.

Under the light of a single, unshielded electric light bulb, with Stalin looking on from an imported Russian poster tacked to the wall, she read to me out of a red paper-covered book. I can't remember the exact words, but I got the idea that I was pledging my life to the Communist Party not only in the United States, but in the Soviet Union and all other countries of the world as well. I was relieved when she didn't ask me to repeat it after her, although under the circumstances I could hardly have felt that I was perjuring myself.

After I was "sworn in" Leona introduced me as Angela Cole to all of the people present. I tried hard to remember all of their names. During the rest of the meeting, I tested myself to see if I could put a name to every face in the room. Only then did I realize that one young man had been introduced simply as a "comrade from the South." He sat beside Leona and apparently did not belong to the branch.

After my induction, the regular business of the meeting went on. A comrade reported on a special press meeting, stating that changes were to be made in *The Daily Worker* to increase its circulation. I learned that the *Worker* had never paid its own way. Comrades frankly advocated more funnies and more sports and better typography to compete with the "Capitalist press," and felt that there should be more articles for people who did not understand Communism, if the *Worker* was ever to build a large circulation. It was shortly after this that the paper adopted the tabloid form.

Leona introduced the nameless visitor as a "comrade who will tell us something about white chauvinism in the South." He gave us a report, apparently gathered at first hand, on the conviction of a Negro in Alabama by an all-white jury. He had secured this information, he implied, at considerable risk, for the sole purpose of acquainting us with affairs which we could not learn through the "Capitalist press." When he got through, Leona presented a resolution to send a small contribution to the family of the convicted Negro. In my new role as a good Communist, I gave a dollar.

The "educational" was given, perhaps in my honor, by a teacher from the Worker's School, an organization housed in the national headquarters building, which existed to train Communists in Marxist ideology. He read excerpts from Marx and Lenin on the role of the trade unions in the revolution. His own sermon on these texts was devoted to their application to the Party's duty in America. According to him, unions existed so that Communists could lead them to Socialism.

At the end of the meeting, Leona gave me my Party card. It was made out to Angela Cole, but I felt sure that she had forwarded my real name to higher authorities in charge of membership records. She told me to take good care of it. It was a small folded piece of cardboard like a report card or a union card, with blank spaces in which to put the stamps you received when you paid your dues. Dues depended on wages, and at that time they ran from five dollars a month down to ten cents for the unemployed. Everyone had to pay something, however, as a matter of principle. Payment of dues, Leona told me, was a monthly reaffirmation of faith in the Communist Party. My dues, based on the twenty-seven dollars a week I was earning at W.P.A., amounted to sixty cents. She also introduced me to the "cell captain" to whom I was assigned. Every member belonged to a cell of five people who could be used as a unit in Party work.

As soon as I got home, I phoned the good news to my agents. They asked me to meet them at a certain room number in Rockefeller Center the next day.

I was puzzled, when I got to the appointed room, to find that it said "Estate of ——" on the door. Could it be the right place? I stood outside for a full minute, wondering whether I should knock or walk right in. Nothing happened. Then it occurred to me that somebody passing by might see me and wonder why I was standing in the hall. I knocked and the door was opened by Ken and Bill. The place was fixed up to look like a small law office.

In the inner room, with one ear cocked for the occasional caller who might take our blind office seriously, I described the ritual of my induction in great detail. I wanted to show them that I had observed everything I thought could possibly interest them, but they kept pressing questions on me.

"Was the book Leona read out of *Peter's Manual?*" Ken asked. He explained that *Peter's Manual* was a handbook of Communist procedure for branch organizers which the Party had officially outlawed so that it would not have to register as an agent of a foreign government—though actually the book was still in use.* I couldn't tell because I hadn't been able to read the title from where I stood. He showed me a copy of *Peter's Manual* which has a red cover and certainly resembled Leona's handbook in its text. I suppose the F.B.I. was interested in finding out whether the Party was still requiring new members to pledge allegiance to Russia.

They also questioned me closely on the individuals present whose names I could recall. They wanted descriptions like those of criminals I had seen in "wanted" notices at the post office: height, weight, age, color of eyes and hair, distinguishing characteristics like scars. These descriptions were very important, they told me, because they often provided the only clue to the identity of the important Party member masquerading under two or three names.

One of the members I described was a woman who later became personnel director of a Federal agency, a handy spot for a comrade. Personnel workers can ease a fellow comrade into a job with access to vital information or policy making. The jobs don't have to be important. Often a secretary can be more valuable than a staff worker with a high-sounding title.

I don't know whether this girl ever used her position in the Government in this way, but I do know that she was dismissed

* See Appendix. The author of *Peter's Manual* is the J. Peters whose name figured prominently in the Alger Hiss case.

in 1948 for failing to beat a loyalty check. She tried to deny membership in the Party and even started a suit in court to clear herself, but she discontinued the action, after I took the stand in the Communist trial. I turned in her Party card number in 1942. By 1948, the F.B.I. probably had a bushel basket of evidence on her.

When I had exhausted my first list of contacts, they brought out photographs, photostats of newspaper pictures, rogues' gallery pictures with prison identification numbers across them. The only one I recognized was a man who had attended the branch meeting to which I had been invited as a recruit. I had a sudden inspiration.

"Would you like pictures of some of these people I've been telling you about?"

"You bet we would," Bill said.

"Any time it's easy and natural to do it," Ken warned. "Don't go out of your way to get pictures. It's safer to let them come to you."

"And we'd like to borrow your Party card long enough to photostat it," said Bill.

I realized, with something of a shock, that the F.B.I. must have a great many plants like myself. Why else would the Bureau hire a blind office? So after my first report, I watched comrades closely for signs that they, too, might be undercover agents. Perhaps I was figuring as a dangerous Communist in some other spy's reports.

Meanwhile, Leona undertook to make a good Communist of me by teaching me "practical tactics." The very next Sunday she took me with her to "visit the masses in their homes." We met in one of New York's West Side slum sections, and started down a shabby side street with ten copies of the *Worker* apiece.

"Let's look in here," Leona said, stopping in the dingy hallway of a tenement. "It ought to be a good house because there are both foreign and American names on the mailboxes."

I rang the bell. A drowsy woman in a house coat answered. The woman took the paper we handed her and stood there

looking at us in surprise. The Party's current struggle was to
free Earl Browder, but Leona didn't think our listener was
ready to be "activated" on Browder. She began with a subject
the woman ought to have been interested in:

"Did you know that they're going to raise the price of milk
a penny a quart?" she asked ominously.

"Oh, dear," the woman sighed. "I don't know what I'll ever
do. Everything is so high already."

"The Communist Party is opposing the action," Leona followed up. "We need your help. . . ."

Leona tried to make herself useful to the people we visited.
She advised idle persons how to get on relief. She knew how to
cope with landlord problems. And always she made her listeners feel that the Communists were their only friends. She
wasn't upset when doors were slammed in our faces. "If they
tell you to get out," she instructed me, "you get out."

So zealous was Leona that she bought a six months' sub-
scription to *The Daily Worker* for a stranger on whom we
called and paid for it out of her own pocket. She believed that
the *Worker* was, as it claimed to be, "the only newspaper that
tells the truth." She advised me that getting subscriptions
would help me to rise in the Party.

Leona, I found, was not very well liked at the branch. One
girl derisively called her a "Jimmy Higgins." The term puzzled
me and I asked Leona about it. She flushed as if I had said a
bad word.

"There was once a comrade by that name who worked very
hard at the distribution of Party literature," she explained.
"Comrades who feel these tasks are menial call anyone who does
them a 'Jimmy Higgins.' But we don't say that any more because it's chauvinistic. There's no chore too small for a comrade!"

Leona loved canvassing, although she was high enough up in
the Party to avoid it if she wished. To her, it was social life. I
hated it. The first time I was allowed to go alone, I dumped
my quota of *Daily Workers* in the nearest ash can.

Early in May, the State Committee of the Party sent me a printed invitation to a rally for new members. A girl comrade collected my invitation as a ticket of admission at the door of the Irving Plaza auditorium. By counting rows and columns of chairs, I figured that the Party must have brought in over one thousand new members in the spring recruiting drive in New York County alone. The hall was packed to capacity.

We started off singing "The Star-Spangled Banner," like any group of loyal Americans in wartime, and then we sang, just as vigorously, the "Internationale."

> "It's the final conflict, let each stand in his place.
> The International Soviet will be the human race!"

Israel Amter, New York State chairman of the Party, made the formal welcome. A recruit as green as myself leaned over to give me a piece of her new knowledge:

"Do you see how pale he looks? He's never been well since the Cossacks clubbed him while he was defending striking workers!" I supposed she meant the police.

I looked around at the faces of my new brothers- and sisters-in-arms. It would have been hard to generalize on the crowd. I'd say the average age was thirty. Looking at the sea of faces, and trying hard to memorize as many of them as possible, I saw that all of them were radiant with hope for the new life. The terrible thing about it was that they looked no different from the people I'd known all my life, people I had imagined could never have fallen for mummery of this sort. It was like a nightmare in which you feel either that everyone else is crazy and you alone are sane, or that everyone else is sane and you alone are crazy. The emotion in the room was stifling. I wanted more than anything else in the world to get out of the place.

I tried to concentrate on the next speaker, an appealing, slight man with an eager boyish face who made his audience feel as if he were personally reaching out to their little hopes

and fears. His name was Gil Green. Seven years later his face
was much older and harder and grim, when I identified him in
court as one of the eleven defendants in the Communist trial.

"From this day forward," he promised, "your lives will be
enriched as much as you are enriching the lives of all man-
kind. . . . The Party is not all work and no play. . . . There
will be fun and social life, too. . . . You have a lot to learn.
Make the older comrades explain the Party to you in language
you can understand. Don't be ashamed of your ignorance.
Pull them down to your level."

On the way out, each of us got a pale yellow envelope of
literature—"The Foundations of Leninism," the "Communist
Manifesto," the "Constitution of the Communist Party, U.S.A."
and some pamphlets by the imprisoned Browder. But the Party
did not leave our education to chance reading. In classes of
ten, at homes of comrades, we new members learned the orthodox Leninist line: class struggle culminating in revolution. I
listened, terrified. Everything seemed ominous.

Our teacher, Joe Prinsky, painted capitalists as predatory fat
men in Wall Street who had come to power by systematically
stealing from the "proletariat," which of course meant us.
Luckily, these thieves were now on their last fat legs. The
slightest shove would topple their shaky system. All that held
it up were the courts, the churches, the schools, the "venal"
press and other agencies of "bourgeois morality." The way he
talked, black was white and white was black. I felt as if I
would have to stand on my head to enjoy the new society. No
wonder Gil Green had warned us to make our teachers talk
in words we could understand!

Puzzled new members tried to ask questions but our teachers
never really answered them. All they did was to promise us that
we would soon learn to distinguish between the "bourgeoisie"
(free enterprisers and all their works) and the "masses" (wage
earners). This would prepare us to work through "mass organizations" (potential diffusers of Communist propaganda) in
order to make their members "politically conscious" (ready to

follow Marx where Stalin led). As we became good Marxists ourselves, we would learn how to avoid the mortal sin of "Trotzkyism" (philosophical differences with Stalin's policies) on the one hand and "right deviationism" (compromise with capitalism) on the other.

Our lessons were studded with such bugaboos as "chauvinism." There was a "white chauvinism," a "male chauvinism," a "national chauvinism"—all kinds. The dictionary says that chauvinism means "exaggerated patriotism." To Communists, it means any sentiment that the Party does not approve.

I learned that in order to be a Communist in good standing, I would have to pay dues, attend branch meetings, "fight for Socialism" and read the Party press.

Joe Prinsky warned us that the revolution might be delayed by "opportunists"—proletarians who turn away from the cause of the people to pick up crumbs from the capitalist banquet. I noted at the time that "opportunists" seemed to be people like myself who wanted to make their own way. As "enemies of the people," the "opportunists" would get theirs, the teacher promised—by "liquidation."

"What would we do if we found a spy among us?" a timid learner asked.

I tried desperately to keep the blood from rushing to my face. I was sure I had already been discovered. But the teacher answered casually:

"We'd kill him."

After that I was careful, believe me. I'd wait until I was alone before writing to the F.B.I., and when I sat down to do a report, I didn't answer the door. I never signed my number until I was ready to walk out to the mailbox. The first few times I was interrupted, I hid the papers under the rug behind my studio couch. Later I found other hiding places—never in a book, of course, which casual visitors might pick off a shelf.

I had been in the Party only six weeks when Leona arranged to get me into the Marxist Summer Day School for "cadre" training. The military term sounded strange, but I recalled that henceforth I was pledged to violent struggle. At Leona's orders, I went down to national headquarters on Twelfth Street to see Elizabeth Lawson, the director of the school. Miss Lawson didn't think I would be able to keep up with the classes, but she agreed, at Leona's insistence, to give me a week's trial. I felt I had had quite enough "education" in Communism but I dutifully acted as if I felt a great honor were being conferred on me.

When I reported the new course to Ken by phone, he said that he wanted to see me right away. "Can you be at Chambers Street and Broadway in exactly one hour?" he asked. "Stand on the northwest corner. We'll pick you up in a black sedan. If we miss connections, neither of us will wait for more than twenty minutes. After that, call in to the office to get new instructions."

I took the subway down to Chambers Street and walked up and down the block, watching everyone on the street to see if they were watching me. I had no reason to believe that any of them knew me, but my short acquaintance with the Communist Party had already taught me that you could never tell. I wondered what I would say if Leona should suddenly appear, and how I would warn Ken and Bill not to hail me.

Exactly on the dot, they pulled up in a car and greeted me as if we had a date. I felt safer, sitting in the front seat between the two men. Soon we were cruising along the East River Drive.

"You're a fast worker, Angela," Bill said. "How did you manage to get invited to the Marxist Summer Day School so soon?"

"Do you really want me to go?" I asked, surprised. I foresaw a hot summer of hitting dull books. It all seemed pointless. If the F.B.I. agents were so interested, why didn't they get books out of the library and read them for themselves? I had no way of knowing then, nor, I think, did the agents, that the lawyers preparing the case against the eleven Communists would need a witness able to testify at first-hand that Communists were systematically teaching the overthrow of the Government.

I explained that I was now working for Hal Phyfe, a portrait photographer on Fifth Avenue.

"How am I going to manage it?" I asked the boys. "I can't ask for three weeks off just after I've been hired."

"Don't worry, Angela," Ken said. "We'll fix it up some way." In the end, I got a part-time job and the Bureau made up the difference in pay.

Our classes met in the now-disbanded Worker's School in the national headquarters of the Communist Party, a drab building south of Union Square. Uninitiates with business at *The Daily Worker* or the Worker's Bookshop there, might easily miss the building entirely, because both its front and back doors look like freight entrances. Even if you're a Party member, you have to have a special pass to get in to the floors reserved for the state and national committees.

It was hard to realize that this inconspicuous building with its peeling olive-drab paint was the mecca of all American Communists. Going upstairs to our classroom on the second floor, awed comrades pointed out members of the American Politburo, their nickname for the top body of the Party, riding up in the old-fashioned exposed elevator cage to the ninth floor to study cables from Moscow and plot Party strategy to match. Some of my classmates hinted that they had even seen "visitors from overseas"—soft-voiced, hard-faced men with Russian accents who assumed names like Williams, Edwards or Michaels —plurals of English given names. (The reason for the choice of such names is obscure, but apparently some advantage was seen in unmistakably Anglo-Saxon pseudonyms.)

If I had elected American History, I would have learned that George Washington believed in violent revolution and that Abraham Lincoln corresponded with Marx. My course, Political Economy, was even more confusing. On the first day, our teacher asked us for a definition of Marxism.

I waited for the gray-haired Party functionaries in the class to answer: "the theory that the proletariat must overthrow their capitalist exploiters," or more simply, "the teachings of Karl Marx."

The teacher, however, rejected both these suggestions. "Marxism is not a dogma," he reproved. "It is a guide to action." I got that one down in my notebook before the bell rang.

After class, the teacher asked me about photography and told me that he was a camera bug himself. At our next meeting, he chose me to check the attendance. I didn't dare write the names down while I had his book before me, but I concentrated on a few every day and phoned them in to the F.B.I. every evening. It did not take long for me to place every member of the class.

In the following weeks, I learned that Marxism was a discipline, like logic or theology, as well as a "guide to action." Difficult as it was to practice, it was the only path to the salvation of the world. In this new "scientific" religion, Marx was the only prophet. Lenin was the saviour who effected the predicted revolution, while Stalin and even our own American leader Browder were apostles or present-day saints—the Communists call them "heroes." Our teacher illustrated from the history of the Soviet Union.

We studied the teachings of these thinkers in cheap paperbound texts published by the International Publishers, Inc.: *Wage-Labour and Capital* and *Value, Price and Profit* by Karl Marx; *The Foundations of Leninism,* by Stalin; *The State and Revolution,* by Lenin, and Georgi Dimitroff's *United Front Against Fascism,* an address to the Seventh World Congress of the Communist International in 1935, which laid down the principle of opposition to Hitler which held until the non-aggression pact in 1939.

We analyzed these thorny texts, word for word, in class. The girl who sat next to me confided that she had failed the course twice and was on her third try. I gave up trying to follow the

twisted reasoning and concentrated on writing down everything the teacher said word for word, running in the names of
class members I was memorizing.

The teacher must have noticed how anxiously I hung on
every word, because he stopped me one day after class to ask
me how I was getting on and whether I thought his lectures
were too hard for the students.

"It's tough going," I admitted with sincerity, "but of course
all of us have gone to capitalist schools all our lives and we
have a lot to unlearn." He seemed pleased with my answer.
Apparently I was learning the double talk. I passed the course.

At the next branch meeting, Leona displayed the little cer-
tificate the Worker's School had given me and asked me to rise.
For a moment I stood up, a shining example to my branch.
The irony of the ovation I received escaped me. At the moment, I felt only the embarrassment of being teacher's pet. In
private, Leona no longer bothered to be ingratiating. She
treated me as if I were a newly commissioned second lieutenant
waiting for an assignment.

I soon learned that the Party is organized like an army. The
working units which actually do the work of propaganda are
the branches, of twenty or more members each, subdivided into
cells under group captains who can be compared to corporals.
The work of a number of branches is supervised by a "section,"
the next higher unit. Sections report to a county committee,
but in New York City, where the structure is more complicated,
there are sometimes other units between the section and the
county. County committees report to their state committee,
and state committees to the National Committee of the Party,
which in its turn is supervised by a smaller executive committee nicknamed the American "Politburo." This small group
keeps in close touch with Communist leaders in Russia through
"visitors" and "representatives" of the international organization of the Party.

From top to bottom, leaders of each body are chosen and
checked by leaders in the next higher body. In fact, the very

existence of branches and sections depends on the pleasure of
the county committee, which is always reforming them for
specific campaigns or to eliminate factional feuds.

Our branch was a tight little world of its own. We were
little more than a score, but of that number at least a quarter
were "officers." As branch organizer, Leona presided at meetings, both regular and executive. We knew in a general way
that she was responsible to "higher authority" for our activities,
and that our knowledge of Party policy must come through her.
As financial secretary, Martha collected the dues, acted as treasurer of the branch's funds, and decided how much each of us
should contribute to the fund drives which came up every few
months. The membership secretary kept the all-important
membership list, issued new cards at the end of every year,
managed the periodic recruiting drives, and checked on our
activities inside the Party and out. On her master list she noted
how many papers each of us sold, what front organizations each
of us attended, and what special talents each of us had. The
educational secretary arranged for outside speakers at branch
meetings, took responsibility for the indoctrination of new
members, and recommended promising comrades for further
education in the higher Party schools. The literature and press
director hounded us all to sell *The Daily Worker* and to buy
the books and pamphlets the Party was pushing at the moment.

These executives ran the branch. Leona invited me to become one of them: "The Party must develop women leaders to
replace members of the cadre fighting on the battle front. You
have proved that you are leadership material. Henceforth, I
want you to attend meetings of the executive committee of the
branch. You will come to my apartment at eight o'clock every
Monday night." She gave me her apartment number and made
me write it down "so that you won't have to ask when you get
there." I felt as if I were really getting behind the scenes.

A usually friendly little Irish librarian from our branch cut
me dead in the elevator going up to Leona's apartment. "Party
members do not recognize each other in public places," she

explained sharply as soon as the elevator door slammed shut behind us.

When we came in, every available seat in Leona's small living room was occupied by comrades chatting in the subdued and self-conscious way of friends who meet at a non-social occasion of some gravity. All the people who talked most frequently in branch meetings were there—the finance, education, literature, membership and press directors, and a few others whom I knew to be cell captains in charge of groups of five members each. I was the only member without portfolio. I found a place on the floor.

Leona called the meeting to order as formally as if she were presiding from a rostrum, with a gavel and a glass of ice water at her elbow, and announced the agenda. It closely followed the order of the programs at branch meetings.

For the inevitable "educational," Joan, the educational director, rehearsed the talk on "democratic centralism" she had prepared for the regular branch meeting the next evening.

"The Communist Party is not a debating society. It is an organization for action in which all members agree to execute the decisions of the majority. The principle of democratic centralism is written into the United States Constitution, but whereas Congress does not attempt to resolve differences, the Communist Party makes decisions and sees that all members execute them. . . ."

Democratic centralism is the exact reverse of democracy. It means that authority is "centralized" at the top. Reports go from cell to branch to section to district or region to state to National Committee and eventually to the international organization of the Party controlled by the Soviet Union. Conversely, directives travel down the chain of command through "stations," or regular meetings of the executives of one unit with their counterparts in the next echelon.

During the educational program Leona asked me to report on my experience at the Marxist Summer Day School. Surprised, I scrambled to my feet:

"I'm a new member, and I won't attempt to repeat the many things I learned at school, but I would like to say that I left with the feeling that I want to go on studying by myself and work harder in my branch." My words rang so corny in my ears that I was sure someone would detect their insincerity. On the spur of the moment, I had simply paid out the line I had been given. But my comrades beamed approvingly. I had made the "right" answer.

During a detailed report on the work each Party member in the branch was doing, I amused myself by matching the names read out with faces I had seen, sometimes only once, at branch meetings. With the whispered help of the girl sitting next to me, I managed to place twenty-six of the list when the membership director concluded her report.

"We have left only John and Elaine," she said. "Comrade Elaine has done no Party work for three months. She has repeatedly broken promises to attend branch meetings since I asked her to recruit her fiancé. The last time I visited her, she was in a very unstable frame of mind. She told me that she wanted to leave the Party.

"I was forced to explain to her that while a comrade cannot quit the Party at will, the Party can and must expel members who fail to do their duty. I pointed out that such expulsions are frequently published in *The Daily Worker* for the protection of other comrades.

"Elaine is potentially valuable to the Party. She earns a good salary in an advertising agency and is well connected in bourgeois circles. I've asked her to appear before this committee at nine-fifteen before referring her for discipline to higher authority. I believe this is a matter we can handle in the branch."

"Know her?" I whispered to my neighbor. She nodded, grimacing. "And John?"

"Don't ask about him. He's a secret member."

No one commented on Elaine, and the membership director went on to give what she called a "composition" of the branch. It consisted of a long list of clubs, unions and associations, some of which were new to me, followed by a figure representing the number of members of the branch belonging to each.

"Only eighteen of the twenty-eight members in the branch are registered in the American Labor Party," she commented, after one item. "As you recall, the Party requires every comrade to register. We also have an unusually large number of members who are not in any trade union."

In the discussion that followed the composition report a florid-faced group captain named Arthur asked why the last eight people recruited to the branch were all white collar workers. "The membership director knows perfectly well," he charged, without looking at her, "that she has orders to increase the proportion of basic workers."

"Can I help it if you all bring in white collar people?" the membership director flared. Apparently they were old enemies.

"All I can say is that we're a fine lot of workers. Look at us! I'll bet there isn't a comrade in this room who gets his hands dirty."

A buzzer interrupted him, indicating someone at the street door. "That must be Elaine," Leona warned, glancing at her wristwatch. "She'll be up here in a minute. Please remember to keep your voices down at meetings. Does Comrade Arthur have any suggestions for securing more basic workers?"

Comrade Arthur muttered something about "never getting any workers as long as the branch was run by a bunch of women."

"Hold on, old man," the press director cut in. He was the only male functionary left in the branch. "We're all of us going off to war pretty soon. This is no time to indulge in male chauvinism."

The apartment bell sounded, and Leona let in a young girl with dark hair and attractive features who looked distressingly like a trapped animal. No one greeted her or made a place for her. She stood awkwardly, clutching her handbag. Leona broke the tense silence.

"We haven't seen you at branch meetings," she accused. "If

you have read your Constitution, you know that it is your responsibility to attend. You can't get the program of the Party any other way. It's bad enough that you don't do your share of Party work. But do you realize that other members of the branch have to take time from the work you should be doing to visit you and find out why you have been neglecting your Party duty? Do you think that is right?"

Elaine had to admit that it wasn't right.

"Do you have anything to say for yourself?"

"I've been so busy."

"You know that it is your duty to share the Party with your friends and family. Remember what Lenin said: 'We must train men and women who will devote to the revolution, not merely their spare evenings, but the whole of their lives.' "

Elaine came to branch meetings after that. In order to make up for her absence, she meekly accepted the chores Leona piled on her.

I began to see that some comrades stayed in the Party simply because they were afraid to get out.

4. I HELP TO OPEN UP A "SECOND FRONT"

I LEARNED TO be a good "soldier of the revolution" at the one time in history when the objectives of the Soviet Union ran parallel to those of the United States. My first year as a spy in the Communist Party was the year when everyone believed that Hitler might conquer first Russia, then England, and then the world.

In the summer of 1942, this menace overshadowed every other consideration in public and private life. The Communist Party was regarded as a believer in the political system of our allies. Franklin D. Roosevelt had freed Earl Browder after he had served a year and a half of his sentence for passport fraud because the action "would have a tendency to promote national unity and allay any feeling which may exist in some minds that the unusually long sentence was by way of penalty imposed on him because of his political views."

At grim branch meetings every Tuesday night, Leona explained the war. Whatever the news of the day—whether Tobruk fell or American warships sank in the Pacific—our lesson always concerned the German offensive in Russia. On our huge map, the battle front edged an inch or so east every week. Rostov fell. The River Don was lost. The Germans threatened Stalingrad. The moral of every lesson was the same:

Open up a Second Front! Hit the enemy on land! Smash
Hitler now! Do to Hitler what Doolittle did to Tokyo! Defense will not win the war! We crossed the Atlantic, how can
the Channel stop us!

In branch "educationals" we discussed the strategy of invasion. Anyone who said we didn't have the ships was lying. Joe
Curran, head of the National Maritime Union, said we did have
the ships. Military experts who shuddered at the human cost
of invading the Continent were "defeatists" who hoped to
negotiate a peace with Germany. "Appeasers"—*The Daily
Worker* likened them to the men of Munich—wanted to see
Russia bled white because they didn't like her political system.
They were the Sixth Column, betraying the people's war in
the interests of their class. For everyone knew that these "bogus
patriots" and "noisy traitors" were getting rich. Profiteering on
war contracts wasn't enough for them. They were exacting as
much tribute from the American consumer as the wartime
market would bear. Any child could see what was happening!
Rents were high. Food was high. Somebody was getting the
gravy, and we could all guess who.

That was the line. I soon found that I would have to work as
hard as the genuine comrades to put it over with the people. In
order to be a good Communist, I had to sell special editions of
The Daily Worker, distribute leaflets at street tables, hold street
meetings, get signatures for petitions to the President and the
generals, write letters to our Congressmen, and cheer at mass
rallies, all aimed at arousing the people to demand an immediate invasion of Europe. Every Communist branch in the
country was doing the same thing. I was to see these standard
techniques used again and again. A seasoned Communist has
done all these things so many times that he needs very little
guidance.

I will never forget the first time I had to stand on a street
corner and hawk the Party line as if I believed in it myself. A
sympathizing labor union, which was conducting its own Sec-

ond Front drive, had planned a series of street tables and asked the Communist Party to supply workers to man some of them.

Leona assigned me to help at a table on the corner of Fourteenth Street and Fifth Avenue intended to appeal to white collar workers. Union workers got the police permit, giving the union as sponsor, and brought a card table with a big sign tacked to the edge: DEAR MR. PRESIDENT.

Two girls stood behind the table with pens and a petition to President Roosevelt and General Marshall to open the Second Front *now*. Two other workers circulated among the crowd, handing out Second Front leaflets and urging everyone to come up to the table and sign. We worked on four-hour shifts and we worked hard.

It takes a certain amount of physical energy just to stand on the corner of Fifth Avenue and Fourteenth Street on a sunny Saturday afternoon. Crowds of window shoppers munch frankfurters from the outdoor concessions. Working girls hunt for bargains. Foreign-born families from the eastern bulge of Manhattan take the air together, getting some kind of elementary social pleasure out of the physical presence of large numbers of human beings whom they don't know. They took us as one of the sights provided for their diversion, along with the street hawkers and candid photographers. We talked to anyone who looked our way:

"Read how you can help beat Hitler this year!" we'd urge, offering a leaflet. Embarrassed and a little puzzled (what were we selling?), they'd look at the literature and throw it away, but it was surprising—and frightening—how many could be persuaded to "step up to the table and sign."

Some signed difficult names with the pride of people who have just learned how to write. Some, I think, were intrigued with the thought that they were addressing the President of the United States. It was the closest they might ever get to people who had their pictures in the papers. Some signed for a lark, as if taking a chance on a raffle. Some signed as solemnly as if they were doing a civic duty, like registering to vote. And a

great many signed just because we asked them to. "After all,"
you could see them figuring, "I've got nothing to lose." At the
end of the afternoon, we had nearly one hundred names.

I shuddered to think how easy it is to get large numbers of
people to support a "good cause" if they can do it without
spending time or money. I felt that we were morally black-
mailing well-meaning people who had less energy than we did.
I waited in fear and hope for someone to ask us, "Why a Second Front now?" or "Why was there no demand for a Second
Front in 1939 when England and France were fighting alone
against the Nazis?" or "Do you think you know more about it
than the generals?" I would have found such questions embarrassing, but they weren't asked. People just took what we had
to say on faith. We talked faster than they did, so we must
know.

At every turn of the news, we bombarded the President, the
generals and even Congressmen with printed postcards ("Keep
your promise to open a second front this year!"), identical except for the letterhead. Each member got a quota to distribute among friends, fellow employees, and acquaintances in
churches, clubs and other organizations. The membership secretary knew all our potential "contacts" and she didn't hesitate
to remind us of them.

There was something a little ridiculous about it: the postcards all came from the same place, they all went to the same
place—I hope the wastebaskets in Washington are large—and it
didn't seem possible that anyone could be fooled into thinking
there was anything spontaneous about the torrent. Yet we kept
on soberly sending them out from as many different sources as
possible. We tried to get as many as possible sent out by individuals under their own letterheads.

Special efforts were required of Party members. At one
branch meeting Leona handed out paper and instructed us to
compose personal letters to the President. "Keep it simple," she
coached, "but use your own words." As if any of us could possibly find "our own words" after the education we had received!

As I sat there dutifully piecing together the expected sen-
tences, I was sure no public official could possibly doubt that
the writer was a Communist. I winced at the thought that
anyone would read it. I even hated to sign Angela Cole. But
Leona left us no escape. She gave us ten minutes to write
our letters and then collected them, schoolteacher-fashion, and
mailed them herself, charging the postage to the branch
treasury.

These activities soon took several evenings a week of my
time—far more than I had anticipated when I agreed to join
the Party as a volunteer service. They also threw me into almost daily contact with the people on whom I was spying.
With mounting horror, I realized that I could not observe
passively. The comrades expected me to be a comrade in fact,
as well as in name. I found that I could not safely turn down
their social invitations without being regarded as a slacker,
because all of them were aimed at "activizing" me further in
Party work.

I almost got into trouble when a woman in my branch asked
me to join the Advertising Section of the Book and Magazine Guild of the United Office and Professional Workers of
America.

"What's in it for me?" I said. "I'm not employed as a photographer by any advertising agency, and I don't want to be.
I want to go into business for myself." My comrade was
genuinely shocked.

"But surely you believe in unions!" she argued. "Every
comrade should *want* to help the cause of the toiling workers."
She talked as if I were very selfish indeed and ought to be
ashamed of myself. I confessed my error and joined.

The Advertising Section of the UOPWA is a tenuous group
which went through regular cycles of reorganization largely
because it had very little real trade union function to hold it
together. At UOPWA meetings, we soundly berated each other
for being second-class members of the proletariat. The idea was
that we weren't really as good as people who worked with their

hands. Yet, we bemoaned the difficulties of recruiting office workers to a union.

"The trouble with white collar workers is that they're snobbish," the argument ran. "They think they can bargain individually. That's why they're getting the short end of the stick while industrial toilers organize and get raises."

Inevitably, some Party hack would interrupt a discussion of ways and means of bringing white collar workers in line with the cost of living, in order to bring up matters of larger importance than the economic welfare of members:

"Higher wages are fine, but if we don't open up a second front, Russia will fall. If Russia goes, democracy will go, and with it the trade union movement around the world. Let us not be selfish and short-sighted!"

There was no danger of "selfishness" in that group. I found myself on committees to send packages to Red Army soldiers with encouraging messages promising "to do everything within our power" to open a European land front in the west. In the fall of 1942, Lewis Merrill, president of UOPWA and chairman of the Political Committee of New York City's C.I.O. Council, could report proudly: "Only those who are for the immediate opening of the Second Front and who give full support to the foreign and domestic policies of the President can get the backing of the C.I.O. Council."

We comrades heard so much about the Second Front that it seemed natural to find it in the forefront of every organization. It came as a shock, however, to realize that the Photo League, to which I had belonged for so many years, was simply one piece in the jigsaw puzzle of Communist propaganda.

I was used to hearing radical opinions at the League, but I had always respected the sincerity of the people who expressed them even when I could not agree. Now, as a "Communist" myself, I realized that my deep-thinking friends were simply parrots. Whenever I went to the Photo League, I felt as if I were returning to a childhood home suddenly made sinister by something I had never noticed before—an unexplained spot that might perhaps be an old bloodstain.

At one session we arranged a lecture by a well-known woman photographer.

"How can I talk about photography," she opened her address, "when they are dying in Stalingrad!" I was hardly surprised when the talk on the art of the documentary for which the audience had paid their money settled into the familiar appeal: Open up a Second Front.

I wondered whether the board of directors knew how the League was being used. All of them were well known in photography: Margaret Bourke-White, Leo Herowitz, Paul Strand, Berenice Abbott, and later, Beaumont Newhall, curator of photography at the Museum of Modern Art. But few of them had time to come to League meetings and see what was going on.

I had new duties thrust upon me in the Photo League. Joe applied for service in the Signal Corps. An Army Intelligence investigator came around to ask me questions about him and I took the risk of referring him to the F.B.I. I don't know whether he followed up my hint, but Joe left for the wars as a Signal Corpsman. He was a great loss to the Photo League "fraction," as the nucleus of comrades within a non-Communist organization calls itself. I was elected executive secretary of the League on an unopposed slate although I myself protested that the League's charter provided for more than one nomination for every office.

As an executive of the League, I had to see that we passed the "right" resolutions, kept the bulletin board posted with Party literature, and cultivated students who might be recruited into the Party even as I had been. I soon discovered that the League had a stormy history of internal factionalism. It had been originally started in the late thirties by a group of film artists, including Paul Strand and Leo Herowitz, and in those days it was known as the Film and Photo League. In 1938, the movie people left the organization to the still photographers.

There were always members who objected to the League's endorsement of candidates for political office and its rather blatant propagandizing, but they usually didn't get a chance to affect policy. A great many of them quit in disgust, and were replaced by more innocent or less conscientious photographers.

When Fred Stein, a refugee from Nazism, wrote a letter of resignation protesting the League's political activities, the executive board destroyed it so that the other League members couldn't see it. Years later, when Fred's application for citizenship was rejected, this letter would have proved his innocent connection with the Photo League, which was listed in 1947 as a subversive organization. After the trial, I was glad to help him clear himself.

From the inside, it was easy for me to see how the League fitted into the master plan. It was a natural rallying point for liberals who would normally be sympathetic to Communist causes. It was an organization whose facilities could be used to spread propaganda. And it was a cultural force which could influence indirectly the millions of people who respond to pictures more easily than to printed words.

I began to worry that my own point of view on the documentary had been unconsciously influenced by the politics of my teachers. Joe had conditioned us to think that a good picture was a picture that illustrated social injustice, even when he was teaching us technique. Once he sent us out to take any picture that would show texture. One student brought in a photograph of tweed material highlighting the tiny hairs. Another did a hand on which you could see the pores of the skin. But the study that Joe admired for its texture was a shot of a hobo who had used a newspaper for a blanket on a park bench. Joe pointed out that you could actually read the finest print in the paper.

It was the same thing when he told us to take a picture of a mother and child. A haggard mother and a dirty child were just better art than a neatly dressed mother playing with a normally healthy baby. Scenes of comfort or contentment were derided as "commercialism."

I discovered how convenient it was for Party publications that we documentary photographers were unconsciously trained to document the seamy side of American life, when *The New Masses* asked to see a series I had done on underprivileged children at Greenwich House. I had pictures of the youngsters drawing, playing games, dancing, and drinking mid-morning milk in the settlement nursery school. The magazine was particularly interested in an informal shot of some little girls playing house. One child was busy "scrubbing" as she had seen her mother do. *The New Masses* ran that picture with a caption suggesting the evils of child labor. To make matters worse, if possible, they never paid me the two dollars apiece they promised. As a Party member, I was supposed to contribute my art to the "cause."

I was good and mad. I longed to ask my former teachers, whose integrity as artists I still respected, whether they felt that a documentary photograph was a valid document if it was captioned all out of context to make a "point."

I was even more upset later on, after the Harlem riots of 1943 in which five Negroes were killed, when social workers friendly to the Party asked the League to assemble a photographic "document" of Harlem life for display in a Negro community house. We had plenty of sordid pictures on tap for them. Students had ferreted out the shabbiest tenement doorways, the seediest gutter crapshooters, the saddest old folk, the most pathetic babies scratching for scraps in garbage cans. There is real misery in Harlem. As Photo League students we had documented every inch of it. Our picture story should have been sent to a city planner, a welfare society or Congress— somebody who could have done something about it. Instead, it was circulated among the very people it documented with a view to rousing them to action against their intolerable circumstances. If a picture could incite to riot, these pictures were just the ones to do it.

I seemed to be the only one who worried about a Red slant in photography. In those days, anyone who suggested that Photo League artists were spreading propaganda would have been called a Fascist, the favorite Commie smear word. The Office of War Information asked the League to recommend photographers to do pictures explaining the American way of life. The League, of course, saw to it that loyal comrades dedicated to overthrowing American capitalism got the paying jobs. I even got one assignment.

When I joined the Party, I worried for fear I should become personally attached to some of the people on whom I was reporting. I had even wondered what would happen if, Hollywood-fashion, I should fall in love with a Communist. In practice, the dilemma never presented itself. Unconsciously, I shrank from intimacies that might have saddled me with a feeling of loyalty to any of the people I was observing. Actually it was easy for me to keep uninvolved because very few of the comrades were people who would naturally have attracted me. These people were a drab and serious lot. A surprising number of them were in the Party because they could find no other social life. They didn't know how to have a good time, and their fanatical emotional attachment to an abstract cause was not endearing. I often felt, listening to them, that they were trying to be Communists first and human beings second. In all my experience with the Party, I don't believe I met five out of a hundred whom I would have sought as companions if I had met them under other circumstances.

One of these exceptions was Martha. Martha was neat and attractive. She always wore stunning clothes, and she was efficient in her job as financial director of the branch. I liked her because she showed a little more consideration for other people than was common in the Party. We used to sit together at branch meetings. All I knew about her, for a few months, was that she had a job as a secretary and a husband, Peter, whom she revered.

When she invited me to a meeting of the International Workers Order, I was glad of the opportunity to know her better. "You'll have to join an IWO lodge sooner or later," she advised me. "Come with me and I'll get you into Lodge 500. It's the best one. Earl Browder is in our lodge, and Elizabeth Gurley Flynn." Elizabeth Gurley Flynn, national director of women's work for the Party, was a very important person in Communist circles. I was eager to get closer to the real leaders.

The International Workers Order is a fraternal association with insurance benefits. It is divided into lodges on a national origin basis. There are Italian lodges, Spanish lodges, Irish lodges. Lodge 500 is a catchall. It meets every other week for a program that combines welfare projects and lectures and social good times about in the proportion you would find in a women's club or a service organization like Rotary.

Although I.W.O. members would vigorously deny Red influence, it was easy for good comrades like Martha to introduce resolutions, circulate petitions and postcards urging a second front, assemble Russian war relief packages and endorse "progressive" (Red-influenced) candidates for political office. You could close your eyes and imagine you were at a Party meeting, and I was often tired and bored enough to do just that.

After one of these sessions, it was a relief to stop at Martha's apartment for a nightcap. Peter was a salesman with a good job. He certainly did not look like the kind of man who could afford to be married to a Communist, and I noticed that Martha never discussed Party matters when Peter was present. Perhaps he didn't approve of his wife's Party activities and she didn't like to rub it in. Unless, of course, which seemed possible but unlikely, he didn't know she was a Party member.

Peter was an attractive and affable man. He liked me immediately, and used to put his arm around me affectionately, by way of greeting. I found both of them good company, and under their sympathetic interest I told them about my ambition for a career as a photographer.

Martha was full of helpful advice. "Peter ought to have

press pictures," she suggested. "The ones he has are frightful.
Would you like to take them?"

I studied my subject carefully in order to make a good job
of the assignment. Peter was not a good-looking man. I would
have liked to take him for what he was, a good-tempered,
friendly man of uncertain age. But I knew that he was sensitive about his appearance and wanted "glamour" pictures for
publication, so I tried to make him look younger and more
dignified than he was.

The pictures turned out well. Martha and Peter were enthusiastic. Through them, I got jobs of photographing I.W.O.
meetings and officers. Party members were always eager to help
each other out professionally, and a great deal of this type of
business came my way naturally. This work was valuable to
the F.B.I., who received a duplicate of every print. It would
prove more valuable still when I had my own studio on a full-
time professional basis, as I shall recount later.

A few weeks after the pictures were delivered, Martha asked
me to help her check the payment of dues in our branch. We
went down the membership list together. "I've paid mine,"
Martha said to herself, as she passed her own name. "And I've
got John's right here." I had noticed John's name on the membership list before, but I had never seen John. He was always
passed over without comment. I recalled being told at my first
executive meeting that he was "underground." However, I felt
that I knew Martha well enough by now to ask her the direct
question against which my agents were continually warning
me.

"Who is John?" I inquired. Martha looked up briefly from
the list.

"Don't you know? John is Peter."

I felt the blood leave my face, but there was nothing to do
but act as though I had suspected it all along. If Peter was a
Communist, anybody could be a Communist. I wondered how
many of the people I had known and liked in the past were on
the books of some Party branch under an assumed name. I had

a helpless feeling that I would never be able to trust anybody again.

I called up Ken and told him I had some news.

"What's the matter, Angela?" he asked. "You sound as if you'd just seen a ghost."

"Maybe I have," I said.

In less than an hour, we were driving uptown. It was becoming second nature for us to meet in cars. The boys would pick me up at a street corner in an unmarked F.B.I. pool car, or I would pick them up in my own car, and we would confer while riding around. We'd look out of the windows to see if anyone was following us, and turn off on a few unlikely side streets just to be sure. If we found a deserted street, we would park and look at the reports or literature I was turning in. We had to give up the "law office" when a Communist trailed another plant there. Actually the car was safer.

That day we went up to the Bronx and had something to eat in a little delicatessen. Ken and Bill explained to me that many Party members go underground not only to protect themselves, but to worm their way into positions where they can influence business organizations, labor unions and Government agencies more effectively than they could if they were known to be Communists. As a plant, I would uncover many of these secret members. I began to feel better when I realized that I had unexpectedly come upon a piece of information that was important.

I resolved never to speak my real thoughts to anyone, no matter how "safe" that person seemed to be on the surface. The most conservative acquaintance might be a secret Party member who would report my heresies. I was sure that most of the people in the organizations to which my new "friends" invited me were not Communists, but souls whom the comrades thought they could save. But how many of them were underground Party members like Peter-John? Even a comrade couldn't tell the sheep from the goats.

I tried to guess who was a member and who was not at these

meetings by watching the audience. I got into the habit of sitting in the back of the room, or in the gallery, if there was one —any place from which I could observe everyone who came in and went out. I watched known comrades carefully. It was safe to assume that at functions of this kind they would try to sit with people who were not in the Party.

During the dull programs, I memorized the faces of individuals who made it their business to know everybody. Often I could even take notes on them. And, always, I looked for an acquaintance who might be watching the show the way I was. I was sure that I had been recommended to the F.B.I. by someone who was an F.B.I. undercover agent, too.

All this while the war was draining men from homes and shops and political movements. Like millions of other able-bodied women, I got a war job in the fall of 1942. I stood, eight hours a day and longer, at a bench in a converted watch dial shop on West Twenty-third Street and burred the nicks out of machine-tooled gun parts. I was well paid—forty-five dollars a week—but my hands were always full of metal splinters and I was ready to drop every night when I came home to take up my number one war job in the Communist Party.

The Party was shorthanded and looking for women leaders. Leona was transferred uptown, and she took me and some others with her. I welcomed the shift. If I was going to masquerade as a Communist, I certainly preferred to do it among strangers. Our new branch headquarters were one block up from Madison Square Garden on the ragged western edge of the theater district. We had two rooms above a dry cleaner at 300½ West Fifty-first Street. To reach them, we had to push open a shaky door of fancy frosted glass salvaged from an Irish saloon and climb a flight of uncertain stairs.

It would have been hard to find more troubled water in which to fish. Our branch was named Melini-Douglass after an Italian and a Negro hero, but our constituency included, in addition, Puerto Ricans, Slavs, Irish, all of whom fought, sometimes literally, for sleeping space in chipped old brownstones and battered four- and five-story brick tenements. The streets were never clear of baby carriages, discarded iceboxes and bottles. Gangs of children intent on their own affairs darted familiarly in and out of dim hallways and corridors, up and down fire escapes and over roofs.

Our businessmen were hardly in the brackets to relish free enterprise, but they knew all about competition: dealers in "New and Pawnbrokers' Men's Clothing" and "Sample Dresses at Factory Prices"; foreign-language grocers; proprietors of five, ten and twenty-five cent stores full of disorder stock; an occasional young electrician or carpenter who bravely called himself a contractor. Along the sullen side streets, where the rent was cheaper, tailors, cobblers and junk men set up shop in basement apartments underneath faded shingles beckoning "transient guests" from Times Square. The most prosperous structures in our whole territory were the bars, bright spots of cleanliness and gaiety that looked as if they had been grafted on to the sick brickwork by an insensitive or downright sadistic plastic surgeon.

In that neighborhood, we functioned as much like Tammany as possible. We gave our foreign-speaking constituents free advice on legal problems along with a shot of propaganda on the second front. We allowed our poorer converts to keep the money they collected when they sold *The Daily Worker,* and we got subscriptions for *L'Unità da Popolo,* an Italian newspaper that often reprinted editorials from *The Daily Worker.* Spanish-speaking people were urged to read *Liberación,* the "progressive" Spanish paper.

Leona and I and several other imported leaders tried to give neighborhood members the impression they were running the branch, but we always decided among ourselves at the executive sessions what the branch meeting would do. Most of the time, we simply discussed how to carry out directives handed down to us from higher authority.

One day Leona came back from a session with "higher authority" with orders to hold an "evaluation" of Melini-Douglass membership. She explained the procedure.

"As comrades, we are dedicated to a voluntary discipline. That means that we cannot grow in Marxism unless we evaluate ourselves constantly. Tonight we are going to evaluate our leadership, just as the National Board evaluates its leadership. If any of you have anything to say, good or bad, about the way I and the other members of the executive board are carrying out the Party program, I want you to say it." I thought Leona was riding for a fall. She certainly didn't expect anyone to criticize her.

A young man with an Italian accent started the ball rolling in an unexpected direction. "I think the Party expects too much of new members," he said apologetically. "I think that the educational director should take into account that not all comrades are at the same level of political maturity." It was quite a speech for him, and he rolled out the new term, "level of political maturity," with pride.

"Perhaps the educational director should choose different materials," a schoolteacher suggested. The educational director said he would try. He did not want to admit that he had to present the booklets and talks and speakers that the leaders above him prescribed.

"I'd like to say that I don't think the leadership takes into account that comrades have other responsibilities besides the Party," a boy called Tim said quietly. "Personally, I resent being asked why I can't attend a meeting. If I could attend, I would."

The comrade with an Italian accent nodded eagerly. "Leona, sometimes she's bossy." There was a titter, but it only goaded him. "This is a free country. We are not children. We are in the Party because we believe. What we do for the Party comes from the heart. You cannot order the heart."

Leona flushed when the rest of us smiled. As a member of the executive board, Martha came to her rescue. "I think we will all agree that Leona is a hard worker who has never asked any of us to do anything she is not willing to do herself."

"Yes, but a leader is supposed to be a person who knows how to get other people to do things. If Leona were a more efficient cadre, she wouldn't have to do so much herself," Tim said.

I drove Leona home after the meeting and tried to comfort her. I had always thought of her as a hard-boiled character who did not care or, for that matter, even know what other people thought of her. But the comments at the evaluation had crushed her. "Am I really like that, Angie?" she asked.

"Of course not," I lied. "They're just jealous of you because you do more for the Party than they do. Don't get subjective about it."

When Leona decided that something had to be done to clear up misunderstanding of Stalin's friendship with Hitler from 1939 to 1941, she elected me to bone up on the subject and prepare a talk for the branch. The idea was that if we ourselves understood the Party's strategy thoroughly, we would be able to get it over to the neighborhood. The thought of "educating" hardened Communists dismayed me, but Leona told me that the practice in public speaking would be good training for my future work.

It was not hard to find the right phrases. They were all available in pamphlets any comrade could buy at the Worker's Bookshop. I cribbed shamelessly from Party "literature" and showed a copy of my speech to the F.B.I. agents before I gave it.

"Do you think it sounds like the real thing?" I asked, anxious as any non-professional with a speech hanging over his head.

"A masterpiece," Ken reassured me, smiling. "We'll put it in the national archives."

"Better cut my name off it, if you do," I begged. "Some file clerk might make a mistake and put Angela Cole down for a genuine comrade." I knew how efficiently the F.B.I. identified aliases. My information had already traced some of the Party names.

I felt a little foolish, but the speech went off rather well. I pointed out that Russia had tried to make a treaty with the western powers before she came to terms with Germany. She signed up only to gain time to equip the Red Army for the inevitable struggle with Fascism. Even so, it was not Russia who had broken the treaty, but Hitler. Hitler had invaded the Soviet Union. Leona liked my report so well that she had me repeat it before the general membership of the branch. She began to trust me with confidential jobs.

I never had any qualms about being one of Leona's favorites, because I knew her interest in me was political rather than personal. One day she confided that she had to go "underground" because she was going to work for the National Council of American-Soviet Friendship, as director of the Speakers' Bureau. I lost track of her when she left our branch, although I heard about her from time to time through other Party members, and always reported these bits of news to the F.B.I.

In June, 1949, after my spying days were over, I was surprised to learn that I wasn't the only F.B.I. plant on Leona's trail. The revelation came during the trial of Judith Coplon, the Justice Department employee convicted of giving secret documents to a Russian agent, when the judge insisted on reading the report of F.B.I. informant "T-1" into the record.

According to the newspapers, T-1 reported that Leona Saron got a job with the Soviet Information Bulletin. T-1 had apparently been able to get hold of Leona's application to the Soviet Embassy for the job. It described her as having attended the College of the City of New York, Hunter College and Cornell. Under the heading of experience, Leona had listed the Council of American-Soviet Friendship, one of the Soviets listening posts in America. The Associated Press remarked that "the report on the Saron woman was so detailed that it told of her arranging at one time to go to Baltimore to 'buy some Polish sausage from a Polish butcher.'"

I thought that this excerpt from a typical report was a little unfair to T-1. It made him look as if he were turning in irrelevant information. As a seasoned plant myself, I suspect

that it was well worth letting the F.B.I. know where Leona was
going and the reason she gave for the trip.

In the winter of 1942-1943 Leona was replaced as branch
organizer by a girl named Diana who was very much like her.
To Diana, the first warm days of spring meant that street meeting time had come again. At one of our branch executive
caucuses she outlined plans enthusiastically. "We'll hold the
meeting in the name of the Communist Party," she suggested
boldly, "and hope the police let us have a good corner."

I learned that in order to hold a street meeting you have to
get a permit from the police and tell them who is the sponsor.
The police didn't dare refuse us because we were Communists,
my comrades leered. But they could find reasons why we
shouldn't hold a meeting on a residential street. For our
purposes, a commercial street was less desirable than a side
street that served as the front parlor for hundreds of tenement
families.

"You'll speak, won't you, Tim?" Diana asked. Tim was
awaiting greetings from Uncle Sam.

"They'll ask me why I'm not in uniform," he objected.
"Don't you think it would be better to have a woman?"

"Don't have any girls with a strong enough voice," Diana
retorted. She was not a good speaker herself. "All right, I'll
get the section organizer. It was his idea anyway. You can help
me set up the stand."

Diana planned the work deftly, making notes in her black
book: see police; see section on speaker; borrow portable stand;
print handbill announcements; cell captains to mobilize for
distribution. "There's been some trouble with the post office
about handbills—evading postage is the charge—but I don't
think they'll bother us if we stuff the announcements under
doors. And do we have an American flag? Ought to have one
for branch meetings in wartime anyway." She made a note:
buy American flag.

"Now all we have to worry about really is the weather,"

Diana said, after we had chosen a time and place. "Angie, you make the motion tomorrow." The fiction of branch initiative had to be maintained among the rank and file. At the regular meeting, all the plans we had made were solemnly suggested from the floor. Only an astute outsider would have suspected that the arrangements were handled a little too smoothly for spontaneity.

I didn't want to distribute handbills, so I offered to bring the gear in my car. I could never have survived the Second Front campaign without Charlotte, the good-tempered Chevrolet station wagon Betty and I had bought for trips to Haverstraw. I have always had a car, even when I really couldn't afford one, and I consider myself a good driver, although my friends don't all agree. Charlotte patiently lugged my camera equipment, my friends' furniture, my comrades and all of the printed material that went with them. She didn't even groan when I stood on her roof to shoot pictures of Communist demonstrations.

Tim and I picked up the equipment at section headquarters. It was a railed-in platform four feet high and big enough to hold two people. It was an amateur piece of carpentry, made out of random two by twos, but hinged to fold flat for transportation. We had a hard time packing it into the bottom of my station wagon because one of the railings was broken. Tim grinned. "Sometimes they knock you right off the stand," he recalled.

Violence seemed improbable as we headed towards Fifty-second Street and Ninth Avenue, the good location the police had let us have after all. The weather was with us, too. The mild evening had filled the streets. Women were resting at the windows. Men home from a day of physical labor sat heavily in chairs on the sidewalk, reading the tabloids. Kids sucked popsickles. Movie marquees winked at young couples hesitating on street corners.

Something purposeful about the little knot of comrades waiting for us had already attracted the attention of passers-by. Some of them advised us how to set up the stand and hang our small flag over the broken rail. Comrades assigned to hand out leaflets ("Get the Real Facts on the War!") took up their posts on the edge of the crowd, where they would not interfere with the speakers. I counted fifty listeners, exclusive of kids, some of whom, I suspected, were trying to smuggle themselves under the stand. As branch organizer, Diana opened the meeting.

"Friends, neighbors, comrades! This meeting is being held under the auspices of the Communist Party. . . ." There was a derisive catcall, but I was much more worried about a small rustling under her feet. I crawled underneath the platform and hauled out a squirming little boy. He sprinted away while the crowd giggled. Diana turned the meeting over to the main speaker as fast as she could. He was a seasoned street orator:

"We in the Communist Party know what you're paying for milk. We know how you're being gouged on rent. We're trying to help you hold the line. But while we stand here talking, the British and the Russians are dying by the thousands. We have the tanks, the guns, the planes to lick Hitler now. What kind of Americans are we to let other people fight for us?"

"Wouldn't the Army have you?" a soldier in uniform asked.

"The Fascist way of imperialism has changed its character and become a people's war. Ever since Hitler treacherously attacked the Soviet Union . . ."

"So you fell out of bed with them, eh! What did your Stalin expect when he cuddled up to Hitler? Serves him right!" The new heckler had an Irish brogue. Our speaker stood his ground.

"A very misunderstood treaty, sir. I'd like to answer your question at the end of the meeting."

Plop! A paper bag full of water, aimed by the little boy I had discovered earlier, drenched a girl in the audience.

"Damned Communists," a man near me muttered. Others took up the cry.

"Go back to Russia!"

There were several soldiers, now, moving in on our crowd.

Tim tugged at my wrist. "I think we can make it to the car if we go now," he said. "That's the police for you—never there when they can do any good."

I did not know whether I was glad or sorry that the police had not sent a patrolman to cover the meeting. As it turned out, Tim's fears were premature. Our audience was unsympathetic rather than angry. We finished the program a little sooner than we expected, perhaps, but we managed to retreat in good order. I was personally relieved that there had been no trouble that might have exposed me to attention in the newspapers.

The one serious close call I had during the Melini-Douglass days blew up without warning. One night, later in 1943, my roommate Betty and I were spending a quiet evening at home. I was finishing an F.B.I. report in the bedroom. Betty, who sensed that I wanted to be alone, was reading in the living room. The bell rang, and I let Betty answer it. Before I could find a place to hide my report, I heard Diana's voice in the living room. The two had heard of each other, but they had never met. If I left them alone even for a minute, they would undoubtedly strike up a conversation which might prove embarrassing to both of them—and to me. I picked up a rubber stamp lying on my desk, marked my envelope "Photographs Do Not Bend," and sailed into the living room.

"Betty, this is Diana from the Photo League," I said rapidly, hoping that Diana would take the hint that she was not to mention the Party. I had told Diana that it wasn't worth while recruiting Betty to the Party because she was too sick to do active work, but I hadn't dared tell her that Betty was a violent anti-Communist.

Diana acknowledged the introduction with her best recruiting smile. "What are you reading?" she asked, picking up Betty's book. Luckily it was a novel without political implications, but I didn't want to get Betty going on literature. I had to get Diana out of the house and I couldn't leave an F.B.I. report lying on my desk.

"I've got to mail some photographs, Diana," I said boldly. "Want to walk down to the corner with me?" I went into the bedroom to get my coat and Diana followed.

"We've got to deliver next year's Party cards," she whispered. "Here are the new ones for five comrades in your neighborhood. You have to hand them over personally. Pick up the old cards and return them to me to be destroyed." She slipped me a little packet from her briefcase, and for a second time in five minutes I looked around my bedroom for a good place to hide papers. Diana followed my eyes. "You have to keep them on your person at all times they are in your possession," she warned. I tucked them in my handbag.

"I'm sorry I can't stay but a minute," she said in a loud conversational voice for the benefit of Betty in the other room. "Here, I'll mail these photographs for you on my way."

I watched with horror as she picked up my envelope. It was addressed to a fictitious cover that the F.B.I. used as a drop. She read the address curiously. It was on the tip of my tongue to tell her that the photographs had been ordered by an out-of-town client who wanted them sent to him general delivery. But no explanation at all was better than an elaborate one.

"Don't you think you ought to put a piece of carboard in to protect the pictures?" she suggested.

"They're just rough proofs," I said with relief. "I'll take them down to the corner myself. I need a little walk."

It was not a very pleasant walk to the corner. Diana carried my report and asked me what I was doing to recruit Betty to the Party. I told her I felt it best to proceed slowly.

"You really ought to tell her about the Party," Diana reproved. "You should let her know how you feel." It was hard for me to hold up my end of a conversation like that when all I could think of was the envelope she had in her hand. Diana finally put it in the post box herself. "Those cards have to be delivered before the meeting Tuesday," she said, as we parted.

I called Bill South from the drugstore so that I would not have to talk in front of Betty. "I've got five Party cards," I reported. "I can only hold them until Tuesday. I'm supposed to keep them with me all the time."

"Whose cards are they?" Bill asked.

"Don't know yet," I said. "They're in my handbag, but I'm in a public phone booth, and I don't want to take them out."

"Never mind," Bill said. "Can you meet me tomorrow morning at eight? I'll get them photostated and back to you the same day."

"Let's not make it too early," I pleaded. I hate to get up a minute before I have to.

"How about eight at the main post office on Thirty-fourth Street? You don't have to speak to me. You can pass the package to me at the writing desk nearest the money order windows."

"Why not the Twenty-third Street Independent subway station?" I countered. It was the stop nearest my work. "It will be full of people at eight thirty. I'll pass you near the change booth on the uptown side and hand you a newspaper."

"Right," Bill agreed. "Uptown change booth Twenty-third Street station of the Eighth Avenue at eight thirty." Agents always repeat the time and place of a rendezvous.

After Betty went to sleep on the studio couch, I took my handbag into the bathroom and looked at the cards. One of them was for a precinct leader of the American Labor Party. His Party card record would be of some importance to the Government if he were ever elected or appointed to a city office.

I got off at Twenty-third Street next morning at exactly eight twenty-eight. Hordes of workers were streaming past me to the exits. I pretended I was looking for a lost coin or something. But you can only do this for so long.

"Lost something, miss?" the man at the change booth called to me between spurts of traffic. I shook my head, put a nickel in the turnstile, and moved out of his range. I mentally kicked myself for suggesting that we meet during a subway rush. In one way, the crowd was a protection. But the more people, the more chance of encountering someone I knew.

When Bill didn't show at eight thirty-five, I walked out of the station, looked over the magazines on the paper stand, crossed over the street and went down the other entrance. Patience is not one of my virtues. I hate to wait for anyone or anything. This was going to make me late for work. I was thinking black thoughts when Bill steamed into view, looking very apologetic. I silently handed him my copy of *The New York Times* and walked past him. It was lucky for him that I couldn't give him a piece of my Greek temper right then and there.

Bill couldn't have been more contrite when I finally reached him on the phone at lunchtime. In order to save me a second trip, he made an exception to the rule and met me practically on my doorstep. The next time I saw Diana I was able to turn in all the old membership cards, none the worse for having been photostated.

The Party's efforts to open up a Second Front grew more frenzied as the battle of Stalingrad intensified. In addition to their own "struggling," Communists had to play audience for the second front agitation of groups inspired by the Party. Our branch received blocs of invitations to dinners—often ten dollars a ticket—to rallies, and to meetings intended to reach special groups and prove to them, by a large and enthusiastic turnout, that "everybody" believed in rescuing Russia now.

We had to go to a youth rally at Town Hall sponsored by the junior divisions of organizations ranging from the Sons of Italy to the Unitarian Church. Their adult advisors were well distributed, too: Paul McNutt, Wendell Willkie, Newbold Morris, Fiorello La Guardia.

On another occasion, we were ordered to bring as many people as possible to an outdoor mass meeting in Union Square. It was timed for five o'clock to catch employees released from offices. Earl Browder, Israel Amter, Vito Marcantonio and William Z. Foster got up and demanded that the United States keep its "written pledge" (Molotov and Roosevelt had discussed the subject once, the papers reported) to open a Second

Front in 1942. One enthusiastic speaker called on the authorities to open a Second Front before the clock struck midnight. Vito Marcantonio shouted, "Are we going to wait for Hitler to open a Second Front?" Forty thousand trade unionists and friends shouted back, "No."

Rallies as big as this were reported in the newspapers, of course, but the F.B.I. was anxious to get its own report in addition. Newspapers seldom carried all the facts that the Bureau wanted: which speakers said what, and who sat where on the platform, and even who was conspicuously absent. I was also able to report comments of comrades which indicated the popularity of the speakers within the Party. Because it was well known that I was connected with the Photo League, I could take pictures of big rallies without arousing suspicion. It was all chalked up to extra Party zeal. Comrades even made way for me when I came through the crowd with my camera.

I was trying to catch all the speakers on the stand at a big meeting at Madison Square park when a woman with a full skirt and a peasant shawl over her head tapped me timidly. "Please to tell me," she said. "Are you Margaret Bourke-White?" Margaret Bourke-White had just published her *Shooting the Russian War*. My questioner was obviously from the old country, but she was politically more sophisticated than many of the dupes in the crowd who spoke perfect English. At least she connected the speakers with Russia! She was so anxious to go home and tell her family that she had stood beside the famous woman photographer that I couldn't help obliging her. I smiled and nodded my head.

After my shots were taken, I joined thousands of other comrades and sympathizers in yelling, "Open up a Second Front, Open up a Second Front," until we were all dizzy, and a little drunk with the sound of thousands of voices, chanting rhythmically in unison. No cheer leaders directed us, but it was easy to know just when to shout. We listened as the speaker's voice grew louder and louder, angrier and angrier. When he reached full climax, it was our turn to howl.

Mass rallies like this depressed me, but they did a great deal to reassure me that my work with the F.B.I. was worth while. In branch meetings, where I saw the inefficiency, the narrowness and the stupidity of individual Communists, I was often tempted to feel that the whole movement wasn't worth watching. But when I saw the same tactics convert thousands of presumably thinking human beings into well-organized robots I realized, with a shudder, that the Communists could do a great deal of damage. I longed to shake my neighbors by the arm and say to them, "Do you have the faintest idea why you are shouting?" But of course they couldn't know. The only way to find out was to go through the boring process of working inside the Party.

When I look back over the seven years I spent in the Communist Party, I can remember waiting for my cue to second a motion better than I can remember the motion or the name of the front organization holding the meeting. I can remember the face of Earl Browder spotlighted in Madison Square Garden better than I can remember what he said. Meetings at which the speaker thundered for the draft of eighteen year olds for overseas service blur in my mind with similar meetings at which the speaker thundered against the peacetime draft. Even though my memory is considered above average, I was glad to have my reports to refer back to. There is a reason for this trick of memory: in the Party the "struggles" change, but the daily duties to promote them remain the same. The very standardization that makes the Party's propaganda effective is a hallmark by which its influence can always be recognized.

5. PARTY ORGANIZATION

THE COMMUNIST PARTY pretends to be democratic. Actually, an ordinary member has as little to say about choosing his leaders as an ordinary citizen in Russia. I learned how a Communist "election" is handled while I was still working with Diana. When it came time to choose new officers, Diana read a slate to the executive board of the branch. There was just one candidate for each office: the present incumbent.

"Won't there be nominations from the floor?" I asked.

"Of course not," Diana said. "The executive *is* the branch." She sounded like the Episcopalian deaconess who had told me in Sunday School that the Word *is* God. And this pattern held throughout my experience in the Party.

I was included in the executive category from the very first summer I spent in the Party. I pinch-hit for branch functionaries as early as 1943. When the Party dissolved and became the Communist Political Association during 1944-1945 (as will be described in a later chapter), I held the specially created post of recording secretary. After the Party was formally reconstituted in 1945, I was literature director, educational director and financial director of the Columbus Hill Branch. When that branch was split in 1947, I became branch organizer of one of its successors. In 1948 I became co-section organizer of the

West Midtown Section as well as organizer of the West Midtown Branch.

Like every other Communist functionary, I was nominated for these posts by the executives of the next higher body, in my case the Columbus Hill and West Midtown sections, later members of the New York County Committee. They chose me strictly on the basis of my achievement in Party work. They got their information about me from regular weekly reports of membership directors, in which the Party activities of every member were detailed down to the number of copies of *The Daily Worker* each had sold in the week. In addition, they had a stack of Party biographies, beginning with the report Leona had made on me when I joined.

Every year, and every time I was chosen to attend a leadership school, I had to bring this basic biography up to date by filling out a new questionnaire on my name, address, age, parentage, work history, education, the names of comrades I had recruited if any, the mass organizations to which I belonged and my work in them, my religion, and the occupations of my relatives. I had to be careful there were no discrepancies.

In New York City, branches and sections are close enough to the county and state authorities so that these written reports can be delivered personally. But the membership secretary of an out-of-town district (New York City has regions instead of districts) had to send his reports to the state membership director by devious channels, usually a mail drop.

When the district leader of Buffalo, for instance, has written his general report and his personnel reports on onionskin paper in triplicate, he mails them to an individual in New York City who has no outward connection with the Party. Many people who are not members serve the Party in this way. Mail drops seldom function for long at a time. It's safer to rotate them. According to an ex-Communist I know, one trusted mail drop was a physician.

As soon as the doctor received the letter, he phoned his "contact" with the Party and talked with him as if to a patient.

At some point in the conversation, he indicated a convenient time for the contact to visit the office, presumably for treatment. The document was always handed over without comment.

One copy of every personnel report goes to the National Review Commission, the agency responsible for Party security against police and F.B.I. agents. Another is retained by the state authorities. For comrades who hold state or national office, the procedure is a little different. One copy of each report on them goes to the Cominform in Budapest. Another goes directly to Moscow. According to an ex-National Committee member of the Party, none of the defendants in the case against the eleven Communists could have attained his position in the Party without the approval of Soviet Party leaders.

I am no authority on the upper echelons of the Communist Party. I took my orders from New York County Committee officials who did not tell me more than I needed to know to carry out my local duties. But I have been able to piece out Party gossip with information from the files of *Counterattack*, a weekly news bulletin of Communist activities published by several former F.B.I. agents who resigned from the Bureau in order to fight Communism by giving the public information on it. The present publishers of *Counterattack* are none other than my very good friends, Ken Bierly, Ted Kirkpatrick, and Jack Keenen who left the Bureau in 1946.

Now that none of us has any connection with the F.B.I., Ted and Ken have been able to make a great many of my experiences in the Party clear. Everything they have told me about the upper reaches of the Party is an extension of what we did in the upper branches and sections to which I belonged.

The prescription for advancement in the Party is basically the same at all levels. Theoretical grasp of Marxism is respected, but the Party isn't interested in promoting "spittoon philosophers" who do not get out and influence the masses. They want red hot agitators. The quickest way up the ladder is to acquire a following in a trade union controlling a basic industry such as steel, mining, shipping, meat packing, automobile manufacture or publishing.

If a comrade distinguishes himself in leading a successful strike or putting over a successful demonstration, the Party will send him to a leadership school where he will be taught Marxism. There are leadership schools at all echelons, from the schools for New York County leaders which I attended on up to the Lenin School in Russia where national leaders are sent for further training.

Most important for a comrade ambitious to rise is the rating the National Review Commission gives him on Party loyalty. Party loyalty at all echelons is defined as zeal in attendance at meetings, work in trade unions and civic organizations useful to the Party, willingness to do emergency jobs for the Party, success in recruiting, fund raising and the sale of literature. The National Review Commission can consult its file of membership reports on any comrade and ascertain his Party loyalty at a moment's notice. It is assisted in its work by State Review Commissions that report to it.

If any comrade is delinquent in his Party duty, fails to attend meetings or do Party work; if he differs from the Party line in public, or expresses any criticism of the Party's policy to any other member, the Review Commission may order a special investigation. Sometimes the comrade in question is called in and reprimanded, the way Leona reprimanded Elaine. If there is any suspicion that the comrade is an F.B.I. agent, however, he won't be told he is being investigated.

The Review Commission keeps close tabs on the membership because it is the duty of every member to report bits of conversation which indicate political instability in any other member. All these conversations are noted on the comrade's file. The National Review Commission uses the methods of the Soviet secret police on which it is patterned.

One of its favorite checks is to get the suspected comrade to fill out a number of different questionnaires at different times.

If they don't agree on some detail, such as birthplace, the discrepancy is filed for future use against him.

Often an older Party member will flatter a suspected comrade by asking his candid opinion of a policy under discussion. If his opinion is unfavorable, his remarks are reported to the security arm of the Party. The same provocative method of getting evidence of Party disloyalty is more easily practiced by a secret Communist. Subtle discussions on general topics can often trap a comrade into unorthodox sentiments he would never express to a person he knew was a fellow Communist.

A suspect is frequently tailed. In an up-state New York city, one comrade saw another go into a police station. He reported it to his district organizer, who asked the comrade what business he had with the police. The organizer accepted the explanation given, but he had the suspect followed. Eventually, his association with the police was uncovered and he was expelled at an open meeting of the Party.

A suspected comrade can be given a piece of misinformation which will turn up in the hands of the police if he is reporting to them. For example, a leader will be told that a secret demonstration at the city hall is planned for a certain time and place. He is warned not to tell anyone else, not even fellow comrades. If there is an extra patrol of policemen at city hall at the appointed hour, the presumption is that he told them.

As the highest levels, clever women operators are assigned to check the Party loyalty of national leaders whom the Communist International representatives distrust or want to discredit for some reason. These hardworking and loyal girls don't stop at going to bed with their quarries. Some of them have made daily reports on leaders with whom they have been intimate for years. It's easy for them to draw out seemingly innocent information which the Review Commission can check against its records. Very few men, even Communists, will remember to be discreet when a sweetheart asks intimate details of their childhood. Yet a query about birthplace or parentage will often reveal a different story from what the member has told on some questionnaire in the past.

The most startling performance of a Communist girl spy was revealed several years ago in the divorce case of a Negro comrade. Before the war, the Party sent him to the Lenin School in Moscow where promising Communist leaders from all over the world come to learn guerrilla warfare, sabotage, espionage and other arts useful to a revolutionary. While he was in Russia, he joined African Negro students at the Lenin School in accusing white students of white chauvinism, one of the Marxist sins. Earl Browder and James W. Ford of the American National Committee went to Moscow to iron out the difficulties. When the man returned, the National Review Commission assigned a white Party girl to watch him. He fell in love with her and persuaded her to marry him, although her bosses in the Party warned her not to. After the marriage she continued her frequent reports to the Review Commission. Her husband strayed further and further away from the orthodoxy required of a national leader.

When the strain of this contrived marriage grew unbearable for the wife, she appealed to the Party for help. One of the Party leaders asked the man to sign an affidavit admitting adultery to facilitate a divorce suit in New York State. He replied that he had not committed adultery and would sign no such affidavit. Aside from the moral issue involved, he feared that the Party might use the document against him in public. Heartbroken—and enraged—he left the Party.

National officers are watched more closely than the lower cadres because they are responsible to the authorities "overseas" or "across," as Communists refer to Russia. "Visitors" from abroad choose the National Committee and the National Board just as section and county officials designate the officers of branches under them. The National Committee is the top governing body of the American Party. Its executive committee is the National Board, which Communists themselves nickname the "Politburo" after its Russian counterpart. When the Government moved against the Party in 1948, the District Attorney indicted all the members of the National Board at the time. Although it is theoretically chosen by the National Committee, it rules the National Committee the way the executive board of a branch rules the branch, and everyone on the Politburo lives in deathly fear of the "C.I. reps" from abroad. These C.I. reps were formerly representatives of the Comintern. Now they are sent from the Cominform in Budapest. Their functions have not changed.

C.I. reps are usually European Communists from the English, French, German or Finnish parties. They often enter the United States illegally and take false, English-sounding names. They say very little, but they listen closely, attend meetings of the National Committee, roam about headquarters at Twelfth Street, and travel all over the country to observe the Party in action. American Communist leaders obey their every suggestion. Through the detailed personnel reports kept by the National Review Commission they are in a position to locate loyal comrades who can help Soviet espionage agents in search of specific information on industry or politics.

Leaders on my level of the Party had very little to do with the members of the American Politburo. We saw and heard them at the big rallies in Madison Square Garden and listened silently and respectfully when they spoke to groups of county and section leaders. They were almost mythical creatures to us, but we had our own opinions of them.

William Z. Foster, chairman of the National Board after 1946, was not well liked. The usual comment on him was that he was not as good a leader as Earl Browder, whom he replaced. The two hated each other, probably because, as everyone in the Party believed, Stalin played one against the other. They were related politically like the man and wife on the barometer. If foul weather drove Browder inside, Foster was sure to come out.

Foster had come up the hard and violent labor union path. He had his heart set on being national leader of the Party ever since Stalin passed him over in the early 1920s, and he had made many trips to Russia. One of his assets, and a handy one in the Party, was a willingness to swallow huge doses of political humiliation. The comrades accepted Foster in 1946, when a revolutionary line was part of Stalin's cold war plans, but they personally enjoyed the war period in which Browder's more "American" orientation was useful to the Kremlin.

Foster could not compare to Browder in the personal magnetism which binds political workers to their standard bearers. He is a repetitious and uninspired speaker, which may have given rise to the story that he gulped whiskey instead of water at the rostrum. He impressed the Party intellectuals as a rough-and-ready fellow, bright but untutored. Some of them maliciously mimicked his mispronunciation of words.

Eugene Dennis, secretary of the National Board and second in command to Foster, is a tall handsome man who was widely regarded in the Party as a lady-killer. He was Foster's man. I used to catch glimpses of him riding in his chauffeur-driven car on his way to work at national headquarters from his home in the Bronx. All the national leaders have bodyguards.

The career of Dennis in the Party is a typical Communist success story. He was born Francis Eugene Waldron in 1905 in Seattle, Washington, a strong labor town, and joined the Party in the twenties. He distinguished himself by organizing workers and the unemployed in California, and went to China in the thirties, visiting Moscow en route. In 1935 he headed the Wisconsin State Committee of the Party, but he left to serve in the Civil War in Spain in 1937. On his return, he was rewarded with a post on the National Committee in New York. He became general secretary of the National Board and the Party in 1946, when Foster came to power.

Ben Davis, who became a New York City councilman in 1943, was one of the best liked of the top brass. I met him when I was working for his election in the American Labor Party. He impressed me as a powerful speaker with humor and more appeal than Marcantonio, the A.L.P.'s loud-mouthed orator. He became a Communist when he defended Angelo Herndon, a

Negro Communist organizer in Georgia who was indicted
under an old slave law. Davis was brought to New York to
assist in the fight for Negro rights. As a Negro graduate of
Amherst and of Harvard Law School, he was one of the defense
attorneys for the Scottsboro boys accused of rape, who have become one of the Party's *causes célèbres,* though they were not
themselves Communists. He is president of the company that
owns *The Daily Worker,* as well as chairman of the Party's
legislative committee.

I was able to identify nine of the eleven indicted leaders
when I testified at the trial. The only ones I had not seen
personally in the course of my Party work were Gus Hall,
chairman of the Ohio Party, and Carl Winter, chairman of the
Michigan Party, both of whom were stationed out of New York
City.

Gil Green, Illinois chairman of the Party, was New York
State chairman at the time I was recruited in 1942. John
Williamson, the Party's labor secretary, taught at Communist
schools I attended. John Gates, editor of *The Daily Worker,*
was a frequent speaker at closed meetings in New York City.
His wife, Lillian Gates, has recently been active in fighting the
Feinberg law requiring New York State teachers to take oaths
of loyalty to the United States.

Bob Thompson, New York State chairman, was frequently
the presiding officer at meetings I attended. He was the Party's
war hero, having won the Distinguished Service Cross in New
Guinea, but he was a veteran of the San Francisco general strike
of 1934 and the Spanish Civil War as well. I remember him as
a sulky character in baggy tweeds, who was so bad a public
speaker that he embarrassed his audiences.

Henry Winston, organizational secretary of the Party, was
elevated to the National Board in 1946 after his discharge from
the Army. He was another comrade whose war record made
him a valuable addition to the top brass at a time when the
Party was in trouble.

Jack Stachel,* the Party's national director of agitation, propaganda and education, wasn't elected to the National Board until 1945, but I had noticed him before that time as one of the mysterious comrades who always hung around the speakers, somewhere on the platform, at big mass rallies. The report in the Party was that he had been handling "European affairs" for many years. I didn't meet him until 1948.

Under these leaders, the Party spread all over the country in state, district, county, section, branch and cell units, all faithful reproductions of the top bodies which are themselves modelled on the Communist Party of the Soviet Union. The largest concentration of comrades is in New York City, which accounts for one fourth to one third of the national membership. In 1948 there were four hundred branches in New York County alone.

This is the core. Around it is a vast demi-world of underground units, front organizations, secret members, "members at large" who function as members without cards, sympathizers, dupes and unwilling cooperators trapped into furthering the Party's ends.

I always worked in a community branch which agitated in a given number of city blocks, as a unit of the Communist Party. Our meeting rooms, when we had them, sometimes bore a sign, "Communist Party Headquarters." I soon stumbled on other branches, organized on a cultural, professional or trade union basis, which never appeared publicly and even kept their existence a secret from other Party members.

When I attended the New York County Convention in 1948, I heard secret reports from these cultural sections. There were branches, and in some cases enough branches to make up whole sections, of doctors, dentists, lawyers, writers, teachers, actors, photographers, social workers, government employees and many other key professional groups. They put out the Party line among their colleagues, infiltrate professional societies, recruit

* Stachel wrote the Preface to *Peter's Manual.*

likely members of their own fields to the Party, and are, of course, in a position to raise substantial funds.

In addition, they all stood ready to contribute their own special services. The girl who got me into the UOPWA was in the advertising department of a large magazine. Barbara, a girl I was later to know very well, was for a time a volunteer psychiatric worker. I don't know what help Barbara gave to the comrades, but I do know that "progressive" social workers often used their positions to obligate relief clients to the Party. As a photographer, I helped to "document" the shocking social scenes which the Party cited as examples of the failures of capitalism. Lawyers in the Party defended Communists when they landed in jail. Even the doctors in the Party were pressed into service. During the civil war in Spain, they examined comrades on their way to fight with the Loyalists.

Understandably enough, individuals prefer to work in a cultural branch where they can utilize their own skills. They get out of most of the Jimmy Higgins legwork. Since cultural branches are secret, members are better protected from the nuisance of being known as Communists. Comrades are always talking about "transferring to cultural." In order to qualify, they have to prove that they are important enough in their own fields to be of actual use to the Party there. Party functionaries are very loath to release anyone who can be made to do the uninspiring daily Communist work.

There is some bad blood between cultural branches and community branches. The underground workers think they are "better" than the community units. This always amuses me, because it was so clear a case of "bourgeois" snobbery, just the thing the Party claimed it was fighting against. Community branches retorted that cultural groups didn't do any work and were ready to run and hide at the first sign of trouble.

In 1948, I declined an invitation to join the photographers' branch on the ground that I preferred the hard spadework of neighborhood work. I managed to sound like a very zealous comrade, but I had my own reasons for declining. I was finding out more for the F.B.I. in community work than I would have found out if I had limited my contacts to photographers.

There are all kinds of loose groups and underground individuals kicking around in the Party. In 1947, when I was branch organizer in Hell's Kitchen, I stumbled on a whole branch that was underground. I was sitting beside Dotty, my section membership director, at a rather dull meeting of section leaders at the Thomas Jefferson Section on West Seventy-second Street. Dotty and I used to write each other notes like kids in school while we listened to the usual harangues. As I leaned over to read her reply to a note I'd written her—I think it was something about a civil service opening that she wanted me to try for—I noticed a Branch X on her list of section branches. As casually as possible, I asked her about it.

"It's a catchall for foreign comrades waiting to go back to Europe," she said. In other words, Branch X was an accommodation for members of European Communist parties temporarily in the United States. Apparently there were enough of these refugees in the West Seventies and Eighties of New York City to make it worthwhile to locate the branch in the Thomas Jefferson Section. I never learned any more about Branch X, but it was obviously working under orders from the international organization of the Party.

Individuals may be transferred from one group to another or may "drop out of the Party" either by secret expulsion or on a secret mission of one kind or another. In order to cover their tracks from other members, they frequently transfer so many times that the membership records get lost. Sometimes the mission is work in a front organization not yet ripe for official members of the Party. Sometimes it is work on an election campaign in which the candidate the Party hopes to keep in its pocket would be hampered by the frank allegiance of Communist workers. Sometimes the mission is espionage for the Party, or even for the Soviet Union. A good comrade who notices that another has disappeared may speculate, but he doesn't speculate out loud.

I've had at least two run-ins with secret members. One day Sue, my membership secretary, checked over a list of members who hadn't paid their dues. I spied an unfamiliar name on the list—clearly a slip-up because I should have known all the members in the branch for which I was organizer.

"Who's Helen Brown?" I asked.

"She's one of the people I have to see personally," Sue said. I tried not to look surprised, but I arranged to go along with Sue when she called on this mysterious Helen Brown.

We went to an apartment house in a fashionable midtown street and Sue pushed a bell labelled Mitchell. Helen Brown was the wife of a leader of the American Communication Association whom the union was trying to expel as a Communist. Both he and his wife were ordered to lie low. Mrs. Mitchell, in fact, smuggled us into the kitchen while a union exec. meeting was going on in the living room. I found later that the Bureau had the proof on Mitchell, but of course they couldn't have told the union even if the union had applied to them. The F.B.I. can give its information only on request from Federal agencies or the courts.

Before Mike Quill, the Transport Workers Union chief, started wavering in his allegiance to the Party, a woman, a secret Party member, was placed in his office as a spy. Quill's transport workers were pressing him to reverse the Party's stand for the five-cent fare, so that they could get a wage increase. Quill probably knew that the woman in his office was a spy, but he evidently kept her on in hope of learning what the Party would do to him if and when he did leave. She notified Party authorities just before he renounced Communism, and the Party was able to reply instantly with a propaganda campaign against him for saddling the workers with a ten-cent fare. They dubbed him "Mike the Dime" and the name stuck.

Fragmentary revelations like these suggested a vast penumbra of shadowy activity. I touched this underworld of Communism directly only when a strange comrade who called himself Ralph visited me and asked me if I would serve as a courier in the underground just before I took the stand in Judge Medina's court. Unattached as these individuals seemed to be, we working comrades were always sure that they were acting under strict orders from the higher-ups, perhaps even from the Communist International itself. We treated them with respect, boasted on the slimmest acquaintance that we knew them, and were careful to avoid any loose talk that might expose them.

Somewhat ambiguous were the positions of national figures like Leon Josephson, lawyer and Communist International leader, who were more useful to the Party in front organizations. Some, like Josephson, admitted they were Communists although they held no regular job in the Party.

Contrary to the general opinion, the Party isn't financed with "Moscow gold" as it was in its early days. It's financed here— and we even send money to Russia through "relief organizations." The actual sums of money spent by the Party are, however, deceptive. Many services and a great deal of the materials necessary to the conduct of a propaganda program are contributed free.

Often it is not necessary for funds to enter the Communist Party treasury at all. One front organization with a heavy treasury can be made to contribute to another with a light treasury which is in a position to do some of the Party's urgent business. The I.W.O. made contributions to many of the lesser fronts. Trade unions with Communist leanings could often be made to contribute to fronts, as did many well-meaning but uninformed non-Communists. Over in Hell's Kitchen, we regularly collected money to send representatives of tenants' leagues and other local groups to Washington. Thousands of dollars might be collected all over the city to send two delegates. When the less permanent fronts folded, no accounting was made of their funds. A good example is the short-lived American People's Mobilization formed to get America into the war when Germany invaded Russia. It took over the substantial assets in leading cities of the American Peace Mobilization which had energetically opposed American intervention when Germany

and Russia were friends. The new A.P.M.'s funds found their
way to sympathetic trade unions and other organizations.

Except in New York City, most branches do not even rent
headquarters of their own, and even here at the present time
they have taken to meeting in the apartments of members.
Branch organizers aren't paid, although they sometimes spend
twenty to thirty hours a week on Party work. Wherever possible, they get on the payrolls of front organizations or labor
unions. I knew many Party functionaries who were on relief,
collecting unemployment insurance, or "studying" on the G.I.
bill of rights. A functionary who actually has to earn his own
living usually cannot stand the load of work very long, and for
this reason branch functionaries are always changing.

The first paid members in the hierarchy of the Party are
section organizers, although the burden of their salary is often
shifted to the branches or the trade unions. Salaries are low,
but Party leaders often find ways of augmenting them, such as
accepting loans which they are not expected to repay. Earl
Browder received only forty-five dollars a week for his services,
but he made many times that amount in royalties on Party
literature which all members were required to buy.

About twenty to thirty percent of the Party's funds are de-
rived from members' dues. Dues are based on the income of
members, but they are assessed on an honor system. They vary
from time to time but have seldom been as high as five dollars
a month for the highest brackets. At least twenty percent of
the revenue from dues is supposed to remain with the branch,
but higher bodies are always raiding branch treasuries. The
section might send the branch a block of unsalable tickets, or
set a fund quota so high that it could not be met, through individual contributions but only through a direct appropriation
from the branch treasury.

Another fifteen percent of the Party's money comes from the
forced sale of Party literature, a very neat publishing trick indeed. Earl Browder's Teheran story is a good example of the
way the same "literature" was sold to comrades five and six

times over, each time at a price which afforded Browder a royalty as well as a return to the Party.

On December 12, 1943, Earl Browder made a speech at Bridgeport, Connecticut, entitled "Results of Teheran." This speech was reprinted in the January, 1944, issue of *The Communist,* the theoretical organ of the Party to which all good comrades are supposed to subscribe. But they also had to buy it in a five-cent pamphlet published by the Workers Library. In April, 1944, the same comrades were asked to buy the same material in a bound edition of a book entitled, *Teheran—Our Path in War and Peace,* International Publishers. In June, 1944, the Bridgeport speech was bundled together with other speeches saying the same things in a ten-cent pamphlet entitled "The Road Ahead to Victory and Lasting Peace."

This repetitious "literature" goes out to all branches, each of whom is ordinarily given a quota. Sometimes each member has to take five or ten copies in order to make good on the quota. Theoretically, these members are supposed to sell the speech to their friends, but actually most of them simply pay for them and give them away if they can.

Over fifty percent of the Party's money comes from fund drives. There were often three a year. One was for *The Daily Worker,* which was continuously losing money. Another could be expected for the Party itself. And a third was always held to meet some emergency. In the past few years there have been as many as three or four "emergency" fund drives in a year.

Every member is supposed to contribute two weeks' salary to each fund drive, although he may raise this money from friends and acquaintances if he doesn't have it himself. Branch executive committees usually decide how much each member can stand, and plan to raise a part at least of the branch quota by some fund-raising activity. Sometimes we would raffle off a book. Sometimes we sold tickets to the Irving Theater, where Russian movies are displayed, and put the profits into our fund drive account. And always there were fund-raising parties at which drinks were sold at a profit. Well-to-do members with connections in front organizations were often able to give parties of this kind to non-Party friends without revealing where the money was going. Wealthy comrades, especially those in the entertainment field, often parted with considerable sums.

Toward the end of a fund drive, when the branch was hounded by section, regional and county finance directors, methods were used which would make a collection agent or a loan shark cringe. I remember getting a dollar out of a woman who hadn't paid her electric bill and was afraid the company would turn off the lights. She offered us a dime, but we turned it down in contempt.

"Comes the revolution," my companion said grandly, "you will get electricity free."

Poor comrades often got loans from their families or friends to meet their fund drive quotas. One veteran I knew had been hounded so unmercifully that he threw his twenty-five dollars on the table at branch headquarters and announced his resignation. But he paid up before he left.

With well-to-do members, we used shame tactics. I once called on the wife of a garment manufacturer at a suite in a fashionable hotel. We had decided to get one hundred dollars out of her. She offered us ten dollars and some liquor for a fund-raising party. She explained that she was contributing heavily to Palestine relief. My companion, Rena Klein, eyed her bourgeois furnishings accusingly.

"You are living in luxury while many workers are starving. We will not accept ten dollars from you." It sounds almost unbelievable, but that is exactly what she said. Our victim explained that she had to live somewhere, but she was very apologetic about it. We left with a pledge for considerably more than ten dollars.

The highest contribution I ever made was eighty dollars, an assessment I succeeded in cutting down from an original estimate I would have been ashamed to ask the Government to contribute. Looking over my past expense accounts, I find that it cost the Bureau something like thirty dollars a month to maintain me in good standing with the Party. The figure includes dues, literature, rally and meeting tickets, special dinners, miscellaneous local contributions, and expenses of my membership in front organizations. When the comrades began running up my phone bill on "official business" I turned in part of it to the Bureau, but I never bothered to count the mileage I put on my car carrying comrades to picket lines, demonstrations and meetings. I charged the Bureau for the materials I used when I took pictures especially for them at mass rallies, but I did not charge them for my services as a photographer.

Like others in the Party, I often complained that I was cleaned of loose change at every branch meeting. It was always twenty-five cents here toward a telegram of protest, a dollar there toward sending a comrade to a Washington convention, or two dollars toward the strike fund of a friendly trade union, whom we wanted to impress.

The Communist Party is an organization of human beings with all the problems of such organizations. It binds its members to secrecy, but so does a high school fraternity. It is run by a few top leaders through layers of local, regional and state bodies, but so are the Boy Scouts of America. It organizes dramatic demonstrations to impress its views on the people, but so does the Ku Klux Klan. It investigates its candidates for membership and keeps detailed personal data about its members, including many items which an American is apt to regard as nobody else's business—but so does the American Medical Association, for instance. The Communist Party has a special interest in foreign countries, but so does the Pan American Union. None of these facts about the Party are in themselves the explanation of its menace or its amazing durability.

The real strength of the Party lies in the sheer audacity of its ambition to change America lock, stock and barrel. As the vanguard of the revolution, the Party regards itself as a kind of sub-state inside America, answerable only to its own leaders. In a way, you could say that the Party has outlawed itself by

tacitly refusing to recognize the premises on which our society
is built. Comes the revolution, it will be ready to take over.
There is a plan, and the embryonic beginning of the machinery,
for a Socialist government.

The Party has its own constitution, laws, regulations and
judicial system. It has its own school system, graduating the
cream of the students to the Russian schools of revolution and
Marxist doctrine. It works with the Soviet embassy and con-
sulate in deciding who shall be granted a visa to Russia, arro-
gating to itself a function of government. Under the names of
underground members, the Party owns and operates real estate
(it once ran a bus company), a printing and publishing enterprise, and an insurance business (The International Workers
Order). It arranges its own courier system so as to be independent of the United States mails both inside the country and
out, and it communicates with Russia if need be through Party
members who come to New York as foreign seamen.

An examination of its arrangements should be sufficient to
warn Americans of what the Party has in store for them.

6. THE WHOLE OF MY LIFE

IT HAS BECOME popular, lately, to think of the danger of Communism in terms of a Guy Fawkes plot against the Government. This view is dangerous, as well as ignorant, because it encourages the defenders of democracy to think that countermeasures can be mechanical and easy.

In the beginning I almost made the same mistake about the danger of being detected as a spy in the Communist Party. I took precautions against every possibility of my reports falling into the hands of comrades. I worried about telephone taps. I avoided observable contact with the F.B.I. I learned to doodle on scratch pads when I had to take notes so that I could conceal key words and figures.

The full annals of the F.B.I. and the Communist Party, U.S.A., if either are ever written, will prove that these precautions were necessary. But they were only the beginning. In order to be really safe, I had to avoid the suspicion of heresy. Everyone in the Party is as aware of heresy as a Salem preacher.

It is hard for anyone outside the Party to realize that Communism is more than a physical or military threat. It is an assault on the minds of men, as the Party prophets claim. In order to do their work, the shock troops of the revolution must be pure in heart. Sins of word and thought are counted, and even the faithful sin. An off phrase could be a booby trap.

A comrade once mentioned the name of a club.

"Is that a front organization?" I asked.

"Really, Angela," the speaker admonished, "you have been reading too much of the bourgeois press."

I should have said "mass organization" even though every newspaper except *The Daily Worker* would have said "front organization." The slip didn't expose me as a spy, but it marked me as a comrade to watch—for my own correction, of course. And the last thing on earth I wanted was to be watched.

Any member of the Communist Party—and perhaps only a member—can appreciate the magnitude of my assignment. Did I enjoy a book? Better not say so. It might have been unfavorably reviewed in an obscure Communist theoretical organ. Did I patronize a Fifth Avenue store? Perhaps I didn't know that it was oppressing its employees. A Communist can even be criticized for the reactionary views of his friends. He can also run into trouble if he is too strict in enforcing Party regulations. That crime comes under the head of "bureaucracy." All in all, a sincere Communist can expect a great deal of comradely interest in the state of his political health. To a conscientious Communist every human experience is political. The possibilities of sin are therefore limitless.

In practice, the Party loads every member with more work than he can possibly accomplish; no contribution, no sacrifice is ever enough. When you join the Communist Party, you pledge the whole of your life. The demands are so categorical that I have heard sincere believers in Communism confess, apologetically, that they could not live up to the rigors of actual membership and would have to help as best they could "from the outside." For every practising member of the Party in the United States, there is at least one ex-member who dropped out, not because he disagreed with the stated objectives of Communism, but because he found it impossible to live in the straitjacket of Communist life.

As a spy, I couldn't afford even the ordinary quota of gossip. I couldn't have operated if any disgruntled personal enemy had instituted a real investigation. Like Caesar's wife, I had to be above suspicion.

It was a twenty-four hour vigil. Every comrade takes it for granted that he is being watched, checked. The more I learned about the underground, the more careful I became. It wasn't safe to assume that I could talk freely anywhere. I didn't know who was a Communist and who wasn't. I kept the secret of my membership in the Party from my oldest friends—every Communist does that—but I didn't dare voice anti-Communist views to them either. They might have repeated them innocently enough in the wrong company.

When I joined the Communist Party, I was living with a girl who was a violent anti-Communist. Because Betty was ill and not very active, I was able to conceal my Party membership from her. One day, early in the game, I had a close call. A Party canvasser sent out to visit every new subscriber to *The Daily Worker* called when I was away. My roommate explained her views in no uncertain terms and physically shoved the visitor out the door.

When I got home, I told her she had done just the right thing, but the consequences could have been grave for me if the canvasser had known I was a card-carrying comrade. A Party member may live with a non-Party member who might be converted, but he is supposed to keep away from reactionaries—the people who will have to be liquidated in the revolution. Article IX, Sec. 4, of the Constitution of the Communist Party, U.S.A., states that "personal or political relations with enemies of the working class and nation are incompatible with membership in the Communist Party." I liked Betty, but it was easier for me when she moved away. Unconsciously, I drifted away from other friends who might have embarrassed me with the comrades.

The Party supplied a hollow substitute for the companionship I lost: a brand-new set of friends I dared not avoid or offend. I had to spend twenty to thirty hours a week with them.

It wasn't only the Party work, the chores we did together

which the membership secretary recorded in her little black book, although there were, heaven knows, enough of them— committee meetings, strike duty, union meetings that couldn't be shirked, and the rest. I had to mix with the comrades socially as well. This is the kind of thing that happened again and again:

A comrade called me on the phone one Saturday morning: "Let's go to the Russian movies at the Irving Theater and then go canvassing afterwards. We can work off our quota in a few hours." I was dying to see a good detective thriller, but no. I had to check myself in for several hours at a dreary Russian film, during which I was neither finding out anything of interest to the F.B.I. nor visibly improving my "credit" in the Party.

A comrade came to the house: "We're going to distribute leaflets on the West Side tomorrow and then go to Coney Island for a swim. Your car will hold six, won't it?" I had to distribute the leaflets, a copy of which I had already forwarded to the F.B.I. for what it could add to their knowledge, but on top of it all, I had to go to Coney Island. The trouble was that I love Coney Island. Nothing would have been more relaxing at that moment than to watch the crowds on the rides and get gypped at the booths, but in that company, of course, I didn't dare to relax.

A comrade caught me after a meeting: "Here are your tickets to the dance for the Yugoslav seamen." I wasn't asked to go, I was told. So I bought the tickets and I went to the dance. I like to dance, but it's more fun if you don't have to watch your small talk for traces of "chauvinism," "Trotzkyism" or "right deviationism."

A Negro comrade tried to make a date with me: "Let's have dinner at the Russian Skazka first. . . ." The Russian Skazka is an eating place frequented by Soviet diplomats, which comrades reserve for special occasions. My comrade could have only one purpose in mind when he suggested dinner at so expensive a place. Bluntly speaking, a proposition. If he had been a white comrade, I would have refused lightly if possible, firmly if necessary. But in this case, I couldn't do anything so natural. It might easily be interpreted as "white chauvinism."

"Look, Walter," I compromised, "I've got to drive a whole crowd up to the rally Monday night. You're going, aren't you? You should go, you know. Supposing I pick you up on the way." And then I had to find a whole car full of comrades to go with us. The Party's attitude towards Negroes puzzled me. I had grown up with them. It wasn't natural for me to treat them like social cripples.

Whenever there was a party, I had either to go or to produce a very good excuse. A previous engagement just wouldn't do. There would be arguments. Couldn't I come early? Nobody would mind if I had to slip away. If not early, then couldn't I come late? Everyone would understand. And why, exactly, did I have to do something else? I parried these assaults on my privacy as gracefully as I could, but I would have loved to shout: "I'm not coming early, I'm not coming late, I'm not coming at all."

I inquired of the F.B.I. agents. "After all, it's just a party. Is it really necessary for me to go?" But I knew that they would say it was safer to go. They told me that they had once had a plant who wouldn't go to parties. He didn't last long. After he differed with a comrade, Party officials announced that they had evidence that he was an agent of the city police. Part of the evidence: a guilty avoidance of Party companionship. I grumbled, but I went.

I soon found that the parties were well worth attending. Often I picked up information I could not have gotten in any other way. Almost always I managed to make "friends" with comrades working in other sections of the Party who might prove useful later on.

Communists never do anything so frivolous as to give a party just for the sake of a party. It's either an occasion intended to draw outsiders, like the "Forum" at which I met Leona, or it's a party to raise money. Fund-raising parties are all very much alike. I've probably gone to over one hundred in my time, and I gave what was regarded as a very successful one myself.

We were raising money for the branch and I wanted to make a good showing. I held it in my studio, but I did everything I could to keep the comrades away from friends and neighbors who might have supplied, innocently enough, more details of my personal life than I wanted the Communists to have. I told the couple who live over my studio that I was giving a party for the Photo League. They were welcome to come, of course, but the other people would all be photographers, and the conversation would probably be a little special. To get customers, I ran an ad in *The Daily Worker,* a paper I knew none of my personal friends read: "Candlelight, jazz concert, drinks. 9½ Jane Street, Monday night, 8 to 11."

The idea in these fund-raising parties is to make a profit by selling drinks. I got the liquor for my affair from a member of my branch who was vice president of a drug company. He was glad to contribute money instead of doing legwork that would have exposed him. With the liquor paid for, I couldn't help making an attractive net on the evening's business. All I had to do was to buy the fixings, rig up a makeshift bar in the studio, collect buckets of ice cubes, and borrow some records to round out my own collection. At eight o'clock on the appointed evening I and my helpers were ready to wait on trade.

My first customer was a reserved young man with a Southern accent. He hesitated at the door when he saw only three of us.

"I see you're on time," I quipped. "What will it be? Whiskey and soda, fifty-five cents. Not the best drink in town, but the longest for the money." He smiled uncertainly.

"Do you have to be a Communist to come to this party?" he blurted. He sounded like a college boy who had been sent down to the party on a bet. Maybe he was being initiated into a fraternity. Unless, of course, he was a representative of the Party taking a good opportunity to look me over. I could never rule that possibility out.

"Heavens, no," I replied. "Stick around a while. It might be fun."

The next arrivals were an over-exuberant foursome—three girls escorting a somewhat bewildered Negro youth who couldn't stop giggling. The girls were good-looking, turned out with the relentless attention to detail—costume jewelry, matching accessories, careful upsweeps—of women who feel it necessary to spend most of their money on clothes in order to hold their jobs. Not sales girls, I felt. More likely office workers, and well-paid ones. My shy customer gaped at what must have seemed to him an unusual social situation. It was less mysterious to me. Since I had been in the Party, I had witnessed many such scenes. It was easy to reconstruct the early part of their evening:

One of the girls had invited the Negro to dinner at her Village apartment. He was probably a messenger or a mail clerk in her office. Maybe the union was trying to organize the office, and he was a holdout. Maybe she was simply trying to prove to her Party friends that she really believed in social equality of the races and wasn't afraid to practice it. Anyway, she had invited him; and he had come, not knowing quite what to expect.

There had been Italian spaghetti, a tossed salad, French bread rubbed with a clove of garlic. There had certainly been a bottle of wine, and someone had inevitably brought along *The Daily Worker*. In the paper, they had found my ad—and an occasion to show that they were willing to be seen with a Negro escort in public.

The college boy looked as if he were sleepwalking in a bad dream from which he might at any moment wake up screaming. I was uncomfortable, too, but for the opposite reason. Where he was shocked to see white girls entertaining a Negro, I was depressed to see the falsity of the situation. The Party girls were exploiting the Negro for their own purposes.

"Our friend here wants to know whether the party is for Communists alone or whether anyone can come," I called,

hostess-fashion, to warn the girls that there was another potential recruit in the house. One of them obediently turned
around and held out her arms to him invitingly without losing
a beat of the rhythm she was tapping with her foot. He started,
blushed and shook his head. A new group swept into the room
and I had to tend bar. The next time I looked up, he was gone.

It was impossible to move, let alone dance. Thirty people
jammed my tiny studio like a rush hour crowd in a subway
train. They were making the kind of noise that reassures a
hostess. I poured out drinks and took in money, catching only
snatches of conversation.

"Don't you know what would happen? The dirty reactionaries would say, 'Gee, all Communists are Jews.' We've got to
be realistic. It's better for Goldstein to stay behind the scenes,
with that name, I mean. We need something like Markham or
Johnson on the masthead."

I had run across anti-Semitism in the Party before. Like the
Negroes, the Jews were often courted with crocodile tears of
sympathy for the discrimination they suffered. Yet everyone
knew that Jewish comrades were encouraged to change their
names in order to be more useful to the cause. A good Communist has a blind spot for inconsistencies like that.

"I could weep for her, shut up in her private room at the
hospital with a day and night nurse while the Russians are
dying. . . ."

"Slept her way up and down the Party . . ."

"His old man's got plenty of what it takes and he isn't looking any unearned income in the mouth. . . ."

"Could profit by self-criticism . . ."

"Takes all kinds to build the Party . . ."

"A little union discipline . . ."

"Talk about police brutality!"

Dotty, a member of my branch, edged through the crowd to
greet me.

"Did you hear what the cops did up on Sixty-fourth Street
last night?" she burst out. "Just stood there and laughed while

the hoodlums tore down our stand. In another minute they'd
have joined the wrecking crew themselves!"

It was the standard Communist reaction to violence Party
members had themselves provoked. Sometimes the comrades
stirred up a little "police brutality" so that they could demand
an investigation that would make the papers. Yet they were so
convinced that the police were always wrong that I sometimes
wondered whether they knew themselves what they were doing.

"What did the boys do about it?" I asked seriously.

"Well, what would you expect them to do?" she shrugged
bitterly. "Those cops have guns."

"God, I hate violence," I murmured involuntarily. Dotty
looked at me as if I were suddenly taken sick.

"You're a queer one. What are you going to do when the
revolution comes?"

"Oh, I expect I'll run and hide somewhere," I retorted.
Dotty was one of the few people in the Party who knew when
you were joking. I could tell her the truth so that it sounded
like a lie and get away with it. She grinned back her polite
disbelief, as if reassured about the state of my health.

"You know what I'm going to do, Angie? I'm going to be
Commissar of Heavy Industry. Bet you can guess who I'm
going to put behind the horses!" She winked and nodded in
the direction of a tense-mouthed woman without makeup who
was climbing on a chair to launch one of the impromptu political speeches that Communists always make at each other whenever more than two or three are gathered together.

" 'Foreign-language comrades do not approve of women in
pants,' " Dotty mimicked in a whisper. I remembered that the
speaker had once reprimanded her for wearing slacks to a
Communist Party meeting for Yugoslavs.

The comrade who opposed slacks wore her tailored suit as
impersonally as if it were a uniform. She was saying a few
words on behalf of Vito Marcantonio, A.L.P. candidate for
Congress. The familiar arguments bounced off the edges of
my mind like a radio not worth turning off.

"Millions of second-class citizens look to him as their only voice in a Congress intimidated by the Ku Klux Klan. Millions of toilers depend on him to speak out against government by the National Association of Manufacturers. The reactionaries have long tried to silence him with the smear of Moscow gold. This time they are enlisting the help of the social Fascists and fuzzy-minded liberals. We must redouble our efforts. We must save the people from Wall Street."

It was easy to tell the difference between a "fuzzy-minded liberal" and a "social Fascist." Both terms referred to non-Communists who advocated the reforms the Party was preaching at the moment. If the non-Communist looked as if he could be recruited, he was a "fuzzy-minded liberal." If he was hopeless, he was a "social Fascist."

The crowd stood awkwardly at attention, like a theater audience during "The Star-Spangled Banner" or a church congregation hearing a well-worn psalm whose words convey a mood rather than a meaning. Other comrades clamored to speak. Prick a Communist anywhere, and he'll start talking. We stood through an appeal for funds for Russian children, an enthusiastic testimonial for Foster's latest book, and a purported eyewitness account of a lynching allegedly suppressed by the New York papers.

I had to get everyone out by midnight, because I was expecting a friend from out of town. She didn't know I was a "Communist" and I didn't want to have to explain my new associates to her. She'd wired at the last minute that her train got in at eleven forty-three.

"Sorry, kids," I called from my post behind the bar. "I've got one of those landlords—you know the kind."

Most of my guests moved on for some food and more talk at the automat on Union Square, a favorite Party hangout. The future Commissar of Heavy Industry helped me wash glasses under the tap in the darkroom. She chattered about the latest branch gossip: our literature director was being relieved because someone in the regional office had caught him going to a

psychiatrist. There was a rule about it. You couldn't hold
Party office while under psychiatric treatment.

"I suppose we've got to have stable people for leaders," I
commented.

"That's part of it, of course," Dotty said, "but they made the
rule when the F.B.I. broke into a doctor's office and bagged his
notes on one of the leaders. They were full of secret stuff."

I whistled appreciatively. Wait until my agents heard this
fairy tale!

"Guess they've got enough on their minds to drive anyone
nuts," I replied. "What are they supposed to do when they
can't stand it any more—the big shots, I mean?"

"I should think it would be all right if they went to a psychiatrist who was a comrade," Dotty suggested.

Dotty left at last, and I was fast asleep by the time my friend
arrived from the station. Next morning I counted the receipts
and found we had made over seventy-five dollars.

My party was a frank fund-raising device. Substitute a Park
Avenue apartment for my tiny studio, add a few Party intellectuals, throw in a stage or screen star or two as a drawing card,
and the stage is all set for a wealthy secret comrade to influence
the influencers of public opinion. The hostess, a well-bred
society matron, would never dream of advertising for guests in
any newspaper, let alone *The Daily Worker*. She collects a
crowd by chatty notes and telephone calls to social acquaintances and casual contacts likely to be flattered by an invitation
to her home. The bait, if it is necessary, may be a well-known
public figure in the arts or professions, or a progressive candidate for public office who would rather be right than elected.

She handles a miscellaneous guest list with practiced show-
manship. If there is a big name, he is installed in a strategic
corner of the huge, professionally decorated living room. Wives
of editors and professors are herded past him wholesale, to be
picked off one by one for retail attention by snobbishly shabby
young men whose function it is to be "interesting" or "idealistic" or "well-informed" or even "brilliant."

The hostess has been careful to procure a few distinguished Negro intellectuals whose accomplishments would make them acceptable to all but the most uncompromising Southerners. Overpoised, overcultivated, they move from group to group like portable demonstrations of race equality. Their children probably go to a liberal private school that is eager to eradicate race prejudice in white children by including at least one Negro in every class. I had the advantage of colored children in my classes when I went to school on the lower East Side, but we never thought about it.

At a propitious lull in the general conversation, the hostess calls for silence as if to announce a parlor game. The guest of honor speaks a few sincere, intimate words of praise for the current "struggle," followed by "spontaneous" testimonials from the lesser talent. In deference to the sophistication of the company, the Party line is less strident than it was at my party. The word "Communism" is mentioned jokingly, if at all, but the general drift is strikingly similar to the current editorial in *The Daily Worker*.

Butlers pass free drinks around on trays, and uniformed maids distribute caterer's canapés worth more than my party raised. Money, of course, isn't mentioned out loud, but the total haul may run into thousands of dollars. Departing guests hastily scribble checks in bedrooms, or enclose them with thank-you notes. They may be made out simply and safely to the hostess, or to one of the leagues, congresses, institutes, associations, or federations which she is using to catalyze the Red-minded into action.

In a gathering like this, it would be impossible to say, "The girl with the horn-rimmed glasses who is studying Russian is a Communist, while the professor of romance languages to whom she is talking is a liberal dupe." Communists are all sorts and conditions of men, and they are careful not to wear their red badges in public.

It was only when I came to know many of them well that I learned the conventions of the secret world in which they live.

My position in that world at first was much like that of an anthropologist who travels to a distant South Pacific island, dons a grass skirt, and burns incense to the idols in order to find out just how it feels to be a primitive. The Communists have their own taboos, their own virtues and their own vices. I had to observe them even when they struck me as hilariously funny.

I have heard well-to-do Communists apologize for living in a comfortable apartment in an exclusive neighborhood. They felt that they should be living in a tenement, although they couldn't quite bring themselves to it. If they were sinful enough to have a domestic servant, they never referred to this employee as the "maid" or the "cleaning woman." It was always "the girl who works for me" or "Mary"; and if you called at the house when Mary was there, you had to sit down and drink a cup of coffee with her, just to prove she was being treated right. This ritual always struck me as very peculiar. I always ate with my Ellie, but I never thought I was proving anything by it.

The comrades have a special code of conduct toward Negroes. If a Negro talks out of turn, you don't slap him down the way you would if he were a white comrade. Good form requires that you act as if it were your fault that he has bad manners or mistaken notions.

I have known Communist girls who loved "high class" clothes, but wore them only for "political reasons." It was necessary, they explained, to make a good impression when "showing the face of the Party" at a mass organization meeting. In the thirties, Communists had flaunted their defiance of bourgeois standards. Girls wore leather jackets, red high-heeled shoes, unfashionable short haircuts, and no stockings. The gesture was satisfying to them personally, perhaps, but it did not build the Party. Communist girls were ordered to dress and act like the people they were trying to recruit.

There is probably no word that Communists use more frequently than the "masses." The "masses" are being exploited. The "masses" must rule. The "masses" are somehow better

than the people who are not the masses. Yet no Communist I
ever met genuinely thought of himself as one of them. Democracy, to them, meant rule "for the people" but not "by the
people." Their attitude was: "We know what the masses need
and we're going to give it to them even if we have to choke it
down their throats."

Marriage was "all right," but it was a little bourgeois to take
it too seriously. Free love went out with leather jackets when
Russia decided to make an uneasy peace with religion and bid
for the support of non-Communist progressives, but a number
of the older comrades were still living in common law alliances
when I joined the Party. I knew of several of these couples—
the man a scholarly Marxist dreamer, the girl a hardworking
little Jimmy Higgins who sometimes earned his living as well as
her own. There was a deliberately casual attitude toward sex.
My new "friends" were more promiscuous than other groups
of men and women working together. The girls who joined
the Party to get a husband—and there were many such—found
it a poor hunting ground.

The striking thing about it all was that no one in the Party
really regarded sex as important. Sex was Topic B in social
conversation; Marx was Topic A. Intrigues were watched because they might have a political significance. Women who
reached the top of the Communist hierarchy were suspected of
having "slept their way up." It was "all right" to go to bed
with a non-Party member, provided you were trying to enlist
him to the cause—young girls did a great deal of missionary
work among seamen—but those who married or mated outside
the Party were in for trouble. Whenever there was a conflict,
the Party always came first.

I always felt uncomfortable with the comrades. Fundamen-
tally, I had nothing in common with them. I found it hard to
work with people who have no sense of humor and no sense of
perspective. A comrade can't differ with his landlord over the
rent without accusing him of crimes ranging from race prejudice to a suspicious attitude toward the intentions of Soviet

Russia. To him, these things are all of a piece. One presup-
poses the other. Are you sick? wife left you? lost your job?
gone broke? flunked out of college? got a parking ticket? The
reason is easy. It's all the fault of the social system! Or, more
usually, it's "their" fault.

"They"—the general enemy—are the bosses, the Government,
the churches, the schools. You're supposed to gloat, to ridicule,
to dig slyly when "they" get into trouble over a strike or an
international crisis or a moral dilemma. You're supposed to
thunder righteously when "they" settle a strike or foil a Communist maneuver abroad. If "they" reject a Negro for employment, they're obviously reactionary. If "they" accept a Negro
for employment, they're just making a token gesture. "They"
are always wrong, and the Russians are always right.

"They" are in league against the Party, and the Party can
only survive if its members give their all. Sacrifice to the cause
is regarded as a privilege, a proof of membership in the elite,
the vanguard of pioneers saving humanity. A comrade is supposed to extend total aid to any other comrade in trouble. This
requirement involved me in a great deal of profitless activity.
I was a photographer. Any Party member who needed pictures
had only to come to me. I used to bill them, but there was
nothing I could do if my bills weren't paid.

I very soon found that my apartment, my car, my phone, my
books, my services, my time and my money were at the disposal of any comrade as if by God-given right. When a comrade
got into a jam, he or she thought first of the Party. Party
members had to help whether they sympathized with the individual or not. I once collected $250 without disclosing whom
or what it was for.

Late one night a girl with high connections in the Party
came to my house. I'll call her Molly. I did not know her well.

"Angela, you've got to help me," she begged. "I've got to
get $250 by tomorrow. I can't go to my family—they'd disown
me."

"What's the matter?" I asked. Every trace of Molly's usual

bravado was gone. She hadn't even combed her hair. I didn't really have to ask her what was wrong. It could only have been one thing. I got her a cup of coffee and made her sit down and light a cigarette.

"What about the man?" I asked quietly. "Can't he help?" She shook her head impatiently, dismissing an unpleasant memory.

"No, of course not. He doesn't have any money. Besides, he's a regular Party guy." A "regular Party guy" is Communist slang for a man who doesn't want to get caught in marriage. I knew the type well. Nothing to be gained there.

"Have you found a doctor?" I asked, to stall for a little time to think. Molly was a valuable friend to me in the Party. Through her, I could get to know Party leaders whose movements were important to the F.B.I. If I refused to help her, she could also be a powerful enemy. I had heard her comments on comrades she didn't like and I did not want to become one of them. But how could I help? I didn't have $250. The investment in my advancement in the Party would be a good one, but I could hardly expect the F.B.I. to underwrite a loan of that kind. I couldn't even tell them that I had anything to do with an illegal operation. This was one of those occasions on which a plant had to use his own good judgment.

"Of course, I don't have that much money," I said truthfully, "I can give you fifty and maybe we can raise the rest."

I went to work on the telephone and called four comrades from my branch. To each one of them I told the same story: a comrade—a girl—was in trouble and needed money. I couldn't give them the details, but I assured them that they would want to contribute if they knew the situation and that I would stand behind the loan. Every one of them instantly pledged fifty dollars. One comrade I called had to cash war bonds to do it. Molly paid the money back afterwards, and no one was the wiser, not even the F.B.I.

I've often thought how much easier, in some ways, it would have been to be a spy in an enemy army. As a soldier, my life

would have been regimented, but even in military service there
are leaves, periods of relaxation. Privacy is so precious in an
army that soldiers find ways of protecting as much as they can
salvage. Of me, as of every other comrade, the Party demanded
not stated duties, but the whole of my life.

It was right here, the agents told me, that many plants broke
down. Many of them dropped out because they could not
stand the "duplicity" of betraying individuals they knew personally, individuals who were trusting them with secrets, the
exposure of which could, and often did, destroy their careers
and their deepest aspirations.

I do not know, of course, in what way I am constituted differ-
ently from the undercover agents who had to give up. I do
know that from the outset I succeeded in separating my deal-
ings with Party people from the rest of me. I avoided romantic
entanglements so well that I'm afraid it has become a habit.
With the Communists, I was playing a role. I was being an
actress, at times a hammy actress, but I felt no more dishonest
about it than if I were simulating another personality on the
stage.

I met sensitive, conscientious comrades, idealistic comrades,
comrades so persuasive and sincere that I would not have
known how to defend our system against their attacks if I had
set out to do it. I could see what the Party did to the individuals in it, however, and my own observation was enough
to prevent me from taking their views seriously. I could not
even have much personal respect for people who allowed themselves to be exploited in that way.

My real problem was the irritation I felt at having to spend
so much of my time and energy on matters of little interest to
me. I felt that years of my life—years I wanted to live in my
own way—were passing away forever.

Looking back on it now, I think I had two weapons against
the crashing boredom of life in the Party. I used to amuse
myself thinking up ways of escaping the comrades for a few
hours, and I tried to keep a firm grasp on my sense of the ridicu-

lous. I consciously cultivated the impression that I was a screwball artist who might go anywhere and do anything. I never promised to be at a specific place at a specific time, and I let it be known that I had a strange phobia against people who dropped in to see me unannounced. Anyone who wanted a cordial reception soon learned to phone first.

Subterfuge is an art, and I became an artist at it. I learned to get out of Party work of little value to the F.B.I. by pleading photographic assignments. I was "sick" a lot. On several occasions, my excuses boomeranged. They counted me out of sudden emergency assignments I would very much have liked to do. I always had to weigh that possibility when deciding against a chore.

It is easy to lie if you think of a lie as a tool. A lie is quite different from duplicity. Duplicity is being two-faced, and I was never that. I believed sincerely in what I was doing. I never had any twinge of conscience about fooling the Communists—how could I? If they succeeded, they would have been spying far more thoroughly on me, on you—on all of us.

7. THE GOLDEN AGE OF BROWDER

I WENT INTO business for myself in 1943 when I was able to rent the basement of the four-story building behind 9 Jane Street for a portrait studio. The situation was ideal—the studio was close to the apartment, but far enough away to insure privacy. As I have described, 9½ Jane Street is reached through an alley paved with flagstones that opens on a courtyard with a garden. The English basement of the back building has its own entrance three steps down from the patio.

When I rented it, the basement of 9½ Jane was a mass of electric and gas meters, but it had a toilet, running water and a fireplace. I dropped a false ceiling under the worst of the piping, built fake cupboards around the meters, and put in partitions to make a bathroom with shower, a darkroom and a windowless little office about ten feet square. The front, with the fireplace and the window on the courtyard, I fixed up as an informal sitting room for taking portraits. I enjoy working with my hands, and I did as much of the construction work myself as I could.

I was determined to have the office for myself, so I installed a Dutch door between the office and the sitting room to remind friends, "comrades" and clients that they were not to go into it without special permission. I always kept the lower half of the door closed. In the office I had a telephone, my typewriter, work tables and file cabinets for my pictures.

To the side of the picket gate entrance on Jane Street I hung a picture box with my hallmark, "Angela and Her Camera." It usually had a photo of a baby or animal in it.

I soon had more business than I could handle. Families were separated because of the war. The photographic business was booming. Ads in community newspapers brought me a type of work I enjoy: portraits of children. After I became a staff photographer for *Tide* magazine, I began to get profitable assignments but they were harder to fit into my Party schedule than portrait work.

I particularly enjoyed doing pictures of babies for fathers overseas who had never seen them. I also did informal picture stories of families separated during the war which we bound in leatherette covers, four by five inches, to fit into G.I. tunic pockets. I tried to take scenes from everyday home life such as turning off the alarm clock in the morning, making breakfast, the family eating a favorite steak dinner. I was amused at one of my clients who asked me to photograph her in a bubble bath, to say nothing of the black-lace-nightgown shots of wives I did to keep up morale on the fighting fronts. I never got any priorities on film or flash bulbs for this type of work, but I often thought that it was as important warwork as magazine pictures for which I did get priorities.

One of the most satisfying jobs I've ever done on children was a series of pictures of refugee youngsters orphaned in the Spanish war whom the U. S. Committee on the Care of European Children brought to this country in 1943 for adoption. My pictures were often the basis on which foster parents chose a child.

I had my hands full with my growing business, but I never dared to use it as an excuse to get out of Party assignments. With a loyal comrade, the Party always comes first. Often I even had to cancel sittings in order to meet some emergency in the branch. Frequently I had to call up the mother of a child

I was scheduled to photograph and plead a cold in the head that might endanger the child's health. I got to be quite an expert at simulating a stopped-up nose over the phone.

It was a rat-race way of life, but I developed short cuts to accomplish all the things I had to do. The car helped, because it enabled me to make close connections in different parts of town. The studio helped, because it was a retreat. Betty easily accepted my frequent absences as photographic assignments. Sometimes, when I was going out to a Party meeting, I'd carry an empty camera case over my shoulder, to suggest that I was doing a job. I fell into the habit of never promising to be at a party. I learned to cut corners by arriving at Communist meetings twenty minutes late. That way, I saved the time that was always wasted waiting for other late members as well as the unpleasantness of pretending a personal interest in my fellow "comrades" during the inevitable chit-chat that preceded getting down to Party business. Timing was important to me. I became a clock watcher, although I hate clock watching.

All through 1943, our prestige as Communists rose steadily with the victories of the Red Army. Russian relief was a popular cause with respectable big names attached to it. We began to look almost respectable ourselves. In order to foster cooperation among the allies, Stalin dissolved the Communist International. *Daily Worker* editorials put in a patronizing good word for FDR. The editors pulled out all the stops when Roosevelt, Churchill and Stalin met at Teheran in December, 1943, and announced that they had made plans for the defeat of Hitler and laid the basis for a peace that would last for "many generations."

In January, 1944, I was chosen as the comrade for my section to attend a ten-day training course on trade union methods at the Worker's School. Our teacher, who had been giving these short courses for years, made our assignment perfectly clear. Workers and employers are natural enemies. Misguided labor leaders who compromised with capitalists to win better wages and hours must be ousted as enemies of the people.

After a few days of this, however, we had a surprise visit from Roy Hudson, then a member of the Communist National Committee. He told us that the war had produced a class of progressive businessmen—he named Henry Wallace and various New Dealing businessmen—with whom it was our duty to collaborate. We would have to learn to distinguish between "good" capitalists and "bad" capitalists.

I'm sure our teacher was completely unprepared for this denial of everything he had said previously, but he did not show his embarrassment. He simply adopted the new dogma as if he had always preached it, and pointed out that the "good" American capitalists would invest their money in rebuilding Russia after the war. No one commented after class. Most of the students had been through the pact with Hitler and back. It seemed natural and proper to them that our teacher should eat his words.

John B. Williamson, the Party's secretary of labor, came down to elaborate the new line for us in person. I watched him curiously, because he was one of the new wheels on the National Board. He talked quietly, with just a trace of a Scotch burr, about the rosy future. As I listened, I amused myself by imagining how much his face looked like a pig's. It was short, square and red, with deep-set small blue eyes, and his sparse blond hair added to the effect. I thought of my rather unkind comparison again when I identified him in court, years later, as one of the eleven defendants at the trial.

I wrote my reports every night so that the agents could get them on the teletype to Washington. From the way Ken acted, I could tell that something big was happening, but I wasn't sure just what it was.

I was invited to a closed meeting for leaders and comrades marked for leadership in New York County. When I told Ken about it, he asked if there was any natural way for me to get another ticket. I knew that Ken wouldn't go himself. Agents working on Communist activities never show their hands. Perhaps he wanted to give the ticket to another plant in the Party.

I didn't promise to get another ticket—they were all numbered —but luck was with me. I was asked to deliver Martha's ticket to her. Martha didn't want to go, leaving me with an extra on my hands. If I had been a loyal comrade I would have turned it back or destroyed it, and I seriously thought of doing just that. It would have been very easy for a Party official to challenge the person who used it, and trace his presence back to me. I decided to take the chance and turn it over to Ken, but I was nervous about it.

My schedule for the day of the meeting was full but possible: 11 A.M., picture assignment in midtown; 1 P.M., meet Ken at Eighth Avenue and Thirty-fourth Street to turn over the extra ticket; develop films in the afternoon; 8 P.M., meeting; 12 P.M., make prints; 3 A.M., bed.

Everything started out routinely enough. My subject that morning, a middle-aged executive, said all the usual things about hating to have his picture taken, but I noticed that he had had a new haircut and a close shave. Also he was wearing a jacket, although the people I passed on my way to his office were working in shirt sleeves. I had allowed myself two hours to take the picture, get lunch and meet the agents at one o'clock. I set up my equipment slowly. It would take some time to get my subject to relax.

"Let's get this over with," he said impatiently. "How do you want me to pose? Shall I hold the phone?" Phone pictures are trite, but I obligingly wasted a few frames on them.

"Why don't you take off your coat and get at some of your mail?" I suggested. "You'll be more comfortable."

"Can't do it," he protested guiltily. "I've got suspenders on today." He set his face grimly.

"Well, then, why don't you pretend you like me?" I pleaded. "What are you worrying about? You've got teeth and hair!" It was corny language, but it always worked. I shot his very human guffaw—then caught the pleasant, relaxed expression that follows a laugh. For the next shot I decided to plug in the floodlights.

Bang! The whole wall spat fire. Impulsively, I pulled the wire out of the wall socket. I wasn't hurt, but I was pretty scared—but not nearly as scared as my client, whom I discovered standing on his desk, looking very sheepish. The actual damage amounted only to a hole in the wall and a burned rug, but my skirt was ruined. I looked like a bedraggled chimney sweep.

After the commotion died down we borrowed another office and finished the sitting. I hurried through the last shots so as to be through in time to get back to the house and change my scorched clothes before meeting Ken Bierly. I didn't want to use my client's phone to warn Ken I might be late, and I was afraid he would be gone by the time I got out to a public telephone booth. At quarter past twelve I was ready to go, and I figured with luck I could just about make it down to Jane Street and back. On my way out, the treasurer of the company sent for me.

"Are you insured?" he demanded peremptorily. "You've ruined our newly-papered wall!"

"I'm insured with Traveler's," I said huffily. "I nearly got killed with your faulty socket and you want to collect from my insurance company! Let's skip it." I stalked out of his office.

It was twelve-thirty by the time I got out on the street and found a parking ticket on my car. The pot was really boiling now. Cutting viciously through traffic downtown, I remembered I had some pamphlets to give Ken. I tore into the studio and did a five-minute rehabilitation job on myself. The pamphlets were too bulky to cram into my shoulder bag. I dumped them into my briefcase with my wallet containing the ticket so that I would have only one thing to carry. The subway would be faster up to Thirty-fourth Street than the car. By running all the way, I got on to an uptown train at one-fifteen. I counted the minutes on the trip, and dashed out at the Thirty-fourth Street station. If I missed connections with Ken, he might not be able to get the ticket in time to the person who was going to use it.

But where was the ticket? I felt for my shoulder bag and

remembered I had taken the briefcase instead. No wonder I had left it on the train! The door was closing, but I pushed it open and held it with my foot while an amused man handed me the missing briefcase.

"What you got in there, lady?" he quipped. "Love letters?"

I grinned and said, "Sure!"

I steadied myself on the iron guard rail. How could I have been so stupid? Inside that briefcase, where anyone finding it would be sure to look, were a stack of Communist Party literature marked ND 107; several reports to the F.B.I. signed ND 107; a hospitalization card in the name of Angela Calomiris, 9 Jane Street; and several business cards for "Angela and Her Camera." It wouldn't take much imagination for anyone to see my whole story, and the story of the F.B.I.'s surveillance of the Party as well.

I thought I was going to be sick right there in the subway. If I fainted, the subway guard would pick up my briefcase. I've got to get rid of it, I thought dizzily. I looked at my watch. It said one-twenty-five—I was twenty-five minutes late, but there was still a chance that the boys were waiting for me. I took a deep breath and sprinted up the subway steps and across the street toward the corner we had set.

A voice from a passing car hailed me. It was the agent who was temporarily taking Bill South's place. He was sitting next to Ken, who was driving. The boys hadn't been able to find a parking place near our corner, so they had been driving around the block for a half-hour. I felt like kissing both of them, I was so glad to see them.

"For heaven's sake, let's get out of here," I said gruffly as soon as I got into the front seat beside them.

"We're tired of the scenery on this block ourselves," Ken said, swinging uptown. "What's happened?"

"Just about the works," I began. I made a good story out of it to cover my nervousness. By the time I got to the subway scene I was burlesquing my own forgetfulness. A fine undercover agent I was, leaving my briefcase in a subway train!

Ken was picking his way through traffic up in the Bronx. We drove along for a while without talking, and I began to think how I could write my reports so that they would not give me or the F.B.I. away if they should ever fall into the hands of a comrade. The thing that bothered me was that I had been writing them in the first person and leaving Angela Cole out of the list of comrades present at the meetings I described. Branch officials would surely be called in to look at any report of mine that fell into Communist hands. They would remember that I was present and, since I was not mentioned in the report, they would easily conclude that ND 107 was Angela. I decided to write reports in the third person and talk about my own doings as I did those of others.

At the meeting that night, I nearly fell out of the balcony trying to detect who was using the ticket. It gave me an eerie feeling to know that there was another spy in the room. The meeting was city-wide and there were many comrades present I had never seen before. Whoever was using my ticket was playing his role well. I concentrated on the explanations Party leaders were giving of the new policy of collaboration.

"We're not giving up Socialism," one of them warned lamely. "We're just recognizing that the United States will continue to be a capitalist nation for some time after the war." The new policy promised peace for years to come. We were also warned that a violent attempt to bring about Socialism now would split progressive forces and put reactionaries in power. The only way reactionaries could save themselves for the long haul was to provoke a new war. For the Communists, the new policy made sense: Russia was in no condition for a new war. That was the reason why we were hearing that "Communism and Capitalism have proven that they can get along in wartime. They should therefore be able to get along in the peace."

Party war horses dutifully propagated the new line. At a rally in Bridgeport, Earl Browder sounded like a super-patriot putting the cause of the allies ahead of Communism. "If J. P. Morgan supports this coalition," he said of the Anglo-Soviet·

American alliance, "I as a Communist am prepared to grasp his hand on that and join with him to realize it." We know now that William Z. Foster protested this intemperate language, but his objections in the plenary session of the Central Committee were not reported in *The Daily Worker* until he came to power in 1945.

The Communist Party existed to overthrow Capitalism. Class collaboration clearly meant the end of the Party. It was not long in coming.

I wish I could have described in more detail on the witness stand the scene at Madison Square Garden on May 25, 1944. All comrades were ordered to attend an extraordinary Congress. With the other members of my branch, I gladly paid $1.65 to sit in the arena. We knew that the Communist Party was going to be dissolved and we expected a good show. Never before had I seen the Garden so gaily decked. There were huge banners that said, "For a Lasting Peace," "Hail to Our Soviet Friends," "For a Democratic Coalition." Most conspicuous, right over the speaker's stand, was a huge poster of two hands clasped in friendship—one obviously the gnarled hand of a worker, the other the white-cuffed hand of a capitalist.

Robert Minor, William Z. Foster and the other old standbys justified the Party's suicide. Then all the lights went out in the Garden and a single white beam escorted Earl Browder from the wing. Around him, in the shadows, you could see his bodyguards and errand boys. The light glittered on his iron-gray hair and his fine aristocratic face. He faced us, a shepherd leading his sheep. In other surroundings, he would have impressed me as a bank president.

Everyone in the Garden automatically rose to his feet. We yelled, stamped, shouted, chanted, whistled and screamed while colored lights played over the audience. A band struck up, "Browder is our leader, we shall not be downed," a Party song chanted to the chorus of "Dinah, Blow Your Horn." But for the slogans on the wall, it could have been one of the Nazi

Bund meetings I had often seen in the newsreels. It took
Browder ten minutes to get the crowd calmed down.

In his quiet, monotonous, but highly dramatic voice, Earl
Browder moved the dissolution of the Communist Party of
America and the adoption of the Constitution of the Communist Political Association. He described the latter as a non-
Party organization of the American working class dedicated to
the traditions of Washington, Jefferson, Paine, Jackson and
Lincoln, under the changed conditions of modern industrial
society. A small group up front burst into "Happy Birthday"
in honor of the new C.P.A.

Elizabeth Gurley Flynn, a big, dynamic Irishwoman, explained that, in the interests of national unity, we would henceforth adopt bourgeois forms of address. Comrades would
become "brothers and sisters" or even "ladies and gentlemen."
Branches would be "clubs" and branch organizers "chairmen."

The Worker's School became the Jefferson School of Social
Science. Our Melini-Douglass branch was renamed the Columbus Hill Club to emphasize the community instead of the
national groups in it. There were fewer directives from higher
authority. Clubs were supposed to operate autonomously. De-
scriptive club names sprouted all over the city. There was a
Lenin Club, and a Henry Forbes Club, named after the first
Communist G.I. to die in World War II. We soft-pedalled
trade union work and signed pledges not to strike. We planned
club meetings to which members could invite friends and
neighbors, and had non-Communist speakers. We even invited
representatives of the U.S. Treasury to tell us how to conduct
our war bond drives.

The new people we attracted were invited to join without
screening. Our club grew to over fifty members and some clubs
had one hundred or more, far too many to handle in the careful
way to which we were dedicated. Membership directors gave
up notifying the membership by telephone or personal visit,
and sent open postcards through the mail. In our club, we had
dozens of new people who had not been indoctrinated in the

principles of Marxism. National membership was over 100,000. Many old-time comrades pointedly stayed away from meetings in disapproval of a policy which they could hardly reconcile with their understanding of the Party's historic mission. We tactfully left them alone instead of investigating the state of their political health. It was not the time for strict enforcement of Party discipline.

The new open-door policy made my work much easier. I took notes in club meetings, even when I had no official reason to do so. A veteran comrade once leaned over my shoulder while I was scribbling down assignments being given members.

"We do too much talking around here and too little acting," I explained, resisting the temptation to push my notes out of his line of sight. "I thought I'd do a little checking on my own. People get assignments and then they do nothing about them and nobody seems to remember what they were supposed to do." It was a good explanation, because it fitted in with his own fear of our new laxity. He nodded, satisfied.

Not long after that, we established the unprecedented office of recording secretary. I was elected to the new post. It made spying a cinch. I simply gave the F.B.I. a carbon copy of the minutes I had to write up, and I always had a sound reason for checking names. The turnover in the club was high—under wartime conditions, old members were moving away, and the new people often came for a few meetings and then dropped out. It was hard to be sure all of them went to mass rallies. Educational programs slipped. People working on war jobs couldn't be reached. In the shuffle, I served for a time as literature director and then as press director.

All of us were working hard at patriotic voluntary work in civilan defense, in war bond drives, in the Red Cross, in the blood banks and in servicemen's canteens, and the clubs encouraged us to put these obligations first. I took pictures of G.I.s in the Music Box Canteen for them to send to their families—a job which my Party comrades thoroughly approved. Our leaders talked about the necessity of winning the veterans after the war.

I took a Red Cross first aid course and joined the American Women's Voluntary Service. It was a relief for me to be able to do many of the things that I would have done anyway and it seemed silly, sometimes, to report these patriotic Party doings to the F.B.I. Whenever I doubted the need for my work, however, I could always remind myself of my comrades' motives, which had not changed. As Communists, they were helping "our great ally Russia" win "the people's war."

Comrades who for years had led furtive, hunted lives now blossomed out as loyal American citizens, and they loved it. They called each other at their places of business, and even used each other's last names. Some of them stayed at home and discovered family life. The Communist Political Association was a golden age for infiltration in business and Government. Party leaders wrapped themselves in the American flag. The C.P.A. preached national unity, increased production within the framework of Capitalism, and a hard peace for Germany. They even went so far as to order comrades to keep the Party out of the 1944 general election for fear they might embarrass Roosevelt by their support.

"We know quite well that the America that Roosevelt leads is a capitalist America and that it is the mission of Roosevelt, among others, to keep it so," Earl Browder said in a burst of frankness. Socialism could come to America only through catastrophe or a new war, he explained, and "we do not want disaster for America even though it results in Socialism. If we did, we would support Dewey and Hoover and Bricker and their company."

In New York City, however, the Party mobilized members to reelect Vito Marcantonio, American Labor Party candidate for Congress. On election night every lodge of the faithful International Workers Order held a rally for Marcantonio. As a good "Communist" photographer, I got the job of taking group shots of these celebrations for the I.W.O. It was a bit of a plum, because the I.W.O. has a treasury out of which I was paid for my work. I drove from one lodge headquarters to another. I took a score of group shots, with a total of hundreds of faces, including many close-ups of I.W.O. leaders. I was able to check many of the names later when some of the pictures appeared in the I.W.O. magazine, *Fraternal Outlook*. The F.B.I. welcomed the set of prints I made for them because they helped to identify individuals like John-Peter who might give one name in the supposedly non-Red I.W.O. and another in the Party.

From the inception of my work for the F.B.I., I thought that I might be able to help by taking pictures. I had read magazine articles on the ingenuity with which the F.B.I. catches crooks red-handed in the lens of a concealed camera, and I was anxious to try my hand at this photographic warfare. I thought up attachments which would have allowed me to take a picture from a hiding place with the help of mirrors, or the possibility of using a periscope arrangement to get a shot while lying on the floor of an automobile. Unfortunately, I never had to try any of these interesting schemes.

The scores of subjects whose portraits I have contributed to the F.B.I.'s extensive gallery of Reds simply walked into my studio and begged me to take their pictures. I had a reputation for taking good pictures and they figured on a comradely discount.

I took pictures of Communist musicians for professional use, pictures of Communist wives to send to husbands in the armed forces, pictures of Communists elevated to posts of authority in front organizations, and just plain pictures of Communists who were not above the bourgeois celebration of Christmas. An extra print of every client who came to me through the Party went to the F.B.I. as a matter of routine. It was that easy.

While Capitalism and Communism were honeymooning in the United States, the armies of the Soviet Union and the Western allies were moving toward each other across Europe. In December, 1944, Russia absorbed the Baltic states and laid siege to Budapest. In January, the Red Army invaded Poland and no one in the United States seemed to care that the integrity of Poland was the issue over which the war had begun, back in

1939 when Russia and Germany were allies. The boundaries were presumably ironed out at the Yalta meeting of the Big Three in February, but the Russian forces kept rolling on. In March, they took Brandenburg and entered Austria. In April, our Ninth Army politely waited sixty miles outside of Berlin until the Russians entered. The war was just about over. Even to me, that was all that mattered.

Like any other citizen, that spring, I began to look to my own affairs. My photographic business was flourishing. I was under contract with a photographic agency, and was getting assignments that were a real challenge. I was able to improve the "cabin" near Haverstraw which I had rented several seasons before in order to be in the Hudson River country where I had camped as a child. Whenever I could get away, even in the winter, I used to drive up there and spend a quiet weekend indulging in the luxury of my own company.

It was a relief for me to do odd jobs around the cabin and make pictorial characterizations of the farmers in the neighborhood who had become my friends. They did not talk very much, but they meant what they said. There was something very solid and reassuring about Rockland County, and there were many times in the city when I was very glad it was in the world. With one or two exceptions, I kept the rule I had laid down for myself: no Communists allowed.

Up in the cabin, I amused myself figuring out ways I could drop out of the Communist Party. Perhaps I could get transferred to the photographers' branch and then fade out of the picture. Membership records weren't being kept very carefully under the C.P.A., and it looked like a good time to get out. I tried the idea on Ken one day just to see what he would say. I told him I felt sure the F.B.I. wouldn't need me any longer. Communists weren't preaching revolution any more.

Ken didn't answer me directly. "We can't make you stay," he said, "but we'd hate to see you leave now that you've worked your way up in the Party. A good plant is hard to find. Can you recommend anyone to us?"

I thought over everyone I knew outside the Party, but no one seemed to fit the bill, and I would have hesitated even if I had a candidate I could conscientiously recommend. For one thing, I wouldn't wish the tedium and frustration of under-cover work on my worst enemy. For another, anyone I suggested to the F.B.I. might later trace the Bureau's interest to me and endanger my secret. I began to see why the agents would never tell me why they had come to me in the first place. But the very fact that they had asked me for names of possible recruits proved to me that I had done a good job.

I could easily see why they were having a hard time keeping plants. It was volunteer work. Volunteers are usually enthusiastic but they seldom have the sticking power to last through a siege like the Communist Party. I imagined that many who agreed, in the beginning, quickly became disgusted when they found that they were not being asked to catch a bomb-laden saboteur single-handed. Few would be willing, I surmised, to sit evening after evening in stuffy little meeting rooms following the endless harangues the Communists call "educationals." I certainly kicked enough about it myself, but I was just determined enough to stick.

I didn't know it then, but the high mortality in plants came about because very few people who would make plausible Communists were stable enough to stand the strain of a double life. It's easy enough, at the start, to realize the need for reporting every detail you learn in personal conversations, but it is harder to keep it up after you have established the intimate relationships necessary to get this type of information. No matter how hard you try, you're bound to feel, at moments, that you are snooping into other people's private lives. I've found out since that many of the undercover agents the F.B.I. employed broke down completely and had to quit. And every plant who cracked up, of course, was a potential danger to the rest of us.

My agents assured me that I was very valuable to the F.B.I., and that my work was of great national and international importance, but they could not go into details. I did not expect them to, but I couldn't help wondering why they were so anxious to keep me.

"I thought I was taking on a war job," I protested. "The way you talk, I may be in the Communist Party for the rest of my life. Isn't the danger just about over?"

"Just wait," Ken said.

I did not have to wait long. Roosevelt died suddenly in Warm Springs, Georgia. Germany surrendered. Less than a month after V-E Day—before we dropped the Bomb on Hiroshima—*The Daily Worker* published a letter from Jacques Duclos, a French Communist, attacking Earl Browder's policy of collaborating with Capitalism.

Comrades who recognized the voice from Moscow knew that the Golden Age of Browder was over.

8. BACK TO THE REVOLUTION

On May 22, 1945, *The New York World-Telegram* forced the hands of the men on the ninth floor. The newspaper reported that Jacques Duclos, a leading French Marxist, had criticized Browder's policy of collaboration with Capitalism in the April issue of *Cahiers du Communisme,* the theoretical organ of the French Party. The National Board was, of course, aware that the European Communist parties were dissatisfied with the policy of collaboration which had been adopted in the United States, even before they had seen the so-called Duclos "letter." But once the news was published by the *World-Telegram* they lost their hope for a gradual transition back to the revolution. The cat had been let out of the bag.

The greater part of the Duclos "letter," as it was immediately called, is a well-documented, factual and surprisingly objective account of Browder's policy. It quotes freely not only from Browder's published speeches and books, but from speeches opposing his policy made by William Z. Foster in a closed meeting of the National Committee in January, 1944, which Foster suppressed in order to avoid factionalism. It notes in passing, without comment, that Sam Darcy, who made the same objections, was expelled from the Party for repeating them to Party members and to the bourgeois press.

After proving Browder's departure from the orthodox

Marxist-Leninism philosophy out of his own mouth, and summarizing the organizational structure of the Communist Political Association, Comrade Duclos makes four terse, numbered conclusions in the French style: (1) Browder liquidated "the independent political party of the working class in the United States"; (2) Browder effected a "notorious revision of Marxism . . . a revision which is expressed in the conception of a long term class peace in the United States, of the possibility of suppression of the class struggle in the postwar period and of establishment of amity between labor and capitalism"; (3) Browder transformed the Teheran declaration of the allied governments which is a "document of a diplomatic character" into a "political platform of class peace in the United States in the postwar period," thereby "sowing dangerous opportunist illusions" weakening to the labor movement; (4) most Communist parties in the world don't approve of Browder's policy. The last, of course, is a reference to Stalin. Since the dissolution of the Communist International in 1943, there had been no organized way of expressing Soviet policy for the foreign parties. Duclos pointed out that the American Communists could have kept out of the 1944 presidential campaign without going to the length of dissolving the Party. He spanked Browder for trying to solve the problem of national unity, a problem presented in even more acute form to the French Communists, by relying on the "good will of the men of the trusts and under quasi-idyllic conditions as if the capitalist regime had been able to change its nature by some unknown miracle."

The American Politburo had no instructions, and *The Daily Worker* ignored the news for two days. Then they reprinted the letter in full with a note from Browder "welcoming" criticisms and lamely suggesting that American conditions were "different." On June 2, 1945, the National Committee published a long resolution entitled, "The Present Situation and Next Tasks," and called for Party-wide discussion of the dilemma. The errors of the American line, it said, sprang from a "failure to draw our full membership into the discussion and determination of basic policies." The plan was to correct this error immediately by a full and free discussion at all levels leading to a meeting of the National Committe which would "clarify" the will of the Party. The memorandum hit Browder's "Utopian economic perspectives," his "false conceptions of social evolution," his "over-simplified, one-sided approach" to postwar problems. It confessed that "non-labor influences" had "unconsciously affected some of our policies."

I tried to read between the lines of *The Daily Worker* editorials. At the Columbus Hill Club, my dear comrades were just as puzzled as I. Older members withheld comment, but it was clear that they expected stormy weather. The first crisis came in an open class in Marxism we were giving for interested non-Communists in the community. A new Party member who was taking advantage of the lecture stood up and asked boldly:

"What does the Duclos letter mean?"

The teacher the county organization had sent us gave him a revealing lesson in Party discipline. "The Duclos letter concerns Party members only," she snapped. "This is neither the time nor the place to discuss it." After that session, the "course" was dropped without warning. We simply "forgot" to issue postcard notices for the next meeting. We were conspirators again.

Ken called me very soon. I was sure he had questions about the Duclos letter, and I had plenty of my own. We met on Bleecker Street and East Broadway. Ken was driving a black sedan and he had another agent with him whom I had never met before. He introduced Ted Kirkpatrick, a tall, soft-spoken Westerner from Arizona who smiled easily. I liked him immediately.

"Where to?" Ken asked. We often played chauffeur and grand lady.

"Up the East River Drive today, James," I said.

"How are your friends taking the news?"

"Boy, it's knocked them off their ears," I admitted. As soon as I started talking with the agents I unconsciously thought of the Communists as "they" instead of "we."

"Listen, toots," Ken said very seriously. "Ted here is going to take over." I didn't realize at first what he meant. During the war, when the Bureau was pressed for manpower, Ken had often been accompanied by an agent who was new to me, and sometimes he had come alone. But I had always felt primarily responsible to him. He explained that he was being assigned to a desk job. It was really goodbye. I swallowed my disappointment.

"Is this a promotion for you?" I asked.

"Not exactly," he said. I knew that Ken did not want to spend the rest of his life in the Bureau. Like many of the other boys, he wanted to go back to his home town and practice law. Ken came from Peoria.

We talked a little about the Duclos letter, and I saw that the Bureau had been expecting an end to the collaboration policy all along. As I feared, the Party was going to get rough. I didn't even mention leaving my work. We cut across the Bronx.

Ken jammed on the brakes at an intersection on Bruckner Boulevard where the traffic was thick. The car ahead of him had stopped without warning. Our rear bumper was rammed by the truck behind us.

"Quick, Angela, get lost in the crowd," Ted whispered, unlatching the car door. I obeyed automatically, slipping out as inconspicuously as I could. The truck was undamaged, but on the ground beside it was the remains of a plaster apple that had been stuck on the radiator cap as a talisman. The big, baby-faced truck driver, was staring at it, tears in his eyes. Ted jumped out of the car and asked what was wrong.

"You——you," the driver spluttered, "you broke my apple!" The sidewalk crowd was delighted, and so was I. What a picture it would have been if I had only taken my camera! A policeman bore down on the group to take the names and addresses of the agents, the truck driver, and the people in the first car who had caused all the trouble. I now saw why Ted had pushed me out. I could see how the newspapers would have written it up if the accident had proved to be serious:

"The driver of the second car, Kenneth Bierly, is an employee of the Federal Bureau of Investigation. With him at the time of the accident was Ted Kirkpatrick, another F.B.I. man, and a girl photographer, Angela Calomiris, of 9½ Jane Street."

Ted got rid of the policeman without showing his F.B.I. card and the boys picked me up around the corner. I promised to make a full report on the discussion at the next branch meeting, where the Duclos letter was sure to come up.

My report on the first post-Browder meeting of my club is, of course, in the F.B.I. files, where no private citizen can see it, including myself, but to the best of my recollection it runs something like this:

"*REPORT ON MEETING, COLUMBUS HILL CLUB, JUNE 7, 1945.*

"The Meeting was held at branch headquarters, 5 Columbus Circle, Room 501.

"Present were: *

Miriam	Leon	Angela
Pearl	Sam	Toney
Molly	Dave	Judy
Bill	Gertrude	Sue

"A County observer was present whom I have never met before. He did not participate in the discussion but took notes on what was said.

"The meeting was chaired by Gertrude ——, our branch organizer.

"This is one of the largest branch meetings Columbus Hill

---

* My report had full names of comrades present. I'm suppressing the last names here because some of them may have dropped out of the Party.

has had in months due to special announcements sent to each member by mail.

"The main purpose of the meeting was to discuss the letter of Jacques Duclos who severely criticized the C.P.U.S.A. and particularly Earl Browder's leadership. The principal attack is that the American Party is deviating from the Marxist-Leninist path; that the Party and its leaders have given up the struggle for Socialism and have adopted instead a revisionist policy. Browder was named as the chief offender.

"The National Board of the C.P.U.S.A. has ordered that a series of discussions take place in all the branches, using as a basis the Duclos letter.

"All other organizational problems were brushed over lightly. No sale of literature took place and the usual *Daily Worker* harangue was omitted.

"Gertrude —— started the discussion by asking if all of us had read the Duclos letter. She went on to say that we all owed a debt of gratitude to the great French Marxist, Jacques Duclos, for pointing out our deviation from the path of Marxism-Leninism. Surely there must have been many, she said, who felt the bureaucratic leadership of Browder was not our proper militant role, but remained silent for fear of causing dissension in the Party. This silence was wrong. Browder should have been exposed and repudiated long ago.

"Pearl —— brought up an important question. 'Why did not the National Board of our Party indicate to the membership its disapproval of Browder? Have they no faith in us? Didn't we elect them because we thought them the best representatives and the best Marxists in the Party? What kind of democracy do we have if the highest board fears one man and keeps the whole organization under his thumb?'

"Gertrude was rather embarrassed, as she had expected the whole branch to take her cue and lambaste Browder. She answered lamely that our Party abides by a majority decision and anyone who disagrees usually is faced with the accusation of being a factionalist. William Z. Foster had written a letter to the National Board disagreeing with Browder, but it had been suppressed in the interest of national unity.

"Sam —— said he thought it was unfair to blame one man for all the mistakes the leadership had made in recent years. He pointed out that the Party had grown and gotten a foothold in many mass organizations which did not admit or recognize Communists before the C.P.A.

"Leon —— said that it was unimportant and un-Marxian to get a foothold in mass organizations unless that foothold was used for the advancement of Socialism. Any other course would be letting the American people down. Under Browder, he insisted, we have become bourgeois and followed Fascist-Capitalistic interests. It had been his opinion all along that the Communist Party died when it was dissolved. It ceased to lead the working class.

"Miriam —— injected an optimistic note by stating that it was not too late to mend our ways, thanks to Duclos and Marxists of other countries who have kept a vigilant eye on the C.P.U.S.A. 'We must clean house, elect true Marxists to leadership, and never again allow our leaders to dictate to us. We must each of us become so thoroughly grounded in the works of Marx, Engels, Lenin and Stalin that it would be impossible to deceive us into following a revisionist.'

"At this meeting, the bourgeois terms of the past years were shed. We spoke of the 'branch' instead of the 'club' and addressed each other again as 'comrades.' No guests were permitted, and no minutes were taken.

"The chair frankly admitted that discussion material had not as yet reached the branch from the National Committee but she hoped it would be available for the next meeting. I got the impression that she was worried for fear something might be said that the County observer would question. I think this is why she cut off Bill ——, when he defended Browder as a human being subject to mistakes, operating in a difficult period of Party history. He tried to hold the floor, but she called 'time,' as is usually done when a rank-and-filer pushes an embarrassing point.

"We were told that the next four to six weeks would be devoted to a continuance of the Duclos letter commentaries, and we were urged to read *The Daily Worker* faithfully for material. We were asked to visit comrades who lived near us in order to get them to attend the next branch meeting.

"ND 107"

At later meetings, comrade after comrade got up and confessed that he had felt all along that Browder was getting too big for his britches. Those who had cheered Browder wildly at Garden rallies now accused him of "chronic tailism" (following in the progressive movement rather than leading it), "enervating revisionism," "opportunistic support of Roosevelt," and "bourgeois errors." A recent recruit to the Party, unaccustomed to the right-about-face of Party-line shifts, stood it as long as he could.

"Aren't you all being too hard on Browder?" he ventured. "The Party has made advances under him. We're accepted now as citizens, as human beings—not as guys with bombs under our beards."

Gertrude cut him short. "The comrade's speech smacks of revisionism. The comrade no longer has the floor." The comrade never got the floor again. In fact, he left the Party in disgust, along with thousands of others. It was exactly what the Party leaders wanted. The real purpose of the "discussions" was to uncover and clean out pockets of "Browderism."

The Communist Party was reconstituted in July, 1945, under the leadership of Foster, but Browder wasn't formally expelled for deviationism until the following February. During the summer of 1945, the National Committee took vigorous steps to eradicate every trace of Browderism. To replace the lost members, they ordered a recruiting drive which would bring in twenty thousand carefully selected new comrades; the re-establishment of Party discipline; the resumption of day-to-day struggles intended to "awaken the masses" to their true "class interests"; and large doses of schooling for Party members to revive their political health. Old times were back again.

In a course entitled "The Theory and Practice of the Communist Party" we re-read the frankly revolutionary textbooks I had first encountered in 1942. The material we studied, mostly holed up in small apartments, was later to become an issue in the trial of the eleven Communists. Although I never dreamed I would testify in any court at the time, my evidence about what was taught in this educational campaign helped the Government to prove that the leaders had taught, conspired and advocated the overthrow of the United States Government by force and violence when they reconstituted the Party. In brief, this is what they told us:

According to Marxism-Leninism, there are two circumstances under which the inevitable revolution might come about. One is an imperialistic war of aggression which the masses could turn into a civil war against their own capitalistic class. The other is the inevitable depression that was supposed to follow all imperialistic wars. Our teachers applied these prophecies to the present scene.

World War II had begun as a classic imperialistic war of aggression, but it differed from those predicted by Marx in that one of the nations attacked had already advanced to Socialism. Because of this accident, the masses in capitalistic nations allied to the Soviet Union had earnestly supported their masters in the war instead of calling the revolution. But now that the war was over, there would inevitably be a depression that would dwarf the great depression of the thirties as ruinously as World War II dwarfed World War I. Faced with this catastrophe, the bourgeois masters would attempt the only solution they knew—a diversion of surplus production to military preparations for another war.

On the basis of this analysis, our teachers made our duty as Communists perfectly clear. We must mobilize all sentiment against preparation for another war—a war which the capitalists would this time direct against the Soviet Union. We should point out that an atomic war would be too horrible to conceive. In order to avoid the wholesale destruction of American cities, we must stop arming now and do exactly what the Soviet Union wanted us to do. We must bring the boys back home from guard duty along the Iron Curtain, stop helping the Greek and Chinese governments repel Communist forces, abolish universal military training, pare military appropriations, and stop sending arms and money to Europe. The American people are peace-loving, our teachers pointed out. All they had to do to enjoy peace was to stop "provoking" Russia.

Our second task was to prepare for the expected great depression, in which our role, as vanguard of the revolution, would be to lead the masses to revolt. The only way to educate them was to use their current miseries as object lessons. The Party must explain the reason for high prices and high rents. It must teach persecuted minorities, such as the Negroes, to realize that the capitalistic system was responsible for their mistreatment. We must show youth, women, Jews, minority national groups, veterans, how Capitalism was oppressing them. If we struggled for them now, they would follow us when the depression drove them to desperate action. (Stalin counted so heavily on a depression in the United States that he temporarily demoted Varga, the leading Soviet economist, for suggesting that there might not be an immediate collapse in the United States after all.)

Our teachers encouraged us to believe that the revolution would take place as soon as the masses felt the depression. Comrades in the class thrilled to the prospect of real action.

"Are we really strong enough to lead a revolution in the United States?" a practical member asked. "Why didn't the leaders call it in 1933 when we had more members? Millions of the unemployed would have followed us."

"We weren't trained for it then," the teacher answered. "We weren't educated. We had numbers, yes, but they were mostly people who floated into the Party because of the depression. It took less than fifty thousand Communists to stage the revolution in pre-industrial Russia, a sprawling country without modern transportation and communication facilities. We could do the job with far fewer in the United States today. All we need is a few thousand disciplined comrades in the right places."

The third assignment of the Party, our teachers told us, was to rebuild the sadly weakened Party so that, when the opportunity came, it would be equal to its historic vanguard role.

I got away from this schooling for a few weeks during the summer of 1945 on Cape Cod, where I did a series of pictures for a children's book on the adventures of a little boy with a dancing fish. Betty, whose health had not improved, had moved to the country, leaving me alone in the apartment. I missed Betty, but it was a relief not to have to apologize for her to my comrades, who accused her of snobbery because she refused to be drawn into their social life. I don't know whether Betty suspected me of being a Communist or not, because we simply never discussed it. After Betty left, I occasionally put up friends who were victims of the housing shortage, but I kept clear of permanent arrangements.

In the fall, I became financial director of the Columbus Hill Branch, the successor to the Columbus Hill Club under C.P.A. There was plenty of work to do. We executives were loaded with directives for getting the Party back into fighting trim. We prodded members to attend meetings, visited them in their homes to plead for back dues, and ordered them out to agitate on the streets as of old. Comrades who had returned from military service resented our officiousness, but we were warned to go easy on them. The Party was anxious to keep veterans because they could expect courteous reception from Congressmen and civic leaders. There was another reason, too, that we never discussed openly. Comrades with military training would be valuable in the revolutionary crisis.

The year 1946 was a low point in Communist morale. Foster charged that "some of our leading comrades often pay scant

attention or none at all to urgent communications sent to them
from the national or state offices." Comrades on our level had
found pleasanter ways to spend Sunday morning than selling
The Daily Worker. Several times I found unsold bundles of
papers in an ash can near branch headquarters on Columbus
Circle. I should have protested, but I did not have the heart
to scold other people for a trick I had long practiced in my own
Jimmy Higgins days.

We held meetings to devise new ways of "activating" the
membership. Dotty, a cheerful woman who had long been
active in the Party, suggested that we take turns giving Sunday
morning breakfast parties before canvassing trips. Dotty was
one of the few comrades I really liked. Her husband Joel had
a responsible job in a factory which had Government contracts.
I felt sorry for Joel, although I had to report his affiliations to
the F.B.I. Joel was in the Party because of his wife, whom he
adored. As financial director, I knew I could always count on
him to make up a deficit in the branch treasury.

Our membership director, Sue, was typical of hundreds of
other girls I have met in the Party. I got to know her better
than the others because she attached herself to me and was
always willing to do my chores. Sue would have made a good
wife for some man, but she was pathologically fat, and not very
bright. She tagged along after the rest of us, trying hard to
make herself useful, and usually succeeding. Most of the time
she was unemployed, and she looked to the Party for friends
she felt she could not make any other way.

We took shameful advantage of Sue, and every once in a
while I became conscience-stricken. I encouraged her to rent
a typewriter and learn to type—practicing on my reports to
county financial authorities, of course—but she was always too
busy doing Party errands to learn a trade. I gave her a pep talk
about her weight and once I sent her to a doctor. He reported
that her obesity was an emotional problem.

When a visitor from the county complained about the appearance of our branch office, I got Sue to help me clean it out.

We had a single room, high up, which cost us forty-five dollars a month. It was long and narrow with casement windows looking out on Columbus Circle. The chairman's desk stood between the windows. On the other side was a big tilt-top Bible stand for displaying literature, and an el-shaped rough board bookcase for our "library" from which every book by Browder had been carefully deleted. Photographs of Stalin and Foster and Party notices were tacked to the wall. A pipe rack at the rear of the room held coats. Behind it, in great disorder, were dusty stacks of unsold Party leaflets which we were supposed to have distributed, and several file cabinets. In the cleanup, I noticed that one of the cabinets had a broken padlock. It was the cabinet in which membership directors kept their lists.

I pulled the cabinet open and saw a gold mine of old Party records—Party cards that should have been destroyed, carbon copies of receipts for dues—the kind of irrefutable evidence of Party membership for which the Bureau was looking. If I could only get my hands on them! I heard a voice behind me.

"Isn't that criminal?" Sue exclaimed. "All that stuff should have been destroyed years ago."

"Don't you think we should sort it out?" I asked, stalling. "Maybe it's being kept for a reason." But Sue was loyal and punctilious. She had been in the Party since her teens and the one thing she did know was Party procedure.

"We've got to burn it ourselves, Angie," she said. "We can't just throw it out."

"Let's make an occasion of it," I suggested. "We'll truck it down to my studio and burn it in my fireplace. How about Sunday morning for the big fire?"

I tried to steal some of the documents the next evening, but Bob, the Negro elevator operator, stood waiting for me to get the briefcase I said I'd left behind, and I didn't dare stop to sort. I just took one folder from the pile and left the rest. I didn't want Bob to have any reason to mention my extra trip to anyone.

Bob was off duty Sunday. Sue and I lugged the filing cabinet's contents down five flights of dingy stairs and packed them in Penelope, the convertible I had at the time. Penelope was a Hudson Terraplane whom I called the Hudson terrible plane, because she sometimes went backwards when I wanted to go forwards. I had bought her from a nurse leaving for overseas and painted her a pale blue. Sue loved the car, and we had a gay ride downtown with the contraband. But I couldn't think of any way to get rid of her long enough to sort that stuff.

I plied Sue with drinks at the studio, hoping to think of a way out. She chattered to me about her father, a bartender in Philadelphia, who wanted her to go back home to live. One by one, we crumpled the records and threw them on the fire. At first, I tried to remember names and card numbers and amounts, but I had to give it up.

I had better luck with the section membership records which were much more important. On one of my trips up to the Thomas Jefferson Section office on Seventy-second Street, I noticed that the membership file cabinet had been left unlocked by some lax functionary left over from the happy-go-lucky Browder days. I volunteered to help the section organizer run off some pamphlets on rent control one night in the hope of getting a crack at them.

My chance came when he took the key to the john and stepped out of the room. I pulled the file drawer open, hunted around, and found what I was looking for—a thick document containing hundreds of names and addresses. I was lifting it out when I heard footsteps behind me at the open door. There was just time to slide the list under a few sheets of loose mimeograph paper.

"Gee, it's getting hot in here," I babbled. "And late, too. How many more do you think we have to do?"

But my comrade hadn't noticed. He went on feeding sheets of blank paper into the machine. I watched, fascinated. Would he run my list through the mimeographer? What would he say? What would *I* say? Who could have been so careless as to leave a membership list on the table? Any investigation would have started with me. I kept telling my co-worker how tired I was.

"Okay," he finally said. "I'm tired, too. Let's call it a night."

"That's a relief," I said, sliding the remaining sheets into my briefcase. "I think I'll take these home for scrap paper."

The F.B.I. photostated that list the next day in a matter of hours. I hung around section headquarters with my briefcase all afternoon until I found a moment to slide it back exactly where I found it. At the next station with the section I accused the membership secretary of leaving the file unlocked.

"We've got to protect our membership these days," I warned. "We're not the Communist Political Association any more." But my superiors were anxious to hush up the breach of discipline. It would have made underground members uneasy to know that membership records were unguarded. I would have been expelled as an enemy of the people if I had been caught.

About this time Louis Budenz, editor of *The Daily Worker,* left the Party and told his damaging secrets to the public. Comrades were stunned and shaken. They no longer knew whom they could trust. And the worst of it was that Budenz was only one of scores of comrades who were doing the same thing. Even a loyal "comrade" like myself could not hope to escape suspicion.

In the midst of the excitement, I discovered that my part-time assistant in the studio was a Party member. I hadn't given a thought to politics when I hired Rita through a photo supply house that acted as an informal exchange for darkroom help, although in retrospect it sounds like the grossest kind of negligence. The only excuse I can give is that I tried to separate my business from my Party and F.B.I. activities in my own mind. I didn't want to become one of those people who delight in finding Reds under the bed.

I took Rita in preference to a medical student I interviewed because she was interested in photography and took good enough pictures herself to handle an assignment for me when

I had two at the same time. The first out-of-the-way thing I noticed about her was that my phone was always busy when I called in between assignments to pick up messages. Rita seemed to have a great deal of pressing personal business. My first clue to its political nature came when she tried to sell me a ticket to a Party rally in Madison Square Garden.

"Where did you get your tickets?" I asked casually.

"Through the Photo League," she said, in a tone of voice that implied we understood each other. She must have known all along that I was a Communist, but that was not where the danger lay. I thought desperately back to the phone conversations with agents I had held in her presence. I had, of course, said very little on my end of the wire. The boys had given false names the few times they had left messages for me with Rita, though false names would have been as suspicious as right ones under the circumstances. Rita had a key to the studio, but she didn't have a key to the lockbox where I sometimes held notes before writing them up for the F.B.I. I was sure that my habitual precautions had covered me, but I hated to have a Communist installed in the studio.

I longed to fire Rita on the spot, but I knew that I would have to move slowly. The important thing was to assure her that I was a good Communist.

"I've got my own tickets," I said meaningly.

The fat now sizzled in the fire. If I scolded Rita or fired her, she would report it to membership authorities in the Party. I might be called in to explain "suspicious" activities.

As an "ardent Communist" I gladly gave Rita the day off to march in the May Day parade. During the war, there had been no holidays on May Day. The Party asked members to stay on the job and produce for Russia and for victory. Now that the war was over, the people were again demonstrating their solidarity. Good "progressive" photographers had to "document" the festival for fear that the reactionary press would overlook it. I got out of marching myself by explaining that I wanted to photograph the show.

I took scores of shots of the parade and developed them my-self while Rita was away so that I could turn over prints to the F.B.I. The Bureau had its own photographers taking pictures at different points along the route to Union Square, and they collected every picture they could find. All were blown up to a uniform eight by ten and carefully bound in a thick "May Day Parade" book with appropriate captions. Every face was labelled with a number keyed to a name or names on the back.

The Bureau used the May Day Parade book in many ways. The arrangement of a parade—which group goes where—is a triumph of Communist diplomacy, and there is a great deal to be learned about strategy and internal Party politics from the final composition. It was also important to find out whether individuals marched with their branches or with their unions. The parade is traditionally the one event which calls all com-rades on stage. Secret members, or members who for one reason or another never appear in public, will march in the May Day parade, although not as comrades.

It took the Bureau weeks to identify the thousands of faces in the book. All undercover agents, sources and plants were called in one by one to name as many marchers as they could. Cross checks clinched many a dubious Party membership. Sup-pose I recognized a member of my branch whom I knew as Paul. Another source, not necessarily a plant in the Party, might know the same face as Joe Doakes, a Federal employee who vigorously denied being a Communist.

Rita knew I was a "comrade," and she pressed her advantage. When the 1946 fund drive was announced, she asked me for a raise:

"Angela, I'm going to need money this month," she stated baldly. A great many comrades work for sympathetic bosses who kick in under their names during fund drives.

"I'm going to be needing money myself this month," I fenced. I wanted Rita to know that I preferred contributing under my own name.

"If you were General Electric, I could understand it," Rita

said bitterly. That really scared me. What if she complained that I was grinding down the face of labor, and a Party member at that? I gave her a $2.50-a-week raise.

The next week I couldn't get the phone all day long. I missed messages. I couldn't reach Rita to have her put a set of proofs in the mail I had promised a client. At five o'clock, I swept into the studio in a towering rage.

"For two cents, I'd rip that phone right out of the wall," I said savagely. I had always shared the dirty work with my assistant, but I determined to make her do the jobs for which she was hired, Party or no Party. The next day she straggled in late.

"You mix the chemicals," I ordered in my new tough-boss role. "I'll do the printing myself." Mixing chemicals is an unpleasant, smelly chore. Printing is fun. When I came back from lunch, I found a little note on my desk. It said "Dear Angela, I quit, Rita."

I was so glad to have the studio to myself that I did without an assistant for several months. I stayed up nights doing my own finishing. Many commercial photographers farm out their finishing work, but I prefer to supervise or do it myself.

I waited tensely for someone at the Photo League to mention Rita. No one did. Months later, when I was doing a report, I reached for a sheet of carbon and found it had been used. I held it to the light. Plain as day, it showed my last expense account to the F.B.I. Had Rita seen it?

I worried for weeks. This was a serious slip on my part. I not only worried about the consequences but was reluctant to confide in Ted about my carelessness.

I had gotten rid of Rita just in time. Communists were growing uneasy, each member fearing for his own skin. Every newspaper reader knew that the Communists were on the wrong side of the cold war, for which Stalin had ordered the reconstitution of the American Party.

In Korea, in China, in Southeast Asia, in Greece, hot little bonfires licked the edges of the Iron Curtain which had enclosed Russia's closest neighbors, while deadlocked foreign ministers kept Europe in a state of tension. At Lake Success, the Russians vetoed. In obedient Belgrade, they revived the Communist International suppressed in 1943 to lull American public opinion. French and Italian Communists rocked their disordered countries to the brink of revolution. The American people took the warning and looked to the Fifth Column within their own gates.

In March, 1947, the Supreme Court upheld the dismissal of a Federal employee because of Communist sympathies, opening the way for wholesale loyalty checks. The State Department, unsettled by rumors of atomic espionage, announced it would clean its own house of potential Reds. Kravchenko, former Soviet purchasing agent in America, told the House Un-American Activities Committee that the United States was "infested" with Soviet political and economic spies. Ex-Communists, movie stars, trade union leaders, and J. Edgar Hoover himself warned the Committee that the Communist Party, U.S.A., was plotting a Soviet America on orders from Moscow.

Leading Communists sullenly refused to answer these charges, and no one was in a mood to humor them. The Government secured indictments for contempt of Congress against Eugene Dennis, general secretary of the Party, Leon Josephson, C.I.O. attorney, and others.

The Party battened down the hatches and prepared for the order to submerge. There were unconfirmed reports that Stalin himself had designated an alternative set of leaders to function if the Party were outlawed. It was supposed to be so secret that the National Committee itself didn't know for sure which of their own members were chosen to serve on it. Foster and Dennis were believed to be the liaison between the two boards.

Cells were revived as working units against the day when it might be dangerous for more than four or five comrades to gather together. The large branches left over from the Communist Political Association were fragmented into cosy, manageable groups which could patrol their members and fade away at a moment's notice. Our Columbus Hill Branch was split in two, and I became branch organizer of one of the successors, the West Midtown Branch.

One of my first assignments as branch organizer was to buy a Speedoprint. Acting on instructions, I went into a designated stationery store near Fourteenth Street, asked for "Sadie" and said: "Morty sent me from the Thomas Jefferson Section." She sold me an electro-mimeographing machine, and I had to take sixty dollars out of the branch treasury to pay for it. Orders to start classes in writing and printing followed, although we never made more than dry runs. The plan was to be ready in case *The Daily Worker* was suppressed. In that event, press officers would get the daily editorial by word of mouth at secret meetings and publish it branch by branch and, if necessary, cell by cell.

In June, 1947, Congress passed the Taft-Hartley bill requiring union leaders to swear that they were not Communists. Opposition to Taft-Hartley—letters, demonstrations, mass rallies and the rest—had been agitated for months. We Communists denounced the bill as an invasion of civil liberties until we were all blue in the face, but it became obvious even to the dullest and most apathetic union members that our protests had an element of self-interest. Leaders who would have to face Taft-Hartley affidavits vigorously denied their Party membership. Union workers on whom we had formerly relied to carry our story to labor were disappearing from the Party right and left, and we often wondered among ourselves whether they had left to serve the Party better or to save their positions with the rank and file. In most cases it was a little of both.

I had seen before, how my comrades handled organizations in which they were a minority, but the Taft-Hartley fight was an all-out effort. Communist "fractions" in every union used the techniques the Party had developed over a generation of struggle in the labor movement.

We took no chances in the United Office and Professional Workers of America, a white collar union which the Communist minority had run without opposition for years. The show-down there came when Local 16, the unit covering all Manhattan, planned a meeting to decide whether the leader-ship should be directed to sign the affidavits.

A great many union members objected to the idea of the affidavits, but there was a growing sentiment that it would be better for the leaders to sign—or elect leaders who could sign, if it came to that—so that the union could continue to repre-sent us in collective bargaining. The issue was crucial, and the turn-out large enough to include a great many members who had not followed union affairs in the past.

We comrades met before the meeting and prepared to handle a grass-roots rebellion. Each of us was ordered to take a certain seat, so that the dozen comrades present would be distributed throughout the hall. The chairman, a Communist herself, knew just where each of us would sit, and she even had a rough speaking order in mind.

The chair graciously allowed the opposition to state the case for signing, before recognizing Comrade One on her speaking list. He delivered a rousing appeal for the union to combat the invasion of our civil liberties. Subtly, he created the impres-sion that anyone willing to allow our leaders to sign was secretly in league with Fascism. "Are we going to connive at red baiting?" he demanded, rhetorically.

Unfortunately the opposition was not very well organized. A troubled member got up and protested that he too was against sin. "I'm not a red baiter. I'm against witch hunts, as much against them as the next man. But I've been a union member all my working life and I've worked hard to build this union. That's why I don't want to see it broken now. Can't we comply with the law and fight Taft-Hartley, like good citizens, at the polls?"

Three comrades, from different parts of the room, waved excitedly for recognition. Comrade Two's retort ought to have been a dead giveaway. "How long are we going to submit to the whiplashes of Wall Street?" he asked, launching into the standard attack. Signing, he pointed out, would betray not only ourselves but all other workers, all the masses. He made you feel pretty small and selfish about saving our poor little union while humanity lay in chains.

The tricks were childishly simple, at least when you knew them, but they worked. We stole the grass roots out from under the majority and took them for ourselves. Bewildered, bored and slightly uncomfortable, the right wing support began to leave for home. Most of them had to get up and work the next day. I was tired myself, and I tried to slip away with them. At the door, a Party goon laid his hand on my arm.

"Going so soon?" he rebuked. "You'd better get back to your seat for the vote!"

I crept back to the hall and sat through speakers Four, Five and Six. Finally, to groans from the audience, the chairman "summarized" the sense of the discussion. She had prepared a fancy speech herself and wasn't going to miss this chance to give it. To judge by the midnight vote that followed, the only people left to hear her were the comrades themselves.

In December, 1947, Attorney General Clark listed ninety organizations as subversive, for the guidance of Federal executives examining the loyalty of Government employees. I was interested to notice that the Photo League was one of them. Perhaps the F.B.I. had other sources of information, but I couldn't help feeling that my reports had been the main evidence. They had been conclusive enough, heaven knows. For once, I rather enjoyed the indignant outcries of my fellow photographers on the executive board.

The League took the listing as a great affront. We wrote letters to "Dear Mr. President" demanding to know why the League was put on the list. Meanwhile, even in the League, there were doubts and dissents. The gang I had known there before the war were older and wiser now. Many of them had come home to responsible, well-paying jobs. They rallied round the threatened League, but privately they admitted that things looked a little different. They were still "progressives," of course; it wasn't that they'd changed their political outlook. They just wanted to keep the League out of politics.

We loyal comrades denounced them as "yellow bellies" and "turncoats" and "opportunists." The Party was better off without people who fled at the first shock of real battle. The Party's purposes could only be fulfilled by members built of sterner stuff than that. In private bull sessions we raked them over the coals, remembering signs of cowardice from years back that we had never noticed at the time.

At a mass meeting sponsored by the League to "clarify" the issue, a well-known photographer attacked the concept of art for art's sake as decadent. An artist—and we considered ourselves such—needs political interests as much as he needs food. Before he got through, he managed to drag in the evils of the Marshall Plan, the warmongers, and the universal military training bill, ending nicely with an appeal to keep the artists of America free.

The listing was taken more calmly in the other front organizations to which I belonged—the Joint Anti-Fascist Refugee Committee, whose chairman had been jailed for refusing to produce records for the Thomas Committee; the Congress of American Women, formed out of two weaker women's fronts as a kingpin in the campaign to disarm America; the International Workers Order, the deeply intrenched, well-to-do insurance fraternity; American League for Peace and Democracy, one of the short-lived paper fronts; and the American Council for a Democratic Greece, a very sporadic group the Party was hoping to use to recruit Greeks and rouse them to oppose aid to the Greek Government fighting for its life against Russian-trained guerrillas.

All of these organizations, of course, had a great many non-Communists in them. If they hadn't, they wouldn't have been worth the Party's trouble. The purpose of a front organization is to start a group of "politically undeveloped" people moving in the right direction. The program usually features some causes related to the common interest which is the organization's excuse for existence, but the comrades are intellectually athletic at the game of drawing in the entire Party program.

The Congress of American Women, for instance, was designed to attract middle class housewives and professionals of the clubwoman species. It urged the education and relief of European children regardless of whether they were in or out of the Iron Curtain. Around this appealing cause, it was easy enough to build opposition to the "discriminatory" Marshall Plan, universal military training, and the rest of the United States' international policy. Invite a Communist to a medical society, a boys' club, a folk dancing group, or a clutch of suburban ladies interested in botany, and he'll immediately outline the "progressive approach" they ought to take. And although the stimulating newcomer modestly refuses to take the presidency of the organization, he is usually only too glad to do the vital but despised secretarial legwork.

The unwitting dupes in the listed front organizations could have asked embarrassing questions of their leaders, but the comrades in control managed to make the very idea of the listing so hilariously funny that only a very brave rank-and-filer would have dared to take it seriously. Wherever Olympian laughter did not quite suffice, there was always the indirect smear: why hasn't Tom Clark listed the Ku Klux Klan? Why, indeed, the average liberal reflects, did Tom Clark omit the Ku Klux Klan? Obviously because he himself is sympathetic with it! (Of course, if anyone stops to investigate, he will discover that Tom Clark *has* listed the K.K.K. as subversive.)

Nevertheless, front organizations were less useful to the Party than they had been in Browder's time. After the listings, the Party developed a tactic which looked forward to the day when the comrades might lose their controlling positions in many organizations and trade unions. The name of the new tactic was the United Front from Below. It meant, simply enough, the mobilization of "progressive elements" among the rank and file of any group against the tyranny of their "reactionary leaders"—the precise reverse of the tactic the Communists use when they themselves are in control. Tactics, it often seemed to me, depended on whose ox was gored.

As a precaution, we comrades stopped "showing the face of the Party" in mass organizations. In some cases, we connived at the election of respectable but naive or lazy non-Communists who could be managed. And always, we were urged to attend every meeting and redouble our watch.

It was at one of these front organization meetings—I'm not going to say which—that I ran across a casual acquaintance I had known before I joined the Party. Acting on some obscure instinct, I shrank away. I did not believe that he was a Communist, and I did not want him to suspect that I was. Later, at the house of mutual friends, I heard him talk guardedly but knowingly about the dangers of Communism. If he were not a comrade or sympathizer, why had he attended the front organization meeting? I wondered if he could be on the same errand I was. I tried to pump Chick Heiner, the F.B.I. agent who had replaced Ted: "Is —— a plant?" Of course, Chick wouldn't answer, but I thought I detected a flicker of recognition when I mentioned the name of my acquaintance.

Recently I have been able to find out that my guess was right. I can't tell you how I found out, or the man's name, because he is still reporting to the F.B.I. and still highly regarded in the Communist Party.

9. THE CLASS STRUGGLE IN HELL'S KITCHEN

ONE FRIDAY IN MARCH, 1948, I received a telegram summoning all branch organizers to report to section headquarters that evening. Other branch leaders were milling around when I got to the Seventy-second Street office, but the only word was that each of us was to deliver his branch membership to section headquarters at 6:30 P.M. on Saturday.

"What's up?" I asked Wilbur Broms, our section organizer. Wilbur was a slow-thinking Irishman with a Swedish name who rated a good job because he had been district leader in Minnesota. When he came to New York City to study music on the G.I. bill of rights, a favorite Communist meal ticket, he checked in to the local Party, but he had a hard time keeping up with the militancy of the New York comrades. In New York City he had as many active members in his section as there were in an entire Midwest state.

"Don't know myself, Angie," Wilbur said wearily, in the tone of voice of a man who has made the same answer to a series of questioners. "Instructions from the County. It's important."

I believed him when he said he didn't know, and that's what scared me. "Important" could mean only one thing—a violent project to break the law that might involve me in a brush with the police. I phoned the Bureau right away, but I didn't have much to give them, perhaps not enough to make it worth their while warning the New York City police. I repressed an instinct to run out of town and started to round up my membership by phone, by telegram and by personal visit. I tried not to alarm them, but the general mystery of the orders suggested something big afoot. Perhaps the revolution itself would begin with orders of this type.

Everyone was tense and subdued at section headquarters on Saturday. A representative from the County Committee gave us a rousing rehash of the case of the Communists hunger-striking on Ellis Island in protest against their deportation. We listened soberly to the familiar story that had been agitated backwards and forwards in the last few branch meetings. The F.B.I. had arrested Ferdinand C. Smith, Communist secretary of the National Maritime Union, for deportation to his native Trinidad. Nabbed also were Irving Potash, C.P. National Committeeman and leader of the furriers' union, Claudia Jones from Trinidad, Charles Doyle and other violators of the immigration regulations. According to the Party line, their arrest proved that the Government was in league with reactionary employers. The arrests were interpreted as attempts to frame upstanding strugglers for the rights of labor on charges of illegal entry into the United States. The situation called for mass action, and that was the purpose of the secret call.

The whole Party in Manhattan was to be on hand for a "spontaneous" protest against the brutal repression of leading trade unionists. That meant, of course, that we had no police permit for a parade or an open air demonstration. I looked longingly at the telephone as details were rehearsed, figuring out ways I could get it to myself for a minute, but it was too risky. An excited group of comrades half carried me out of the building to my car. We were to filter into Times Square in twos and threes. I could only take five in my car, but everyone wanted a lift down from section headquarters.

Exactly at the signal—when the big clock on the Times building struck seven-forty-five, while theater-goers were filling

Broadway restaurants—we unfurled the banners we were hiding
under our coats. Some of the banners said: "Free the Five."
Another, which took ten people to manage, said, "Jailing
Progressive Trade Union Officials Is Fascism." We formed
ranks quickly and marched four abreast on the sidewalk, arms
linked, as we chanted, "Tom Clark is in the dark." Passers-by
backed into the gutters and gaped. There wasn't a policeman
in sight.

A few veterans swiped at some of the ranting comrades. In
a moment, there were fist fights going on all around. I kept
marching and singing with Sue on one arm. She was having
the time of her life. Excitement, action, danger—this was the
Party life she had always wanted.

Then, out of nowhere, a detachment of mounted police rode
down the sidewalk in front of us. For a moment, I saw Sue,
looking like a frightened bunny, then I ducked into the lobby
of the Paramount Theater to keep from being trampled under-
foot. A policeman rode his horse right after me, up behind the
ticket window. I couldn't think of anything except that the
soft nose of the horse nuzzling my back was the biggest and
most beautiful thing in the world. I slid out of the lobby and
ran half a block down a side street before I realized that it was
safer all around for me to stay with my gang and see it through.
Everything was under control when I got back.

The whole demonstration didn't last more than half an
hour. People read about it next morning in the newspapers,
shrugged, and threw the paper away. I'm sure the immigration
authorities weren't impressed, but that wasn't the point. The
demonstration was an exercise in Party discipline, a fire drill
for the revolution. From the point of view of the Party, it was
a huge success. It proved to the men on the ninth floor that
they could mobilize two thousand comrades on twenty-four
hours' notice. The rank and file had recovered from the laxity
of the Browder era. The Party was again mobile.

Awkward as the Communist Party looks on an organization
chart, with its cumbersome and overlapping echelons, it is

really a slick machine for moving the membership around a sharp curve at ninety miles an hour. The pyramid structure means that orders can travel out from the top with the speed of a geometrical progression. All state committees can be activized at a meeting of the National Committee, which in normal times includes at least one representative from every state. And since the state committees themselves are made up of the key leaders of local units, the word often doesn't have to be passed to more than a few chiefs in any area. Party discipline is enforced so that the organization can operate like an army.

The brief show of force at Times Square was good for Party morale.

It took only a few minutes at the special National Convention in 1945 for the leadership to order the Party back to the revolution by unanimous vote. It took longer to rebuild the fighting spirit which Browder had dissipated in almost a year of cooperation with the "class enemy." Shout and order as they did, the leaders could not get the revived branches and sections to propagate the appallingly long list of Party struggles to their neighborhoods. Branch functionaries twitched at the familiar voice of command like tired work horses who have no real intention of straining at the stuck wheel. In the winter of 1947-1948, when the very existence of the Party was threatened, the New York County Committee reorganized the Manhattan machine for more selective action. The new keyword was to be "concentration" on specific objectives.

The plan called for a rifle rather than a shotgun use of the Party's firepower. The membership was to be divided into a larger number of branches and sections, and each was to be given a specific propaganda target to "concretize" its work. Geographical coordination was to be handled by a new echelon between the section and the county, to be called the "regional committee."

For this purpose, New York County was divided into four regions, the most significant of which was the lower West Side quadrant south of Seventy-second Street, and west of Eighth

Avenue. This area was and is of strategic importance to world Communism. It has what it takes to make a revolution: the docks, railroads, freight yards, teamsters and warehouses that feed the island of Manhattan, the citadel of world Capitalism; a Balkanized population of Italian, Negroes, Yugoslavs, Puerto Ricans, Spanish, Greeks and Irish who retain the nationalistic passions of Europe; and a larger number of disciplined comrades than any other comparable plot of ground in the United States.

I learned of the new system at a regional meeting of all branch organizers. The region was to be divided into six sections, each of which was to "concentrate" on a national group and a basic industry, determined after a year's thorough research study of its neighborhood. Two hundred comrades in the Greenwich Village Section were to work with teamsters and Italians; the two hundred and fifty members of the Upper Village Section to Fourteenth Street and the one hundred and ninety members of the Lower Chelsea Section from Fourteenth to Twenty-third Street were to concentrate on teamsters; Upper Chelsea's ninety-three members were to work with railroad men; Thomas Jefferson, stretching from Fiftieth Street to Seventy-second Street, with its Negroes, Spanish, Irish and Italian populations, was to work on the railroad yards. The Hell's Kitchen Section, to which I belonged, ran from Thirty-eighth to Fiftieth Street. It was to operate from the Yugoslav-American Home on West Forty-first Street and pay particular attention to Yugoslavs and packing house employees.

The Yugoslav-American Home, Inc., was a typical foreign-language association in New York City. Its eight hundred stockholders had contributed $200,000 to buy and redecorate an old Polish church into a clubhouse. The church proper, with its old-fashioned gallery, made a fine floor for folk dancing. The parish house rooms were let out to friendly organizations, among them the Communist Party. The restaurant in the basement, decorated with murals glorifying the working class, was a meeting place for Yugoslav seamen while in town. During the war, members of the National Committee often dropped into the Yugoslav Hall when ships from eastern Europe were in dock. I suspected that the seamen brought messages from the Motherland of Socialism, but I was never able to prove it.

The reorganization of the Party left me as branch organizer with a compact little gang of my own. It seems a little weird, now in retrospect, to remember how I flattered and cajoled loyal comrades into doing their Party work, but Party secrets are told only to those who earn them by hard work. I was out to make a showing as a leader, and I knew that the sheer weight of detail would floor me if I didn't get the cooperation of my branch members. The human material at my disposal was often hard to handle. At one time, four members of my branch were undergoing psychiatric treatment. And there were times when I thought every branch member should have had his head examined. I got to know some of my comrades well enough, up in Hell's Kitchen, to wish I could say, "Look, you're being exploited. Why don't you get out of the Party and think for yourself."

One of the self-confessed neurotics was Barbara, a well-educated, serious girl with long stringy hair whose favorite remark was "Gosh, I look terrible." My photographic eye could see her as quite attractive if she would take the trouble. She would always say no if I asked her to do a chore for me, but I could generally talk her into saying yes, and, more important, carrying through on the job.

Barbara could always get well-paying secretarial work, but she was subject to enthusiasms and piques, and changed jobs rapidly. I knew that she had been a stenotypist in a Government agency in Washington during the war. At the time I met her, she had thrown herself into psychiatric social work in Harlem and was keeping company with a young clerk employed in the Immigration Department, whom we can call Lynn. I lost no time in assembling everything she told me about her boy friend for the Bureau.

Barbara lived with Lynn's married sister, Louise. Louise's husband had been a Federal employee for ten years, but in 1948 he had become eligible for a better post and had been assigned to a Western city. The couple were delighted with the promotion. Barbara, who was very fond of their two-year-old daughter, insisted that I take pictures of the child before the family left town.

Barbara went with me for the sitting. Louise met us on the stairway. "Barbara," she whispered, "I've got a visitor with me, so please don't mention 'the Party.'" It was the first I suspected that she and her husband might be Party members too. I was introduced along with Barbara to Louise's caller, a trained nurse, who was on the point of leaving.

My subject was a lively little imp, not pretty, but full of amusing pranks. I saw at once that I'd have to catch her in action to get a picture that really looked like her. I can remember how I hated to have big grownups pounce on me when I was a child, so I always go slow in getting acquainted with children, and if possible, restrain overanxious mothers from dragging out toys and other stimulations that confuse the baby. Nine youngsters out of ten will find my photographic equipment more interesting than any toy. A pre-school child seldom needs a birdie, but I usually carry a dog with floppy ears or a rubber doll for occasional crises of shyness.

None was needed with this child, who expressed the excitement of her parents over the move to the West by climbing over packing boxes, jumping on chairs, and investigating the operation of the telephone and my light cords.

I was reminded of the well-known photographer of children who told me that he put little girls in a long dress and tacked the hem to the floor so that they would hold still. I shuddered to think how this would have worked out on this little girl.

It was a little bit like covering a fast football game, but we got a number of appealing shots of the little minx in various kinds of mischief best known to a two year old, one of which her parents sent to the *Daily Mirror* "Beautiful Child Contest."

Because Louise and her husband were friends of Barbara, I gave them the Party discount: three pictures for ten dollars instead of three for twenty dollars.

I reported the conversation on the stairs to the F.B.I. The remark did not, of course, prove that the couple were Communists, but it was enough to alert the Western agents to investigate further. It took them over a year to get positive proof, but Louise's husband was a Communist all right, and in important Government employ. He was fired on a loyalty charge just before I took the stand in the big trial.

Besides Dotty and Joel and Sue, we had Tom, a radio editor; the woman who had done the job of spying on Mike Quill; and Clara, an energetic worker who knew how to handle longshoremen but was too dictatorial for much executive responsibility in the Party. When anyone fell down on a chore, Clara would scream, "What kind of a Bolshevik do you think you are?"

We also had a quiet, somewhat mysterious older man, a dentist who went under the name of Cupetz. Cupetz liked me, although he never favored me with any confidences. He had handled literature for years in one Party branch after another and seemed to enjoy the exacting work. In 1948 he simply stopped coming to meetings. A regional membership director to whom I reported his laxity commented cryptically that he was no loss to the Party, so I did not track him down as I would ordinarily have done. I always wondered why he had not joined a dentists' branch. Usually professional men were anxious to get out of community work because of the risk of exposure.

Outside of this nucleus, we had a shifting membership, including our share of the handicapped, the unemployed, and the clearly useless deadwood that drifted in after recruiting drives and stayed just long enough to find out that the Party was not a relief agency. We regulars hated to get these unactivized recruits, brought in by zealous comrades anxious to roll up credit for recruiting. They couldn't work for us, and in addition they created work because they had to be visited and checked as long as they were on the rolls.

In the summer of 1948, our branch spent most of its time and energy on the waterfront. Shipping was the most important basic industry to the Party. Control of the seamen and the longshoremen meant control of every ship that came in or out of New York harbor. Control of shipping throughout the world would be crucial in the event of another war. Our leaders told us that the Party simply had to win the waterfront. The work was so vital that the Party assigned an ex-member of the National Committee, whom I shall call Len, to supervise the waterfront "concentration" work personally.

The Red battle for the docks was going very badly. Joe Curran, the National Maritime Union Leader, had cooperated with the Party under Browder. After the Party returned to the revolution under Foster, the anti-Communist forces in the N.M.U. gained ground. The struggle was carried on with violence and terror. There were broken heads and unsolved waterfront murders in 1948.

The situation in the longshoremen's union was even messier. Their leader, Joe Ryan, was hated by the rank and file of union members, who accused him of racketeering. Joe Ryan was anti-Communist. Our game with the longshoremen was to prove to them that we were their real friends and to encourage them to overthrow their anti-Communist leadership. It was a complicated situation. The Irish, who regard themselves as the aristocrats of the longshore, were traditionally opposed to Communism. We had some support among the Yugoslav longshoremen because of Tito, and we worked feverishly at the Yugoslav Home to enlist their help.

The waterfront struggle came to a head in June, 1948, when Communist leadership was ousted from the N.M.U. At the same time, the longshoremen were threatening to strike. Our game was to come to the aid of the striking longshoremen and prove to them that we were more interested in their struggle than their leaders were. Actually, of course, we were hoping to convert individual longshoremen to Communism and eventually gain control of the union. The longer the strike lasted, the better chance we had to get a toehold. At a briefing of waterfront branch and section functionaries in June, we were given explicit instructions for handling the crisis. I took careful notes in my little black branch-organizer's notebook:

"Maritime strike. A maritime strike ties up shipping on a national scale, even if only one union strikes. If three or four go out, it means 20,000 men on the beach. Three-quarters don't live in New York. We must provide for them and give them public support.

"Demands. 40 hour week, increase in wages, increase in manning scale, welfare program, maintain the hiring hall. This last is most important. Hiring hall instituted a closed shop. Rotary system of hiring. No discrimination.

"Program of Action. 1) Mobilize community adjacent to waterfront—mainly Yugoslavs and Puerto Ricans in longshore. 2) ALP conference. Get comrades active in mass organizations to get their members to attend this conference. These mass groups will get literature to the public. Sound truck. Collect food, money.

"It's not the business of the Party to replace the trade union in this struggle. We will not discuss the internal struggle in N.M.U. We will not tell longshore what to do in relation to strike, but let longshore union tell them. Our job is to give political leadership. Our main weapon of political mobilization is our party press.

"Press program. 1) Every morning, 1000 papers to longshore. Communists in N.M.U. will take care of the seamen.

"2) *Daily Worker*—Quota to be doubled in branches to reach community. Each branch to send two people canvassing in morning and two at night.

"3) Canteen at Chelsea and waterfront."

During May, June and July, I had to organize at least three longshore "mobilizations" a week. It meant getting up at the crack of dawn to hand out literature to the sullen groups of dock workers who gathered, waiting for work, around piers at which ships were being loaded or unloaded.

I used to drive comrades to within a block of one of these "shapeups," as they were called, and park my car where the men couldn't see it. Communists, of course, aren't supposed to have money enough to buy cars. We would start out on foot in couples to sell *The Daily Worker* and to hand out leaflets. We never tried to recruit on the docks. We just gave them reading matter, and tried to get their names and addresses so that we could follow up at their homes. The longshoremen had to brush us off at the shapeup for fear they might not be chosen for work. They might even get beaten up by anti-Communists in their union.

We went in couples because a man and a woman comrade were better protection for each other than two men or two women. The tough guys on the docks weren't so likely to knock a woman down, but they used to amuse themselves by passing out rough remarks.

"Sure, I'll join the Party," a hairy-chested Irishman said to me when I approached him with as much dignity as the circumstances allowed. "I don't believe in any of your Commie stuff, but I do believe in free love."

My East Side upbringing stood me in good stead on the docks. I usually gave the bullies back as good as they handed out, and most of the time they respected me. Once a jeering longshoreman backed me up against a pillar as if to assault on me on the spot. Tim, who was canvassing with me, thought I was really in danger and he socked my attacker in earnest. We managed to get away without trouble. I thanked my champion in private but told him it was strictly against orders to bring on an "incident."

Unfortunately, we didn't have enough working class comrades to man all the longshore mobilizations we were ordered to make, and we had to press white collar members into the work. They were a danger to themselves and the rest of us. I remember one schoolteacher in our branch who dressed up for the occasion as if she were going to a high tea. She wore a gray silk dress, high heels, and a floppy hat that showed off her dyed red hair. She was a prim girl who had probably never spoken to a longshoreman in her life, but I would hate to say what she looked like. I didn't want to go with her, but I knew she would need some protection, and none of the boys had shown up that morning.

"Here's something for you to read," she said to an appraising group of silent men, as she navigated the cobblestones in her impractical shoes. They snickered among themselves, but made no move to take the leaflet she offered them. She ignored them and walked down the line to try another prospect.

"What kind of a Communist are you?" Someone called from behind her back. Another grasped her by the wrist. She struggled to free herself. Longshoremen were gathering around now to watch the fun. "Oh my," one of them mocked in a falsetto, "what a pretty dress!" Flustered, she tried to escape. Someone grabbed her skirt, tearing it down the front. She left on the run, and I was never able to get her to return to long-shore work.

When there was talk of settling the longshore dispute without striking, Len ordered our entire section to visit longshoremen in their homes and encourage them to continue the fight. I stayed at the Yugoslav Home to help dispatch the canvassers. Len was afraid our people would tangle with the union goons. He kept ducking in and out of our office all evening to see how things were going. At nine-thirty he turned to me:

"I'm going to take a little tour," he said. "I ought to be back by eleven. Will you hold on to my notebook?"

I had to think quickly. I didn't know how much there would be in the notebook. I wouldn't dare even to look at it in the building, and I didn't see how I could take it away long enough to copy it.

"Of course," I said, "but I have to leave soon. I have to be at home to get a phone call at ten-thirty."

"Never mind," Len said, handing me one of the small black notebooks which all Party functionaries keep. "I'll have a comrade pick it up at your house."

I got home as fast as I could, tiptoed past a sleeping house guest (she knew nothing of my Party or F.B.I. connections, of course) and closeted myself in the darkroom of my studio before I turned on a light. With trembling fingers I opened the book to read the secrets Len feared might fall into the hands of an anti-Party longshoreman.

It was all in code! With sweat pouring down me in the stuffy little darkroom I copied out the signs—little triangles and circles and boxes with figures in them and occasionally an illegible word. When I returned to my apartment from the studio, my friend wakened long enough to tell me that a man had been looking for me. A few minutes later the appointed comrade rattled again at the gate. I tossed the little black notebook down to him without a word.

I've often wondered, since, if the code experts in the Washington office of the F.B.I. could make anything of my transcription, and whether the secrets it contained were worth the time and the risk I ran in getting them. Len was probably snooping on the progress of the inter-union fight in order to plot the Party's strategy. Obviously he didn't want union members to know what he was doing. The notebook may have added to the F.B.I.'s knowledge of Communist infiltration methods, but I don't think they could have made any direct use of the contents. I was getting used to the incompleteness of my job as a spy.

Longshore mobilizations had first priority, but they were superimposed on the full agenda of campaigns I had to make in the neighborhood. As branch organizer and later acting section organizer in Hell's Kitchen, I had to run a recruiting drive, our quota of a half million dollar fund drive, a *Daily Worker* fund drive, and open air meetings to protest high rents.

My notebook also tells me that we collected funds to send a delegation to Washington to protest the Mundt-Nixon Communist registration bill, conducted street tables for Henry Wallace, and picketed for the packing house workers, the stock exchange union and a bus union.

I grew increasingly disgusted, that summer, with the people we duped. What was the matter with them, I used to think. Can't they see what the Communists are after? Here I and my "comrades" were working like beavers to unsell them on America, while they took the bait or passed us by as harmless visionaries. Our leaders told us that the Communist Party had its back to the wall, and a great many sympathizers began to feel sorry for the "persecution" we were getting at the hands of investigating committees. The Party bravely ordered us to augment our ranks with new recruits. The slogan of the recruiting drive in 1948 was "Build the Party to Defend the Party."

Our regional quota was one hundred new members, fifteen of whom had to come from our section. In order to make our local headquarters sound more attractive, we renamed it "West Midtown Section." We felt that the name "Hell's Kitchen" was chauvinistic, despite its color. My notebook entries for May and June are full of reminders to check members who had promised to sound out likely prospects.

With the middle class professional people, the standard recruiting technique was to invite a prospect to a mass organization meeting and start ridiculing the loyalty checks, the Mundt-Nixon bill, and the investigations of Communists. If he smiled with you, you went on to find out if he favored peace with Russia, better housing, lower food prices, equality for Negroes, and a strong, united labor movement. When he said yes, as he usually did, you disclosed the startling fact that he was a Communist and didn't know it. It is surprising how often you could get away with this nonsense. If you couldn't get your prospect into the Party itself, you could probably get him into the American Labor Party, which was almost as good. The

A.L.P. did a great deal of our agitating for us, and they spear-headed the Wallace campaign.

Most of the time, we had to work with typical Hell's Kitchen people—poor, uneducated, foreign born and often unemployed. To them, the Party offered sympathy and help. The standard technique was to try to sell a seedy-looking man a *Daily Worker*. If he said, "I'm on relief and can't even afford to buy a paper," you would give him a shrug and a smile and say, "So what? I don't have a job either and I'm not on relief. I'm working for a better life for everybody. Communism will get it for us." If you said it with enough conviction, you'd shortly find yourself exchanging confidences.

One prospect told Sue how badly he had been treated in his last job. "And on top of what these goddam bastards do to you, I've got to go home to a sick wife too."

"Sure," she sympathized, "I know all about it. Under Communism you wouldn't have to put up with all this injustice. Now you're beating your brains out for what? Who cares?" Sue asked him what was wrong with his wife, put in a few more plugs for the care, rest and medical service Communism would provide for his wife for free, and was off with one less *Daily Worker* under her arm, and one more prospect on her list.

A great many of our prospects understandably got the idea that the Party was a social agency that would give them money. We talked the good life so vividly that they expected it to appear before the end of the week.

The most unscrupulous appeal we made was to the foreign born: You'll get deported if the American Fascists stay in Power! Even the Puerto Ricans, who are American citizens, could be scared into thinking the Party was their only defense. Actually, of course, only non-citizens who joined the Communist Party risked deportation.

One way to draw in new members was to mention the Party's championship of a minority group or an individual suffering from what looked like discrimination. In order to attract Jews, we picketed the British Empire and protested its policy on Palestine. In order to attract Negroes, we publicized "lynch terror" and "police brutality." These crusades, often centered about an individual martyr, were a very economical way of stirring up unrest that might lead to revolution.

We made special efforts to recruit Negroes, whose struggles had been neglected under the national unity program of Browder. The Party deliberately assigned white girls to canvass Harlem. If a white girl asks a Negro to come to a meeting, he's likely to come. We were directed to invite Negroes to front organizations and to parties. We held special recruiting meetings for them in their own neighborhoods.

We packed several hundred Negro prospects into a small hall in Harlem and brought in specially prepared speakers from the National Committee to give them the works. One after another, our speakers got up and talked about the poll tax, discrimination in employment and in right wing labor unions, the Ku Klux Klan, high rents and gouging food prices in Negro sections. We discovered that housewives in Harlem actually paid more for food than housewives in other parts of the city, and we made the most of the evidence.

Our speakers explained that, as citizens, Negroes pay taxes for low-cost housing projects in which they are not allowed to live. They were told about incidents of racial tension at public playgrounds and swimming pools which the "bourgeois" press refused to report. They were told that it was unfair that Negroes in some states are not allowed to marry whites, and they were given to understand, in a tactful way, that several prominent Negroes in the Party had white wives. Pressure methods like these brought in Negro members, but they left as casually as they joined.

The most effective way to recruit was to dig into the community and get behind its purely local problems. It wasn't necessary to show the face of the Party at once—as a matter of fact, it was probably better to wait until we had accomplished something to which we could point with pride.

Regional officials handed me a juicy project of this kind on
April 22, 1948. My notebook for that date reads:

"Bus Terminal. City to build a bus terminal from 8th to 9th
Avenues between 40th and 41st Street. Families to be evicted.
No place to go. Fight to have rehoused by City in their community. Check A.L.P. for boarded-up houses, get number of
kids also. Demand city renovate these houses and open to tenants. Organize tenants in a tenants' league to fight. Composition: Puerto Rican, Chinese, Greeks, Negroes. Start canvassing
at 320 West 40th Street. Petition in name of Tenants' League
to Borough President and Department of Housing and Build-
ings. Action: 1) Make leaflet. All evictions to be stayed. All
families to be rehoused. 2) Delegation to Borough President
and demand open hearing at Board of Estimates. If club doesn't
help now we'll never get a foothold in the community."

I got the names of the families to be evicted through the
A.L.P. and the Party. Tom, our radio editor, went with me to
call on them in person. We manufactured a front for the
occasion: "West Midtown Tenants Council."

Our first prospect was a cheerful Irishwoman who didn't
seem to be at all worried about being put out of her home.
"They're finding us a much better place with a private bathroom for the same rent," she told us happily. "They're looking
now. They've moved some of the veterans first, and that's no
more than right. But there's a kind gentleman in an office
down on Ninth Avenues does nothing but look after us
tenants. And he's not taken a penny's worth of rent since the
City bought the building."

"Are you sure that's safe?" I asked, for the benefit of Tom.
"They can put you out if you don't pay rent."

But it was no go. The kind gentleman seemed to have
thought of everything. We may have planted a few seeds of
discontent here and there, but we finally had to bury the West
Midtown Tenants Council as honorably as we could. It was a

perfectly beautiful bust and I for one enjoyed every minute of it.

We fared little better trying to win the striking packing house workers, although we picketed with them, and sent donations of food and money to their strike headquarters at 453 West Fortieth Street in our neighborhood. We even gave the strikers a "banquet" to prove our sympathy for their struggle. A few joined but dropped out soon after. Party labor leaders wanted us to support the strike because they had led the union to expect help from the Communist Party. At the very end, after the discouraged union had decided to go back to work, we turned up in force to prevent hired strikebreakers from breaking the strike. Win, lose, or draw, the Party was always for prolonging a strike. A strike provides a fine sounding board for class antagonism. Lenin once said that no strike was ever lost.

Actually, almost any issue of interest to the people around us would do for an opener. At one branch meeting, we discussed a number of possible subjects for street meetings—better playgrounds, nursery schools, demand for a guaranteed annual wage, elimination of the sales tax, retention of the five cent subway fare. If I remember correctly, we decided instead to hold a meeting protesting universal military training. I called up the police station to get the license.

"Who's sponsoring the meeting? The Communist Party?" the hard-boiled police lieutenant wanted to know. Demonstrating against the draft was getting to be a touchy subject, one on which the Party hoped to have a lot of "liberal" company.

"Oh no," I said quickly. "It's the Mothers' Committee of the Lower West Side." A Mothers' Committee can get away with more than a Citizens' Committee.

Like every other unit of the Communist Party, Hell's Kitchen spent a lot of effort trying to boom Wallace for President. Our branch took a straw vote of sentiment in our neighborhood. Each of us got a quota of cards which could be marked for Truman, Dewey, Eisenhower, MacArthur, Vandenburg or Wal-

lace. The idea was to buttonhole the right people, so that
Wallace would come out ahead. Then the list could be used
later to get the "right" vote to the polls.

The Communists had been talking about a Third Party that
would unite "progressives" behind a policy of "peace" with
Russia since 1946, but most New York comrades assumed that
the Party would throw its weight behind the A.L.P., in which
most of us had been working for years.

We learned otherwise at a secret meeting of New York
County functionaries in 1947, before Wallace announced his
candidacy from Chicago. John Gates, the young editor of *The
Daily Worker,* against whom I was to testify at the trial, told
us that the National Committee had agreed to endorse Henry
Wallace for President. Wallace would not run on the A.L.P.
ticket, but head a new Progressive Party. The very name was
borrowed from the term we habitually used as a cover up in
front organizations. A few die-hard A.L.P.-ers in the audience
tried to protest that the Party was departing from its militant
role, but Gates shut them up. In a few months, we were all out
working for Wallace.

The new Progressive Party did not shrink from open ties
with Russia. In March, 1948, Glen H. Taylor, Wallace's running mate, welcomed the new Soviet ambassador at a dinner
given by the National Council of American-Soviet Friendship,
which was on the Attorney General's list of subversive organizations. The Council is an organization which exists to further
better relations and the exchange of cultural information between Russia and the United States. It entertains visiting
Soviet dignitaries, collected funds for Russian war relief during
the war, and sponsors other "friendly" international gestures.

The F.B.I. was particularly interested in its affairs because
it was a natural liaison point between the American Communist
Party and officials of the Soviet Union. A Soviet spy who
wanted a specific piece of information about American life
could turn up at the Council and meet Party members who
might pass him along to sources who could help him, usually

without even realizing that they were serving an espionage chain.

I still have my notes on the dinner at which Glen Taylor spoke, from which I can reconstruct the report I made to the F.B.I. The original, of course, is in the F.B.I.'s morgue:

"REPORT ON DINNER OF NATIONAL COUNCIL OF AMERICAN-SOVIET FRIENDSHIP
"March 23, 1948

"The National Council sponsored this dinner at the Hotel Commodore to welcome Alexander Panyushkin, Soviet Ambassador appointed last October. He made his first public speech at the dinner.

"The following guests of honor were introduced by name:

> Canada Lee
> Muriel Draper
> Eleanor Gimbel
> Jerome Davis
> Mr. and Mrs. Glen H. Taylor
> Ella Winter
> Jessica Smith
> Corliss Lamont
> Abraham Pomerantz
> Frieda (an industrial designer
>   whose last name I didn't catch)
> Sorokin (acting Soviet Consul General)
>   and Mrs. Sorokin
> William Howard Melish
> Richard Morford
> C. A. Baldwin
> First Secretary of the Soviet
>   Embassy in Washington
> Alexander Panyushkin
> Charles Haywood
> Vladimir Kosakevich
> Theodore Beyer

Largest ovations were for Canada Lee, Glen Taylor, Richard Morford and Corliss Lamont. Enthusiastic applause whenever Wallace or Stalin were mentioned.

"*Melish speech* Melish apologized that dinner was given in the East ballroom instead of Grand ballroom as originally planned. He pledged Council support for Wallace and Taylor in the fight for peace and introduced Corliss Lamont, praising him for his devotion to the Council's work in furthering good relations between the United States and the Soviet Union.

"*Lamont speech* Lamont welcomed Panyushkin. The theme of his short speech was that America must be mentally disarmed of the belief that Russia was getting ready to fight. The Truman doctrine and the ERP are warmongering. The administration is indoctrinating soldiers in Germany by issuing pamphlets slandering Russia. He urged everybody to keep calm, resist the Fascists, and work to have the atom bomb shared. He introduced Glen Taylor to a tremendous round of applause.

"*Taylor speech* Taylor told how just before dinner his four-year-old son had taught "Home on the Range" to a Russian child, who had, in turn, taught his son a Russian song. The two children sang the songs on the spot. The point: Americans and Russians could get along together if they started friendly relations as children.

"Taylor went on to assure Panyushkin that mistakes in American foreign policy would soon be corrected. He praised Lamont, who, despite the fact that he was born with a silver spoon in his mouth, rose above his wealthy background to help the people. He cited Pomerantz for his work in the Nazi trials and Dick Morford for his fight against conviction for contempt of Congress arising out of his testimony before the Thomas committee.

"Main points of his prepared speech, which was handed out

to newsmen, was that Wallace could prevent another war by sitting down with Stalin and working out an honorable compromise on the differences between the two countries. Wallace understood the Russians. The Russians weren't tyrants and dictators. On the contrary, they spend more money for education than we do. He claimed that Russia had been misrepresented, and was innocent of the crimes of which she was daily accused in the press.

"Truman and his advisors were Fascists who said the same things the Nazis used to say. The phrase 'iron curtain' was not coined by Churchill, as is generally believed, but by Goebbels.

"Taylor spoke of himself and Wallace as the true heirs of Roosevelt who were championing the people against a few economic royalists who wanted war for their own selfish interests.

"Ten thousand dollars in checks and pledges were collected after the speech.

"Panyushkin's speech Panyushkin delivered a prepared speech in Russian, Kasokevich interpreting. He denied that Russia was intervening in the affairs of other countries. Stories to that effect were vicious slanders spread by international reactionaries who did not want the American people to know about the wonderful things that were happening in Russia under Socialism. These reactionaries were responsible for the Iron Curtain.

"The Russians had borne the brunt of the war. All they wanted now was a chance to rebuild their country and cooperate with other nations toward peace. They had a five year plan which they hoped to finish in four years.

"Panyushkin welcomed a public opportunity to set the United States right on the Czech crisis, which he said was shockingly misunderstood in this country. All changes in the Czechoslovakian government had been made strictly in accordance with the Czech constitution."

Taylor and Lamont could not have done better at the Party line if their speeches had been written by the National Board. In a way, it would have been less alarming if they had been. I'm afraid that the truth is that Party terms have been insinuated into the natural vocabulary of millions of Americans who simply do not recognize the mint in which they were coined, nor the current Soviet purpose they are made to serve. As I sat there, taking the familiar language down, it seemed almost incredible to me that the dupes could fail to recognize that they were selling their country short in an international crisis. Relations between Wallace and Russia were to get closer very soon.

On May 11, 1948, I had to mobilize the membership of my branch and as many friends and relatives as they could individually muster to attend a mass rally at Madison Square Garden, at which Henry Wallace read an open letter to Stalin proposing the solution of differences between the Soviet Union and the United States by mutual adjustment. Wallace implied that ordinary diplomatic means had failed because our Government was wrong. Truman and company *wanted* a war to save the Capitalist class. The only way to get peace was to accede to Russian demands. The crowd, nineteen thousand strong, chanted a jingle we had prepared.

> "One, Two, Three, Four,
> We don't want to go to war.
> Five, Six, Seven, Eight,
> We want Wallace in Forty-eight."

Three days later, at a "station" with a Party political expert, we work horses got the political blueprint for our campaign. My notebook for May 14, 1948 reads:

"Wallace movement. In New York State, seven million will vote in '48. We can get three-quarters of a million upstate if Truman is Dem. candidate. Wallace will carry N.Y. State.

Manhattan must get 400,000 votes. Negro votes most important. Italians, Poles apathetic to '48 elections.

"Organize: Vets for Wallace; Teachers for Wallace; Professionals for Wallace; Businessmen; Youth; Women. Set up Wallace committee in section and branch. Maritime Committee for Wallace. Establish Wallace committee on each ship. Recruiting booths like Army and Navy to recruit for peace and Wallace. 2000 students to work in rural communities for Wallace during summer. P.C.A. and A.L.P. must merge to support Wallace. All Communists to vote for merger. Wallace letter to Stalin is a positive step toward peace between U.S.S.R. and U.S. Main issue of campaign is peace."

On May 17, 1948, Stalin publicly answered Wallace that he'd be glad to sit down with him and settle the cold war by face to face discussions. Stalin obligingly gave us a chance to present Wallace as the man who could settle the Russian question singlehanded, by a personal visit, the way Roosevelt might have done.

The A.L.P. spearheaded the Wallace campaign in New York City. Comrades worked from A.L.P. headquarters on the inevitable doorbell ringing, registration checking, literacy classes and other legwork of a political campaign in a big city. But in our own inner circles, we were always careful to distinguish between the Third Party and the Communist Party. At a conference on youth work I attended in June, there was lively discussion on the question whether we should revive Marxist-Leninist Youth Clubs at this time, or wait until after the election for fear of diverting leadership from the already organized Youth for Wallace Clubs. Said one speaker: "If Wallace loses, youth will be disheartened. If Wallace wins, youth in the Youth for Wallace clubs will be prepared only with bourgeois ideology and they will have to be educated anew to bring Socialism to the people." It was decided to work within existing organizations to give them a more decided Marxist-

Leninist cast without diverting from the number one job:
electing Wallace.

By June, 1948, it was obvious that Hell's Kitchen Communists were a huge success from the point of view of the
Party. The West Midtown Section went over its fund drive
quota, earning me a reputation for being a good money-raiser.
We had sent more than one third of our membership to Washington to protest the Mundt-Nixon Communist registration
bill. We had organized a Yugoslav youth organization from
which nineteen had been recruited into the Party in a period
of four months. Since I had been assuming active direction of
the section, I got the credit for all these accomplishments and
began to reap the rewards in invitations to policy conferences.

State and county observers attended our new section's first
convention, at which I made the main address. It was probably
the high point in my Party career. Breathing fire and conviction, I urged my comrades on to their "immediate tasks" in
the traditional double talk:

"It is necessary to expose Wall Street's imperialistic chauvinism in its fraudulent claims that its drive for world domination
is motivated by high moral considerations, that it is merely
asserting 'leadership' in the world and that it fights for 'Western civilization' because of its alleged 'superiority' over other
civilizations, that it fights against 'anarchy' and totalitarianism,
and that the 'white Christian Anglo-Saxon' world is entitled to
top position and 'to lord it' over everybody else. This theory
is borrowed from the Nazi racist theory which was ideologically
prepared by German monopolists for the war to conquer the
world. . . .

"We must everywhere in our work expose the destruction
of the Bill of Rights in the name of Constitutionalism. . . .

"We must expose the anti-Communist 'Foreign Agent' Myth
employed by the monopolists to confuse and disarm the people's
struggle. This 'foreign agent' myth is not new. Jefferson was
called a French agent, Lenin a German agent, etc., and now

the U.S. Communists are called 'Russian agents.' This cry is ironical coming from Wall Street, which maintains a widespread spy system in every country as its 'Project X.'

"The immediate task of the C.P. is to help the people's coalition to realize its immediate tasks, but in so doing, comrades must present to the masses the objectives of the struggle and the movement. In this connection, we must guard and struggle against left sectarian errors which would result in our failure to rally the masses around the immediate tasks of the coalition in the interests of the higher struggle to come. The immediate struggles are basic preliminary steps toward the higher struggle of achieving Socialism and are inseparable from it. We must guard and struggle equally against the right opportunist mistakes which would result in the abandonment of the struggle for Socialism and a betrayal of the working class. We must continue to cleanse our Party of those conscious right opportunists who would have us struggle for the immediate needs without seeing the ultimate aim of Socialism."

It was a fine Red speech. I labelled opposing concepts "myths" and referred to the Constitution as "Constitutionalism." As I talked, I could not help thinking about the tricks all Communists use. They create more "ism" words than any other group of theorists. And they give their own violent purposes away by projecting them on their enemies. The Communists think they are superior, so they have to accuse the West of a superiority complex. The Communists have an international spy system as a Project X, so they must attribute it to "Wall Street." The Soviet Union hopes to conquer the world ideologically and politically, so to them it follows that nations who resist absorption are themselves "imperialistic."

Every situation has its stock phrase. Translated out of the gobbledegook, my speech meant simply this:

"America must give in to Russia or face war. But war isn't necessary. The United States is a democracy, in which the Government listens to the people. The American Communists

can win the people to a policy of appeasement and tie the hands
of the diplomats who understand that the Soviet Union wants
to dominate the world. There are so few American Communists that the only way they can do this huge job is to get
the help of a great many other Americans by fighting their
local grievances in 'day-to-day struggles' such as campaigns for
Negro and labor rights. But in so doing, the American Communists must stay pure in heart themselves. They must never
forget that these struggles are just a means to an end. To
advocate them only for themselves is to commit 'right devia-
tionalism.' The Communists must remember that their goal
is the revolution."

Our section convention was one of many being held by
sections all over the country. It was followed by a county and
a state convention, leading to the National Convention of the
Party in August. Their real function was educational rather
than deliberative. The resolutions to be passed at the National
Convention had been circulating for months in mimeographed
form as "draft resolutions" so that they could be thoroughly
"discussed" at every echelon.

I was a delegate to the 1948 New York County Convention.
On Friday, July 9, we convened at the Irving Plaza Hall near
Union Square, but we met at the Renaissance Casino in Harlem
on Saturday and Sunday in deference to Negro members. The
atmosphere was grim. Security officers went over our credentials at the door. Three people ahead of me were turned away.
I was glad that I had not attempted to get extra invitations for
the F.B.I. to give to other observers. I estimated the crowd
at five hundred. Since each delegate was supposed to repre-
sent 25 members, that would have made the New York County
membership 12,500, but the estimate could not be accurately
made because some delegates represented smaller cultural,
labor and national groups.

George Blake, secretary of the New York County Committee,
opened the convention on a conspiratorial note by cautioning

us against discussing facts and figures outside the convention hall, even among ourselves. If we wanted to jot down reminders for our own use during the sessions, we could use the paper provided and destroy the sheets before leaving. Big, bored-looking Party goons hulked around the sides of the hall to keep a sharp watch on notetakers.

I had to take notes on the long speeches and on as many of the panels as possible, and get them home with me, so I sat with comrades from my section doodling on the sheets of paper as was my habit. When I'd marked up one sheet I'd crumple it as if to throw it away, wait for a moment, and slip it into the pocket of my dress. Once or twice I lost a sheet on the floor. Then I had to wait a good opportunity to retrieve it. Several times I dropped a pencil on the floor. When I picked it up I also got my notes.

The F.B.I. was very much interested to see if the national leaders would mention Tito in any of the long ideological speeches. Two weeks before the convention, the Cominform had reprimanded Tito for being "anti-Party" and uttering "anti-Soviet opinions incompatible with Marxism-Leninism." Instead of crawling apologetically and begging forgiveness, Tito had tartly labelled the charges "contrived falsehoods" and threatened to organize a Balkan federation hostile to Russia. My comrades were as anxious as I to get instructions on how to handle the questions we knew the Yugoslav members would ask us. If we lost the Yugoslavs we might never win the waterfront.

We strained our ears for a policy line, but the leaders seemed to be just as much in the dark as we were. They contented themselves with safe sentiments: we must guard against the attempts of "Wall Street" to use the breach as a pretext for the war they have up their sleeves. The real lesson to be learned from the affair is that a good Communist must keep a constant watch on his own political health.

There was no lack of self-criticism at the convention. Comrade after comrade got up and zealously analyzed the Party's

mistakes. The Party could have beaten Taft-Hartley as it did
the Mundt-Nixon bill if it had seized leadership of the forces
opposing the bill earlier. The Party should have tied up the
cause of Israel with the peace campaign in order to get Jewish
votes for Wallace. Tenants' Council work had been left too
much to women. Trained leaders had been diverted from the
crucial long-range task of building youth clubs. The county
had recruited only one hundred Negroes in the past year. It
had not attracted the Italians, either. There were only three
hundred Italian members in the county and eight hundred in
the state. New members were rushed into Party chores before
being educated to realize their importance. Too many new
members were dropping out, and so on. The breast-beating
was largely confined to things the Party had left undone that
it ought to have done.

I tried to get as many exact quotes as possible. Phraseology
was important. Members accused of "errors" might be re-
deemed, but any name linked with the adjective "Trotzkyite"
was down in the Party's book for future liquidation. In trying
to listen to several conversations at once, I managed to get a
hodgepodge of ponderous and trivial comments:

"Who do you suppose leads the Parent Teachers Associations?"

"What would America be like without the Communist
Party?" (Ben Davis)

"The C.P. is all the Puerto Ricans have left. If we can only
get them past the literacy tests in time for the elections!"

"Why doesn't *The Daily Worker* report the liquidation of
Communists in Spain?"

"We ought to have a Negro woman on the County Committee."

It was a broiling hot July weekend, and even Communists
are human. I skirted the edges of a panel which Blackie Myers,
the Communist N.M.U. leader, was trying to keep to the
agenda. "It's hot and we want to get you all out of here as
fast as possible," he was pleading, as all of us had at one time

or another pleaded with branch meetings which threatened to go off the track. Some Communist in the group, resenting the use of a familiar speed-up-shutup tactic on himself, murmured, "Why can't we get an air-conditioned room, then?"

There was exciting gossip. Blackie Myers, in his role as diamond in the rough, had cut off a long-winded lady comrade with the ungallant suggestion: "Women talk too much." The lady and her friends wanted him brought up on charges of male chauvinism, but they were placated by a resolution reprimanding Comrade Myers and the establishment of a county commission to eliminate male chauvinism within the Party by giving more important posts to women and urging that married comrades share baby sitting. Our own section was flustered over the rumor that Dottie had voted against Rena Klein, our regional organizer, on the supposedly secret ballot for the county slate.

By the end of the first day, my dress pockets were bulging with crumpled balls of hot notes: the exact county membership of 10,120, an increase of 1947's 6,500 members, broken down by precinct, occupation, national group and sex; the policy on testifying at investigations of the Communist movement; plans for getting the department store union to demonstrate in Gimbel's; a report on a Harlem group called "A League to Violate Civil Obedience" which was going to urge resistance to the draft law until segregation was abolished in the armed forces. If I were caught with this dope, I would have had a hard time explaining why I had taken it down in the first place, let alone attempted to smuggle it out. Many of the subjects were far from my concerns as a section organizer.

When I stood up, my pockets almost overflowed. It seemed inevitable to me that someone should notice. I looked longingly at the door—but it was blocked by a chatting group. They were being held up while a strong-arm guard searched a comrade. I had a panicky moment during which I thought of dumping my loot, but it would have been more conspicuous, I figured, to pull papers out of concealment than to brave it through. I attached myself to one of the waiting huddles and engaged in a lively post mortem on the convention until the door was unblocked. With a county official on each side, I sailed past the guards unchallenged and assumed my usual role of taxi driver. I kept my eyes on the traffic while some notes tumbled under my companions' feet in the crowded front seat. I was relieved to get home undetected, but I did not know at that time that the whole course of my life might have been different if Rena had so much as picked up and read one of the crumpled sheets. Even if she had not thought about it that night, she would have been sure to remember it in the weeks to come.

10. COMMUNISTS AT BAY

THE COMMUNIST PARTY claims that it practices "democratic centralism," a much higher form of democracy than the "pseudo-democracy" of America. It makes elaborate provisions for funnelling mass opinion to the top leadership. According to the Constitution, all units of the Party elect their own officers, and criticism of the elected functionaries is a duty of every comrade, no matter how humble he may be. All units hold regular "evaluations" of their officers, at which rank-and-filers are supposed to criticize any habits of their executives which may affect their efficiency as agitators, from their choice of words to their choice of hats. These criticisms are supposed to be given and taken "objectively," as political rather than personal.

Long before I reached echelons in the Party where the pretensions to democracy are contemptuously laid aside, I understood that "democratic centralism" was an Aesopian word for a system that worked very much like the "leadership" principle of Hitler. I had also seen, at second-hand, the lengths to which comrades carried personal vendettas and feuds. How could internal politics be other than cruel and bitter in a hierarchical, conspiratorial group with more than its fair share of unstable personalities? But up to the summer of 1948, I had lived a fairly charmed life. I was known as a reliable comrade, a good leader. The trouble was that I rose to a position worth critical attention at the time when the Party was fighting for its life and when the personal exposure of scores of leaders to legal action lent a sinister cast to their incessant intrigues.

The story of my battle with the Party and the personalities in it during the last half of 1948 is not a pretty one, and it is as confused and as inexplicable as human relations can ever be outside of fiction. But so much of the story could have happened only inside the Communist Party when it was at bay that it may be worth setting down.

To begin with, I had a half dozen or so loyal comrades whom I thought of as "my gang." I had begun to gather them in 1947 at Columbus Hill, and we managed to stay together through successive reorganizations. We stuck together against arbitrary directives and interference from regional and county authorities who didn't understand us or our local problems. My position as branch, and later section, organizer was much like that of a good army sergeant who has to interpret the orders of brass hats he hates as much as his men do.

I remember, for instance, the time when Dora Deutchman, regional membership director, got wind of the fact that Pat, my educational director, was undergoing psychiatric treatment. She had come to visit us and was snacking after the meeting with some of us at Child's Columbus Circle restaurant, one of our favorite places for transacting informal business. Someone complained that Pat couldn't make his fund drive assessment because his psychiatrist cost him a large part of his salary.

"But he can't hold office if he is going to a psychiatrist!" Dora exclaimed. "Angie, you'll have to demote him."

I nodded, but I took no action. Pat was as good an educational director as I could hope to get. His wife was sympathetic to Communism as a theory, but against joining the Party. Marriage to an anti-Communist merited a full investigation, but I contented myself with making her leave her apartment when we held executive meetings there.

Dora, however, didn't let the matter drop. She cornered Pat, who was shy and nervous, and told him he'd have to choose between his job in the Party and his analysis. I don't know what she said, but it brought him to the verge of tears. I had to find another educational director, but I didn't bother to tell Dora that Barbara, my financial director, was in touch with a psychiatrist too.

After the regional reorganization, our West Midtown Branch reported to the West Midtown Section under the leadership of John, a big, magnetic Yugoslav. John was the nearest thing to the ideal proletarian leader of Communist fiction that I ever encountered in the flesh, and I got along with him famously. He was handsome, in his forties, with graying blond hair, blue eyes, and a rugged face, bronzed from outdoor work, that broke into dimples when he smiled, which was often. He was a powerful speaker. Although his English was limited, he had a ring of sincerity that held his audience. If he got his words backward, he would laugh with the crowd and start over again a little shyly. He had been a longshoreman, which made him very useful for our "concentration work." He once organized the comrades to load the Yugoslav ship *Radici* which the anti-Communist longshoremen refused to handle.

John was a carpenter by trade. For two years he had been trying to get transferred from community work so that he could spend all his time on the United Front from Below in Hutcheson's A.F.L. union, which bars Communists from membership. He had accepted leadership of the new West Midtown Section only under pressure. The front job exposed him to discovery and expulsion by the union, which would have meant starvation for his wife and three children, as well as the end of his work in a right wing labor group the Party had been trying to infiltrate for years.

In May, I was made co-section organizer with the idea that I would free John of as much administrative detail as possible. I told George Blake, the county chairman, that I didn't really feel equal to the responsibility—actually I didn't want the front

job either—but I piously explained that I wouldn't turn down
any post the Party wanted me to fill.

According to the standard hierarchical setup, John and I
reported jointly to Rena Klein, the organizer appointed by the
county to set up the Lower West Side region. Progressing up-
ward, the line of authority ran from branch to section to region
to county.

I had first run into Rena back in 1942, when I had been
sent down to help with the clerical work of organizing a morgue
for *The Daily Worker*. I disliked her the first moment I laid
eyes on her. She had a long, thin, concave face with a jutting,
pointed jaw and near-sighted eyes that squinted. If the occasion seemed to require warmth, she screwed up her face into
a compulsive smile that vanished almost immediately without
a trace. I wrote her off for a pinched, ambitious girl who
would never rise very far for all her driving ways. But that
was back in 1942, when I was new to the Party.

I never got a full biography of Rena, but I was able to supply
the F.B.I. with a few suggestive scraps of information. Rena
had been on the Party payroll for years. Before the regional
setup she had been assistant to the county organizer. She was
on intimate terms with leaders of the Italian Communist Party
who visited New York. She was married to a Tass press representative at the United Nations. This last tip appeared to be
particularly interesting to the F.B.I., possibly because it was
well known that the Soviet Union was using Lake Success as a
listening post.

I'm probably prejudiced, but I don't see how anyone could
really have liked Rena. At least, I never met anyone who did.
As an executive, she was a menace. She wanted to do the work
of the six section organizers under her. She would butt into
our branch room at the Yugoslav-American Home while we
were meeting, glare at the speaker, fidget impatiently, and
finally break up the meeting by interrupting with a tactful
remark like "Your approach is absolutely incorrect."

When she spoke herself, she had a curious way of repeating the last phrase in every sentence:

"The Communist Party is the vanguard of the working people. The working people."

"We must form a picket line out there that will show everyone the Communist Party is behind the strike. Behind the strike."

It made the hackneyed phrases sound like a lesson she had learned by rote. At first, I thought it was a nervous habit, but I found out later that she had copied the trick from Blackie Myers and other N.M.U. leaders without putting the punch in the tag line that warned you it was meant for emphasis.

Rena patronized the lower cadre almost beyond endurance. It was always "cookie this" and "honey that"—all of which saccharine nonsense did not prevent her for one small moment from ringing me out of a sound sleep at two in the morning if she happened to think of a better way for me to do my own Party business.

"Don't you ever get tired from all the work you do?" I asked her once, blandly enough. But like many professional Communists, Rena was strangely insensitive to verbal barbs of this type.

"No, I just love it," she replied without guile.

John liked to tease her, particularly if I were around to appreciate the situation. Rena wanted desperately to show her authority over John. Once she bustled up to him importantly to summon him to a special meeting to "discuss" some general problem.

"If there is anything you want me to do, tell it to me now so I can do it," he replied innocently, catching her off guard. He knew that Rena had nothing to tell him, and he also felt he was far too big and old and male to be bullied into attending trumped-up meetings by an officious female. Another trick of his was to get up and leave the room as soon as Rena came in to see him. But Rena lacked a certain kind of pride. After that, she tried to get at him through me. To save my face, I would have to urge him to call her.

"I don't want to see that woman, Angie," John would say bluntly. "She doesn't understand anything. I do all the things she says if they are humanly possible. Otherwise, not."

On one occasion, he made a counteroffensive that penetrated even Rena's atrophied consciousness. She had been outlining to him enough work for six supermen. When she was through, he just stood there grinning slyly.

"Tell me, Rena, does your husband ever get to see you?"

Rena winced, but she was afraid to answer back even if she knew how. John was the most valuable man the Party had for handling the Yugoslavs, and Rena wanted to keep him from transferring out of her organization to undercover work in the union. But she found her own weapons for revenge. On the next recruiting drive she tackled him on the subject of his wife, who was not a Party member.

"She takes care of the children," John explained. "She cooks my supper. I come home and eat it and put on my hat and go out to work for the Party. Why should she join? I am the Communist for both of us!"

"That's male chauvinism!" Rena tried to make the serious accusation lightly.

"My wife does not speak English. She could not work for you."

"We don't want her to work, we want her to join." Rena was her usual self again. "If you don't recruit her, I'll send someone else to do it."

"In that case," John said slowly, "I shall forbid her to join."

And that was the end of that. John could get away with it because he was an old and valuable Party worker.

Rena and Barbara took a violent dislike to each other at first brush. I wasn't there when Rena made a flying visit to our branch and questioned Barbara about the progress of the fund drive—which Barbara was handling brilliantly—but I heard about the encounter from both of them.

"Who does that woman think she is?" Barbara asked me.

"She's only the regional organizer," I said, expecting Barbara to cringe.

"Well, she doesn't bother me. I've seen hundreds of Party hacks just like her."

It didn't take Rena long to find out that Barbara was getting mental therapy. Perhaps her regional membership secretary, Dora Deutchman, had made a thorough check of the membership after discovering Pat. It was standard technique to get some violation or other on every active member to hold in reserve.

"You'll have to get rid of that girl," Rena ordered me. "She's visiting a psychiatrist. You know the rule."

"All right, then send me someone else to do her work. She's the most reliable membership and financial secretary I've ever had. I don't have anyone else who could begin to do as well."

"If you don't have a cadre," Rena repeated sententiously, "then you'll have to develop one." But she did not try to push the matter further. Instead, she got Dora Deutchman to work through Sue, who was membership director of our section, and theoretically boss of Barbara, who was membership director of the branch. Actually, as everyone knew, Sue wasn't able to take elementary care of herself in a crossfire like that. Sue almost broke down when she called Barbara, whom she liked enormously, and asked for the books.

"All books have to remain in the section now," she explained lamely. Barbara knew it was a lie, but Sue couldn't bring herself to tell Barbara the real reason for her demotion. When I explained it to Barbara, she was furious at Rena for getting Sue into a spot like that. I began to worry a little about Barbara. She seemed to grow more nervous and more outspoken every day. I wondered if she was getting ready to leave the Party. My F.B.I. advisors took a great interest in Barbara. They asked me to watch for evidence that she was actually bolting.

A week or so after her demotion, Barbara called me up and

begged me to come over to her apartment right away. I found her on the verge of hysteria. She looked out of the window and into the hall and asked me if anybody had seen me come in.

"I've got to tell someone, and you're one of the few people in the Party I can trust," she wailed. "Angie, the F.B.I. is after me!"

I was genuinely shocked, and for a moment thoroughly alarmed. It was like a nightmare. Did she know about me?

"How do you know?" I shot back with a concern I hope she did not see. But Barbara was beyond subtlety.

"Two F.B.I. men called yesterday," she whispered. "They knew just where to find me. They asked me a lot of questions about people I knew in Washington, when I worked there."

I thought, more calmly now, of the thick stack of reports I had turned in on her. Obviously the agents had gotten her present address from them, but I had been able to report only the veiled hints she had dropped from time to time of important work she had done and important Communists she had known in her past. Recently, Chick Heiner, the F.B.I. agent who had replaced Ted Kirkpatrick, had been asking me all sorts of questions about her, which had obviously been referred to him by other agents—questions about her jobs, her relatives, her present and past residences, description and age. All of them had been answered in my early reports. Somebody in the Bureau was on Barbara's trail, but I was sure it could not have started with my information. I watched her with some interest. Perhaps she had been in espionage work. Whatever she had done, I could not help feeling a little sorry for her now. What a dope she had been!

"Angie, it may be dangerous for you to be here now. Are you afraid?" she asked, imploringly. I concentrated on reassuring her, in hopes of learning more.

"Nonsense!" I said crisply. "I don't see that you're in such trouble. Remember, you don't have to answer if they don't subpoena you."

"That's what they told me," she said. "They were as smooth

as cream. They wanted to get my cooperation, they said. Angie, do you think they'll subpoena me? Do you think they are following me? Do you think they'll search the apartment?"

She waved helplessly at the row of Communist books on her shelf. "I'll have to get rid of all that. I burned my Party card as soon as they left and flushed the ashes down the toilet." I smiled to myself. I had turned her card number in to the F.B.I. long before.

I helped her make plans. She didn't want anyone in the Party to know about the F.B.I. except Sue and me. She couldn't come to any more Party meetings, of course, and she left it to us to explain her absence. We worked the psychiatry rule and told everybody that Barbara was much too ill to work. The Party is very fearful, of course, of what members may tell their psychiatrists while under treatment. The branch accepted the story without question.

Barbara wanted to get the advice of Mrs. Leon Josephson, who was living with her mother in New Jersey during Leon's jail sentence for contempt of Congress. We decided to pack all the incriminating papers in the back of my car and burn them down there. There were dozens of manila folders of correspondence, notebooks, address books, pamphlets and books.

Lucy Josephson and her mother, a retired schoolteacher and a Communist too, shared a comfortable house outside Trenton. Barbara seemed to be on very intimate terms with Lucy, and she poured out her whole story without reservation. The two of them panned the Foster-Dennis leadership in a way which did honor to their confidence in me.

"They've made a martyr out of Leon," Mrs. Josephson said bitterly. "They didn't even try to save him. They acted as if they *wanted* him to go to jail. The thing for you to do, Barbara, is to steer clear of the Party lawyers and get yourself a good conservative attorney."

In the afternoon, we burned the papers in the Josephson backyard. It was a sad occasion, and something told me that it was not the first of its kind on that spot. We stood watch to see that everything was thoroughly destroyed. As the flames turned the pages I wondered what secrets I could have uncovered if I had been able to reverse the process and resurrect the pile of old ashes in the bottom of the wire basket incinerator.

Barbara handed me a package of Communist literature with real regret. "Angie, I can't bear to burn these. Will you take them as a present?"

Barbara lay low after this, but she kept in touch with me by telephone. In order to protect me from the F.B.I., we arranged that I would never call her at her home or her place of business. She always called me from a pay station.

The rift in our section became very obvious at the county convention in July, 1948. John, Dotty, Sue, Clara and I sat together. Clara kept Rena informed of our conversation, including our disapproval of Caroline Scollen, a Yugoslav girl Rena was pushing for office. Caroline Scollen, an I.L.G.W.U. member, had done some educational work at the Yugoslav Home, but was not effective there. We resented her as an outsider with no executive experience in Party leadership. The point was that Rena was getting desperate for Yugoslav leadership. John was the only comrade who might have held the Yugoslav concentration through the developing crisis over Tito's disaffection, and Rena knew that she couldn't keep John in the section much longer.

At the first region-wide meeting of sectional functionaries after the convention, I knew that something was definitely wrong. Rena did not speak to me. As chairman of the meeting, she addressed all questions about our section to Clara. And she went out of her way to elicit opinions from Caroline Scollen, who held no section post and really had no business being there at all. I tried to speak, but Rena interrupted me as if I were a block of dead air. So I was going to be next on her little list!

I had seen the maneuver before. Ignore a comrade. Let him examine his soul unaided until he is ready to believe he has committed Marxist crimes too foul to mention. Then he'll be only too glad to accept any blow. There is no defense against the silent treatment, and it always brought the proud low.

I decided to check my status right away. The very next day I called Clara and asked her to head a longshore mobilization in the community one evening that week.

"Can't go, Angie," she said fliply. "Have to go to a meeting of section organizers that night."

"But there isn't any meeting of section organizers this week," I said. "If there were, I'd know about it. And whatever it is, how come you're going?"

"Rena asked me. I'm running the section now until she finds someone to replace you. She's looking for a Yugoslav."

"Did Rena tell you to tell me?"

"No. I thought you knew."

"Well, I don't know, and furthermore I don't believe it. If Rena is replacing me, she can tell me so in person."

Neither Sue nor Dotty had heard a word about a new section organizer. Sue, the lamb, wanted to know why there hadn't been an election if it were true. "Is Rena running our section?" she asked bitterly.

I looked her straight in the eye. "Sure," I said. "But she's going to have to face me about it. I'm going to that meeting!"

Nobody kicked me out of the meeting for coming uninvited, but then you don't usually expel a ghost. I learned that policy on the Yugoslavs was to be cautious: play down the differences in mass organizations, never mention them at all to the Yugoslavs, but discuss them thoroughly as a lesson in Marxist self-criticism at all Party gatherings. Rena mentioned an editorial on the subject in *The Daily Worker* which I had not read, so I slipped out of the room and went upstairs to the library to look it over.

On my way down, I ran into Rena. She was alone, and she couldn't, after all, walk right through me.

"Hullo, Angie," she said, with her convulsive quick smile.

"Come here," I said. "I want to talk to you."

It was as if a hand had wiped the smile off her face. Probably no one in the Party had ever spoken to her like that, much less a subordinate. While she was still reeling from the shock, I took her by the arm and pushed her into a chair.

"I don't mind being deposed, Rena, but I expect to get the news first hand. Now there are a few things I want to say."

I told her off. I proceeded to make a speech I must have been unconsciously preparing for years. I called her all the bad names that Communists reserve for each other. I told her she was "undemocratic," "chauvinistic," "bureaucratic." That she didn't "politicalize." That she didn't understand the workers because she had never been one. She had never held a job outside the Party and had never been elected to one inside the Party either, for that matter, and with good reason. Nobody would ever elect her to anything. I told her that she was a miserable failure as a leader, and that there was talk of bringing her up on charges to the county. I wish I could remember all the things I told her. I was utterly stupid to do it, but I let myself go once and for all, and I felt better afterwards.

Rena sat there and took it, her thin chin sticking out at an ugly angle. "You're being very subjective, Angela," she commented finally when I was thoroughly out of breath. "This isn't a personal decision of mine. It's a political decision. Your work has been splendid, but you just don't happen to be a Yugoslav."

"Why didn't you tell me first?" I insisted. But Rena didn't think this was worth answering. Caroline Scollen took my place as co-organizer of the section, much to the confusion of John.

I was beginning to worry about my outburst, during the next week, when newspaper headlines announced what sounded like the end of the trail: the F.B.I. had thrown a cordon around national headquarters of the Communist Party and arrested most of the top leaders. They were looking for the rest of the National Board. That day, July 20, 1948, all were indicted for conspiring to teach the overthrow of the United States Government by force, in violation of the Smith Act of 1940.

The news sounded very good to me. If the leaders were going to jail, my work in the F.B.I. was done. But the Party had just begun to fight. Clara called. In her excitement, she forgot to watch her language over the phone. "Special press mobilization. You're to pick up the papers for our section in your car." *The Daily Worker* was getting out a special edition on the "frame up" of the twelve leaders, signalling the "beginning of the police state in America."

The basement of the grimy old building on Thirteenth Street was crowded with comrades from all over Greater New York who had come, like myself, to pick up bundles of papers for distribution in their neighborhoods. The old *Daily Worker* printing plant groaned and thundered under the strain of the extra stint, and we got the papers literally hot off the press. Brooklyn sections were served first, because they were farther away. John Gates, editor of the paper, hadn't been caught. We whispered together, wondering where he had hidden himself, and whether he had managed to escape arrest so that he could write the editorial for the extra. Next day he turned himself in under his own steam. *The Daily Worker* made him look quite noble.

Over the years that I had observed the Communists, heard them explain their aims inside the Party and out, and seen their methods, I had often wondered how much evidence the Government needed to prove that they were aiming at nothing short of complete control of the United States in the interests of Soviet Russia. What was the Government going to do with all the evidence it was accumulating? Agents had told me that there were legal difficulties. At first, this was hard for me to understand. If you sent a threatening letter through the mails, the F.B.I. would catch you and get you convicted and sent to jail. But under our laws, you apparently went scot-free if you only devoted your life to plotting the abolition of all our laws and to misleading other people in helping you do it. It didn't make sense to me. Chick shared my indignation, but he often smiled, as a trained lawyer, at what he regarded as feminine rather than legal logic.

He and other agents who came with him pointed out that in this country you can't jail a man for his opinions, however unpopular or dangerous. I appreciated the glories of free speech, but I had spent so many hours listening to Communists who hypocritically wrapped themselves in the Constitution that I am afraid I had become a little suspicious of people who constantly feared that their democratic rights were in danger. I often tussled with the dilemma in private: how can we preserve our civil liberties against the threat of Communism without doing away with our civil liberties in the process?

Legal attempts to solve the problem had previously relied on denying certain privileges, such as naturalization, immigration and Federal employment to persons "advocating the overthrow of the Government by force and violence." But the laws didn't cover all Communists and had hard going in the courts. The current obstacle was the Schneiderman decision.

In June, 1943, the Supreme Court of the United States ruled that William Schneiderman, Communist organizer on the West Coast, could not be denaturalized on the ground that he was a Communist. This invalidated an amendment to the naturalization laws made in 1940, when Fifth Column methods were being demonstrated for us abroad, which made it possible to cancel the citizenship of a person who had obtained it by fraudulently swearing that he was attached to the Constitution of the United States. The most dangerous Communists were those who came from Europe to assist the revolution in the United States, and the Government had long sought to deport or deny entrance to as many of these unwelcome visitors as possible.

The Department of Justice had tried to prove that, as a member of Communist organizations, William Schneiderman could not possibly be "attached to the principles of the Constitution" as he had sworn when he became a citizen. The Supreme Court, reversing lower courts, held that belief in the dictatorship of the proletariat was not "necessarily incompatible with the general political philosophy of the Constitution." It went on to say that you couldn't prove what a man believed by the policy of the organizations to which he belonged. And it was pointed out that the Supreme Court had never decided whether the Communists actually did advocate "the overthrow of the Government by force and violence."

If they didn't, then the other anti-Communist laws using that language didn't apply to Communists either, as the F.B.I. and the Government had been assuming. There would even be doubt about the application of the Smith Act of 1940, which made it illegal to conspire to advocate or teach the overthrow of the Government by force and violence.

Involved as the legal tangle was, I understood that the indictment of the twelve Communists was the Government's attempt to open the road to legislation curbing the real but recent danger of subversive activities carried on by methods the founding fathers had not anticipated and hence not provided for.

But the indictment was only the beginning. Evidence of the Communist conspiracy was turning up from other quarters. On July 30, Elizabeth Bentley, self-confessed Red spy, charged that the War Department and the State Department were honeycombed with Communist agents. On August 2, Louis Budenz, former editor of *The Daily Worker,* testified before a Senate subcommittee investigating Communist activities that there were many subversive spy rings in the country, and perhaps thousands of members of the Russian Fifth Column in Government jobs. On August 3, Whittaker Chambers, a confessed ex-courier in the Communist spy ring, named eight high Federal officials as leaders in a Communist underground apparatus which had sought to infiltrate all Government departments.

The Government was getting the goods. Comrades tried to laugh it off, but they began to think about their own skins. Everyone was on edge, wondering who the next traitor would prove to be.

I began to worry a little myself. It didn't make me feel one bit safer to know that the Party was getting desperate. In that hysterical atmosphere, a gentle push off a subway platform might well have been my first and last notice that the Party had discovered my work with the Bureau. Any comrade who stumbled on my real motive for being in the Party would have recoiled from me in horror. How he would have reacted to the discovery of such sacrilege was anybody's guess, and I was not anxious to find out.

I scanned the list of Government officials dismissed for disloyalty to the United States to see if any of them could have been traced to me. Luckily for my peace of mind, none of the dismissals that could have been based on my reports came to public attention until after my testimony was safely in. But I hated to think of my tiff with Rena.

Barbara, too, grew steadily more nervous. The F.B.I. agents continued to question her. She feared that she might be involved in the proceedings against Communists. To me, she openly criticized the Foster regime which she felt was responsible for all the Party's troubles. "To think I might have to go to jail for those guys!" she beefed in what amounted to a confession. I reported Barbara's dissatisfaction with the National Board to the F.B.I., who continued to be interested in her state of mind. But if they hoped that she would leave the Party and turn state's evidence, they were wrong. Barbara quit her job with an insurance broker who sympathized with Communism for fear the F.B.I. would investigate him as her employer. She was disgruntled with the leadership, but seventeen years of loyalty to the Party had made covering-up a habit.

I did not know at the time that Barbara was more afraid of Miss Bentley than of the indictment. It wasn't until June 6, 1949, that I learned what Miss Bentley's confession must have meant to her. On that day, Elizabeth Bentley publicly named thirty-seven Federal employees, six outsiders, and three employees of foreign governments as persons involved in transferring data to Russia. The girl whom I am calling Barbara was on that list. Miss Bentley had been feeding information to the F.B.I.

for at least a year before she broke with the Party. It was only then, after my appearance in court, that I learned that the agents who visited Barbara were following leads Miss Bentley had given them.

The official Party line was to play down the disclosures. When anyone worried out loud, some functionary was sure to stop him. But we leaders quietly adopted the normal security measures that Communist Parties all over the world adopt when they are in danger. The phrase for it is "going on the alert."

Meetings were held in homes instead of at public meeting places such as the Yugoslav Home. People didn't like to be seen going to and from Communist meetings. Attendance dropped off. I held a number of meetings in my studio, which had the advantage of being cool in summer.

Word came down that we were to watch our language over the phone and in the mails. Members were always accusing each other of "carelessness" in the face of "Fascist persecution of liberals and progressives." Clara complained because someone mentioned the A.L.P. over her phone. One comrade became almost hysterical because I had phoned him and asked him to come to "section headquarters." "Anybody listening in would know that the Communist Party is the only organization that has sections. Why didn't you tell me to come to Seventy-second Street?" Mailed notices of meetings were as cryptic as "See you on Tuesday."

We tried to keep cell meetings going all summer, in case the Party needed that most secret unit, but it was hard work getting people to attend. We visited the fearful, exhorting them to rally to the Party now that "Wall Street" was trying to intimidate the "workers." The franker ones pleaded business and social ties. One woman explained that she wanted to transfer to a lawyers' section because her husband was in it. We checked and found that the lawyers' section had never heard of him. I think many of the "white collar" comrades had some gimmick in the back of their minds for easing themselves out of the Party in a pinch.

My own ambiguous position with Rena continued to drag on. I knew that Caroline Scollen would never rest until she had deposed me as branch organizer too. She got very little cooperation either from John or the rest of us in the section, so she struck out to find new friends among the rank and file. She began to "develop" Martin, a shy, pimply boy who had tried unsuccessfully to date me. I surprised them sitting in my car one evening after a meeting, and it seemed to me that they acted rather awkwardly when I greeted them.

A week later, Caroline asked me to come to her house on Monday night. I thought it was the regular briefing of branch organizers for the Tuesday branch membership meeting. When I arrived, I found her sitting stiffly with Dora Deutchman.

"Where's everybody?" I asked, looking around for the other branch organizers. Caroline cleared her throat.

"We just wanted to talk to you," she said in a strained voice.

"What about?" I looked from one to the other and they certainly looked like a pair of conspirators. Evidently Dora was there to do Rena's dirty work. She had mousy brown hair and loved to deliver long ideological speeches quoting from Marx, Engels and Lenin.

"We would like you to drop out of the Party," she announced.

"You would WHAT?" I shouted. My genuine alarm was exactly what Dora would have expected of a good comrade. Expulsion is the worst thing that can happen to a Communist. Some commit suicide over it. Others go insane.

"We would like you to drop out of the Party," she repeated. "It has come to our attention, and I'm not going to name any names, that you are anti-Party, that you have been associating with anti-Party people, and that you've been heard making anti-Party remarks. As you well know, that's ground for expulsion under the Constitution."

I was shaking with fear and anger. Maybe they had me on the F.B.I. deal and didn't want me to know. I just stood there for a moment looking at her, and I thought to myself, all right, I'm going to call your bluff. If you really know, I want to see just what you're going to do to me. I've got to find out who told you and how much you know. I controlled my voice:

"What do you mean by this? What anti-Party remarks? What anti-Party people? Where? When? Who?"

"We're not going to name any names," she repeated. "But we have proof, evidence and witnesses."

"You have, have you?" I said. "Well, that's fine, because you're going to have to produce them. The Party means as much to me as it does to you, and I will fight any attempt to expel me. I demand a trial!"

"There'll be no hearing," Dora sneered.

"There will be a hearing," I insisted, "if I have to go to the National Committee to get it. I've given nearly seven years of my life to the Party and the least it can do in return is to show me some of its fine super-democracy. It says right in the Constitution that charges against a member have to be made in writing."

Both of them were at a loss. They had not expected opposition. I went home and read over the section of the Constitution of the Communist Party which states the charges that can be brought against members. They are:

"Conduct or action detrimental to the working class and the nation, as well as to the interests of the Party, violation of decisions of its leading committees or of this Constitution, financial irregularities, or other conduct unbecoming a member of the Party, may be punished by censure, removal from posts of leadership, or by expulsion from membership. . . .

"Adherence to or participation in the activities of any clique, group, circle, faction or party which conspires or acts to subvert, undermine, weaken or overthrow any or all institutions of American democracy, whereby the majority of the American people can maintain their right to determine their destinies in any degree, shall be punished by immediate expulsion. . . .

"The practice or advocacy of any form of racial, national or religious discrimination shall be grounds for expulsion from membership. . . .

"Personal or political relations with enemies of the working class and nation are incompatible with membership in the Communist Party."

The significant rubrics were "actions detrimental to the working class," "personal or political relations with enemies of the working class and nation," and "conduct unbecoming a member of the Party," a classification as elastic as "conduct unbecoming an officer and a gentleman." The provision for punishing members who undermine American democracy is sheer window-dressing added in 1945 to silence critics who pointed out that the Party owed its first allegiance to Russia.

The next morning I went to see John Lautner of the State Security Commission and demanded my constitutional right to a formal accusation and a formal hearing with witnesses. He tried to calm me down. He asked me a lot of questions about my service in the Party.

"We need Greek comrades badly now to help integrate refugees from Greece. They don't understand what the American Party is trying to do. Would you like to work in a Greek concentration?"

I told him I didn't want to work with Greeks.

"We need good reliable workers like yourself in the photographers' section," he suggested. I knew that the photographers, always a turbulent group inside the Party, were now accusing each other of "opportunism." If I had been a sincere Party member, I would have chosen to serve in my own profession, but as an F.B.I. observer I knew there was less to be learned from the Greeks and the photographers than in the community sections.

"I don't want another job," I said. "I want to clear myself on the job I've got. And I think the least you can do right now is to call in Rena Klein and hear what she has to say."

Lautner asked her to step into the office, and I could see right away that he was afraid of her. She wouldn't give any details about the accusation while I was there, and Lautner didn't press her very hard. He didn't seem to get the hang of the case, and that encouraged me somewhat. If Rena had discovered my relations with the F.B.I., he would have taken the charges more seriously. He seemed only interested in getting rid of me.

"I'll investigate the charges and let you know as soon as possible."

"Investigate anything you want," I raged. "I've always done my job. I've raised money for the Party. I've never been criticized, let alone brought up on charges. My private life is an open book. I'm pretty well known professionally. Investigate anything you want, but investigate and clear me."

I couldn't afford to have security officers in the Party on my trail. The only way to call them off was to force a formal hearing which would dispose of the charges against me or disclose enough about them to warn me that the Party suspected I was a spy. Far from reassuring me, Rena's reluctance to talk suggested that she really had some damaging evidence. A week after our confrontation in Lautner's office, Rena asked me to go to lunch with her as if nothing had happened.

"What about the trial?" I greeted her. But she ignored all reference to the trial. She hadn't had time to go into it. She acted as if the whole idea of a hearing had been a bad dream.

Over lunch, Rena told me that she wanted me to go up to one of the A.L.P. Clubs and do a job of spying. The suspect was a member of my branch, but the Party was afraid that he might make a deal with the regular Democratic machine. I was supposed to observe him and report whether he was pushing Wallace and in general following the Party line so that the county committee could be warned in time if he threatened to bolt. The obvious weapon they had over him was that they could have exposed him as a Red to his anti-Communist constituency, ending his political career and making way for a more obedient A.L.P. leader.

I felt that Rena was brushing me off. I would never be in the clear until I got open reinstatement. I suggested that she use someone else for the A.L.P. job. One way to look at it was that Rena would never have set me spying for the Communists if she seriously thought I was spying on the Communists. But I insisted that I wanted a trial and reinstatement as a member in good standing before I could consider other Party assignments.

When I arrived at the next meeting of the West Midtown Branch, Martin had been appointed branch organizer in my place. Apparently elections were going out of style in my corner of the Communist Party. When I refused the transfer, Rena had been obliged to depose me openly. I wasn't out of the woods yet.

I told Lautner that I had been deposed as branch organizer without cause and threatened to carry the case over his head if I did not get action. By this time, Dora Deutchman was denying that there had ever been any charges. "There are accusations, but no charges," she kept repeating.

Chick and his partner from the F.B.I. told me I was doing fine, but they warned me to take care of myself. I took good care of myself, all right. I kept my door locked at all times. I kept away from lonely subway stations. I weigh ninety-four pounds and it would have been easy for me to "fall" off a platform. People embarrassing to the Party have "fallen" that way before. I never went out alone at night, even if I had to get Sue or the still-shaken Barbara to go with me.

Sue, Barbara and I spent a lot of time together that fall of 1948. One of the reasons was that Sue and I were the only comrades besides Lucy Josephson and her mother who knew that Barbara was under surveillance by the F.B.I. Somewhat against her conscience, Sue had agreed to keep it quiet, although as section membership director, it was her duty to report the incident to the security arm of the Party. Barbara didn't want them to know because she didn't trust the leadership. She was sure that they would muff any attempt to protect her. She called Johnny Lautner a "blockhead," railed against Foster and Dennis, and lamented the golden days of Browder's early regime.

Sue agreed with Barbara that the leadership was behaving badly. To hear the two girls talk, you would think both of them were on the verge of leaving the Party. If anyone put in a good word for Foster, it was myself. Actually, however, they were angry at the inefficiency of the National Board rather than at the Communist movement. It was interesting to me to see how loyal both of them really were. When the F.B.I. finally served a subpoena on Barbara ordering her to appear before a secret grand jury, Sue announced that she could no longer withhold the facts from Johnny Lautner, and Barbara bore her no ill-will for telling. Sue was simply doing her duty. Lautner transferred Barbara to Marcantonio's headquarters in order to get her out of active Party work for a while.

Barbara pleaded vacation plans to get a postponement of her appearance before the grand jury. Meanwhile, the F.B.I. agents quizzed me about her family and her projected vacation trip to Chicago. I knew that she was going to visit "friends," but she never told me why it was so important for her to see them before she testified. If I had been Barbara, I would have wondered why the Government agreed to the postponement so readily. I kept the Bureau posted on her trip. I hope they trailed her out to Chicago to find out who her mysterious friends were. For all I know, they could have been Party leaders whom she wished to warn.

When Barbara got back, I helped her buy a suit for her date with the grand jury. She wanted something demure, with a Peter Pan collar, that would disarm her inquisitors. It turned out to be a brief ordeal: the good, conservative lawyer she had hired advised her to refuse to answer on the ground that she might incriminate herself. Later, I found out that the grand jury before which she appeared was sifting evidence turned in by Bentley.

To Barbara, my futile demands for a trial simply proved the evils which Foster, Dennis & Co. had brought on the Communist Party. "I'm going to get you straight to the top," she promised. "You and I are going to see Paul Crosbie." He was the state treasurer and a comrade who has contributed great sums to the Party. Barbara certainly knew the brass hats.

As a member of the State Review Commission, Paul Crosbie must have been a very harassed comrade in the fall of 1948, but he rose with bourgeois gallantry to greet us when we were ushered into the private office where he worked at a battered oak desk with several telephones on it. I judged him to be about sixty-five, but he was still the ladies' man—charming, slightly built, well-dressed, and jolly, with blue twinkly-steel eyes and an engaging goatee.

"Well, well, girls, what can I do for you today?" he greeted us. He took our visit as a rather amusing joke, and I thought there was something mocking about his sympathetic concern at my recital of unsubstantiated accusations and arbitrary demotions.

Our conversation was interrupted briefly when Robert Thompson, New York State chairman of the Party, one of the defendants I was to confront in court, burst into his office without knocking. "I'd like to get my pay check a little early," he demanded surlily, without paying the slightest attention to the two strange women in the room. Thompson's manner indicated clearly that he regarded Crosbie as a figurehead, and a none-too-useful one at that. I felt myself that we would make little progress with Crosbie.

Like a good bureaucrat, Crosbie got rid of us by suggesting that I write a formal letter to the State Security Commission, forwarding carbon copies to county and regional authorities. As we left, he warned us not to call in by phone. "The F.B.I. is tapping telephones, but here at headquarters we know which ones are tapped and which aren't. Naturally we never say anything over the tapped lines." He showed us how to unscrew the bell box of a telephone instrument to check whether it has a recording device in it. According to his story, some of the new taps were so good that they picked up conversations carried on at some distance from the phone.

Barbara and I got my letter off on October 13, 1948. We

translated the whole story of my loyal Party service and shabby
Party treatment into dignified Government English, conclud-
ing with a demand that I be informed of the charges against
me, as provided under the Constitution of the Communist
Party. If there were charges, I had a right to an immediate
trial. If there were none, I ought to be reinstated as organizer
of my branch. We must have done several drafts of this important letter.

By this time, there really wasn't much point in asking for my
old job back, because the West Midtown Branch had fallen
apart under its new leadership and been abolished. I allowed
myself to be persuaded into working at the A.L.P. Club, where
we volunteers worked several evenings and afternoons a week
in a cold water flat. We sat on wooden folding chairs at impro-
vised tables made by laying planks across saw horses. A.L.P.
clubs are as bleak and as shabby as Communist quarters, but
they are usually swept out once a day and they always have an
American flag draped beside the blown-up photographs of
candidates.

I was an insignificant member of the volunteer staff which
was concerned with mailing lists and routine door-to-door canvassing, but our suspect knew I had sharp ears and would
report bits of conversation to Party officials. The newspaper
disclosures on Communist spy activities didn't make him very
happy, and I'm sure he cursed the day he ever became a Party
member. He occasionally grumbled that he had never received
the political support from the Party which he had hoped to get.

I felt at moments that I was doing a little too much spying all
around for comfort. My service at A.L.P. added nothing to the
Bureau's record—I had turned in our suspect's Party card number and activities years before—but I was able to satisfy Rena
with reports of his current doings. Just for good measure, Rena
had me check on Party members who said they were transferring out of branch work to help the campaign. It became very
popular, that fall, to get into the safer duties of front organiza-

tions, and we rightly suspected that many of the comrades were using them as an excuse to get out of Party work of any kind.

I spent election night, 1948, running a breakdown of the vote by precincts from A.L.P. headquarters to the headquarters of the Communist Party at 35 East Twelfth Street. Communist headquarters were lit up from top to bottom, but full of gloom over the miserable showing Wallace made.

Meanwhile, Rena had gone to the hospital to have a baby and left my case in Dora's hands. Apparently as a result of my letter, Dora had been asked to supply a Party biography of me. She called me on the phone and asked me about my personal and Party history. I suspected that Rena and Dora were stalling off a trial which would give me a chance to clear myself. When I hung up, I thought of a way to get my case more attention.

The people at national headquarters implied that they didn't have time for what they regarded as an insignificant family squabble, but I knew they were scared to death of telephone taps. I drove down to national headquarters and told Lautner and Crosbie that Dora had asked me about my Party record over the phone. Anybody listening in would have had positive proof of her Party membership and mine. They were both furious. It was a good maneuver, for anyone in my position, because it presented me as a red hot Communist concerned about Party security at a time when the Party's conspiratorial methods were being widely revealed.

11. SPY UNCOVERED

MY BATTLE WITH RENA was fought during the Christmas rush at the studio. I fell into the very bad habit of leaving my dark-room work for the night. I'd come in from a Party meeting around midnight, put a pot of coffee on the single burner in the studio, and work through till dawn, pecking out my report to the Bureau while I had prints washing. It was the only time I could be reasonably safe from the telephone and the doorbell, but it always left me low in body and spirit around five o'clock the next afternoon. For a serious photographer, portrait work is potboiling, and accordingly I resented the hurry-up pictures for Christmas gifts. After a few such nights, I'd get to thinking of the photographic work I would have been free to do if I could have left town on magazine assignments. At such times, I wondered why I had ever become involved in under-cover work and how much longer I would have to serve.

I was still finishing pictures and very tired of it one dim November afternoon in 1948 when Chick called me and asked me to meet him within an hour.

I changed, took the subway down to Chambers Street and hopped into the Pontiac with a brief greeting. Passers-by prob-ably took us for a young couple embarking on a date after work. Chick headed east to Mulberry Street and up to Canal past crowds swarming home through a murky gray drizzle. I could tell that he had exciting news.

"Angela," he said finally. "This is it. The boys in Washington want to know if you will testify at the trial of the Communist leaders."

"Why, of course I will," I said quickly, without quite realizing what it would mean. I was honored, and a little surprised. I had assumed that my reports would help the Government in its case, but I never dreamed of taking the witness chair myself, even if only to swear to the truth of my reports.

I knew the case was the biggest thing that had ever happened to Chick and the other boys at the "B" whom I can't name because they are still in the Internal Security Unit. The F.B.I. doesn't pay its G-men handsome salaries, but it treats them with a great deal of consideration. Chick was responsible for me to the Bureau, and I think he expected me to do him proud. He was very pleased that I would testify, and rushed back to the office in the Federal Building—an office I had never seen in all my nearly seven years' connection with it—to get my answer to Washington.

It wasn't until the next day that the full significance of the thing dawned on me: I was going to get a chance to tell the world just where I stood. I was going to be able, after seven years, to serve my country openly. All the Communists I had ever put up with would know it; all the friends who thought I was piling up a fortune because I was "busy" day and night; business associates who may have stumbled across my membership in front organizations and questioned my loyalty to the United States—all these would know the truth at last. I pictured the face of the old farmer who rented me my cabin when he read the papers.

At last, I was going to enjoy some of the freedom I had gone undercover to protect, the freedom that comes closest to home—my freedom to be Angela Calomiris, photographer, instead of Angela Cole, Communist, and IS-342. (After the war, my number was changed from ND-107 for National Defense, to

IS-342 for Internal Security.) The drama in which I had played both Dr. Jekyll and Mr. Hyde was in its last act.

I became positively cheerful. For several days I didn't mind Barbara's whining. I didn't mind the inanities of the Wallace campaign in Hell's Kitchen, then in its last lap. And I thought my run-in with Rena was the crowning joke of the century. I was going to have a little fun of my own with that. I imagined Rena's consternation when she discovered that she had set an F.B.I. spy to spying for the Communist Party. And Johnny Lautner—what kind of a watchdog would his superiors think he was, when they discovered that he couldn't catch an F.B.I. operator that plagued him every other day? I forgot, for a moment, that the Communist Party is a resourceful and vigilant network, and that I had not yet successfully defied it.

A mysterious telephone call cut my giddy daydreams short. A man, who called himself Ralph, asked me if I had heard from Clarissa Michaelson, an aristocratic Boston girl who was a section organizer in lower Manhattan. I told him I had not seen Clarissa for a long time. He paused for a moment. Apparently Clarissa was supposed to have given me some message. But he decided to go on just the same.

"I'll be at your studio in ten minutes," he said precisely. "I'll need exactly twenty minutes of your time." He didn't wait for an answer. He just hung up.

Something steely in his voice scared me, but I didn't want to cry wolf to the F.B.I. I decided to stand my ground and find out what Ralph wanted. As a precaution I phoned a police-woman friend who lived in the neighborhood and told her that I had a suspicious character coming into the studio for pictures. She knew that I had had a few nasty sessions with male clients in the past. She agreed to call me back in fifteen minutes. If I made social conversation, she would know that everything was all right. If I said, "Wrong number," and hung up, she was to come right over.

Ralph arrived, in ten minutes to the dot. In my report to the F.B.I. I described him as a well-built, good-looking man in his

early thirties, dressed in tweeds, five feet, nine inches tall, curly
black hair, olive skin, large brown eyes. I showed him to a seat
and he just looked me over without saying a word for a full
minute.

"I'm from the National Committee," he announced. "Your
name has been given me as a comrade whose loyalty is unques-
tioned. I would like to know whether you are able and willing
to help the Party more than you are now doing."

"The Party means a great deal to me," I said gravely. "I will
never turn down any assignment I am given." That note had
always made a hit in the past, and it seemed to reassure Ralph.
It was the "right" answer.

He asked me the usual personal questions. I told Ralph that
I had no family, that I was single and not planning to marry in
the immediate future, that I was not widely known as a Communist; that I was a photographer; that I could come and go
without arousing suspicion; and that, in short, I was free to take
on an extra-curricular Party assignment. All of these answers
were "right" too.

"You know that the Party will have to operate in secret ways
if we lose this case against the twelve," he began cautiously. "In
that event, we would like to use you for special work."

The damned phone rang. My friend was braying into it,
"I've got my gun Esmeralda and my gum-soled shoes. Do you
want me to come over?" I got rid of her as quickly as I could
for fear Ralph would hear her from across the room.

"I have a car at the disposal of the Party," I offered, trying
for information.

"No, I don't think we'll need your car," he answered. "You
would work directly with me between midtown Manhattan
points. You would be notified in advance, and you would only
be needed for an hour or two a day. You would go on with
your regular life, but you would have to drop out of the Party
as discreetly as possible. A series of transfers might be arranged."

So he wanted me to carry messages for the underground Politburo of which we had heard rumors! I visualized myself X-raying envelopes covering secret documents. I was overwhelmed, as I had every right to be. Ralph watched my reaction narrowly. "Do you live alone?" he asked. I nodded. He looked around the studio. It was furnished like an informal apartment with a studio couch, a Mexican leather and cane chair by the whitewashed fireplace, bookshelves, a radio phonograph for music during sittings, and an exhibit of portraits around the wall. I told Ralph that the studio was a place of business. My residence was at 9 Jane Street, the front building.

"We will need meeting places, a great many of them, because we won't be able to meet twice in succession in the same place," he explained.

"You are welcome to use the studio at any time," I said, thinking how easily it could be wired for sound. "But I would have to have some notice in advance to be sure you would not be disturbed."

Ralph changed the subject to photography, as a signal that the business side of the meeting was over. He told me he had a movie camera made in Switzerland for which he couldn't find film. I called up a supply house I knew while he was there and told him he would have to bring the camera in to them. He may have been checking on me further, but I doubt it. He was a stiff and correct fellow and I think he was trying to be friendly.

I had never known a Communist quite like him before. From the nature of his questions on my Party record, he seemed unacquainted with the New York County Party machine. I asked him how he had come to me. He told me that he couldn't tell me even if I happened to guess the comrade's name. If he had had a trace of foreign accent I would have taken him for a European Communist. As he left, he promised to let me know about my new assignment within a few weeks.

He was no sooner safely out of the studio than I called the F.B.I. Chick was out on a case. I called the supervisor and gave him a rough sketch of my visit, and he promised to call

Chick in from the field. It wasn't until 10 P.M., however, that
I managed to get together with my advisor.

Chick and I drove up and down until midnight figuring the
thing out from every possible angle. Ralph did not impress
either of us as a pushover for a game of cat and mouse. There
were three possibilities. The first was that the Party knew that
I was going to testify for the Government. After all, I was still
suspected of being anti-Party. I hadn't been tried or expelled,
but from the point of view of the Party, there were probably
better ways of handling a known spy than immediate expulsion.
If they knew about me, Ralph's offer could be a trap. The idea
might be to put me on work so hot that the Government would
be reluctant to waste me on the stand. Ralph could always give
me phony messages to carry between phony points. We didn't
like to think about the possibility that the Party would use my
new work to lure me to locations where it would be easy to
erase me once and for all.

The second possibility was that the offer was a test of my
loyalty made in the course of the investigation I had demanded.
It would have been very easy to give me a phony message and
trail me to see what I did with it.

The third possibility was that the offer was genuine. We
knew that the Party was so disorganized at the time that Ralph
might know nothing of my inner Party troubles.

On balance, we decided that it was more important for me to
help win the Government's case than it was to have me in a
position to deliver secret messages in the underground the Party
might set up if it were outlawed. We decided to keep this com-
plication to ourselves until after the legal staff had determined
whether or not they wanted to use me as a witness.

A few days later, Chick called me up and told me that "someone wanted to see me." I was sure that the someone would be
from the Attorney General's office. Chick was to pick me up at
the foot of Jane Street near the Hudson River. I walked back
and forth on the pier, watching every car that approached.
But no Chick. After the allotted twenty minutes, I went back

to the apartment and phoned the office. There was an apologetic message from Chick asking me to be at the rendezvous thirty minutes later, so I started back. By this time, I had loitered long enough on the waterfront to attract some attention from off-duty seamen, but I stuck it out for another twenty minutes. Good and mad at being stood up again, I trotted back to the studio, whipped off my good clothes, and started to salvage what remained of the afternoon for darkroom work. Chick caught me on the phone before I had barely started. There was nothing for it but to climb out of slacks again. I was in a weary and discouraged mood when Chick hailed me from the wheel of a big black Buick.

I hopped into the back seat with a gentleman whom Chick introduced as Eward C. Wallace, a special assistant to Attorney General Clark. The dark man in front with Chick was another lawyer, Irving S. Shapiro, another attorney from the Department of Justice. Chick didn't give them my right name. He simply called me Anna. An F.B.I. man automatically keeps the identity of a contact even from fellow members of the force. There was still a chance that the lawyers might not want to use me on the stand, and there was no point in telling them exactly who I was until it was necessary.

Mr. Wallace was very tired. He seemed a man in his late forties. Later, at the trial, I was surprised to see how much younger he was. Preparing the trial was a man-killing job. At our first session, he asked me the questions that were later put to me on the stand: Where were you born? How old are you? How long have you been in the Party? What offices have you held in the Party? Why did you join it?

I answered briefly, catching on to the game. "How much does the F.B.I. pay you?" Mr. Wallace asked, assuming for the moment the role of cross-examiner.

I told him I received no pay for my F.B.I. work.

"Do you mean to say that you do all this for nothing?" he pursued, as a defense attorney might have done in an attempt to shake my credibility.

"It all depends on how you look at it," I said. "I'm a citizen of this country. Somebody has to find out what the Communists intend to do with it."

"What do you think they are going to do?"

I answered carefully, "As soon as there is a proper 'revolutionary situation,' they will try to overthrow the Government."

"How do you feel about testifying?" he wanted to know. I assured him that I was honored to testify for the Government.

"Think: have you ever done anything they can use against you as a witness? Have you ever been arrested? Do you have any enemies?"

"Well, of course everybody in the Communist Party will be my enemy if I testify," I pointed out. "There's nothing specific, I think." I told him about a few parking tickets, and I described my feud with Rena. "You can count on Rena to trump up anything to discredit me that she thinks she can get away with. Communists don't stick to the truth."

Chick told me afterward that Mr. Wallace said I would be able to handle myself on the stand. Apparently, I looked like a good witness. Thereafter, Chick chauffeured me on many automobile rides. He would come armed with a sheaf of my old reports which I tried to read and clarify as we lurched in and out of lower Manhattan traffic. The sessions were frequent, but often too short to make it worth while to drive out into open country, where we might have been more comfortable.

Occasionally, Chick would find a quiet place on a street of warehouses where we could stop long enough to look over papers, but he kept a sharp lookout and didn't like to stay in one place very long. He worked out our routes so that we did not repeat streets very often—there are more streets in New York City than you realize before you start to count them—and he used different cars from the pool. We had to be careful whenever we were stopped alongside of other cars at a red light.

We all agreed that I should continue as a loyal Communist until the very moment of my appearance in court. Surprise would be my best defense against attempts to smear me on cross-examination. We wanted to shake the Party to its core—and we did!

After the presidential election, the branches in the West Midtown Section went through another frenzied shakeup—this time, I think, for the purpose of splitting me away from Sue and Dotty. Barbara was already in Siberia up with Marcantonio. Branches are frequently merged and split to break up cliques. The Party reason is "avoiding factionalism." I was assigned to a new branch headed by my old enemy Clara, and made financial secretary, a very busy post at the time. The Party had announced that it would raise a quarter of a million dollars to finance the trial. The new drive came on the heels of several others that year, and it was hard to get the money out of comrades who had already been bled white. But we had a good argument: the life of the Party is at stake, it can now depend only on its faithful members.

My assessment, based on my estimate of two weeks' income, was set at $125, but I got it scaled down on the promise that I would raise money from other sources. In the end, the Government paid only fifty dollars, through my expense account, to the defense of the criminals against whom I was to testify. I brought in close to two hundred dollars, however, by putting the heat on well-to-do Party members. Some of them raised the money in the name of innocent charities.

As financial director, I reported to Joel, who was at that time financial director of the West Midtown Section. Strictly speaking, all reports were supposed to be oral. The new ruling was part of the "alert" which had been sounded through the Party. But it was next to impossible to keep records of dues in one's head. I used to write out an account of funds received, and slip it to Joel between sessions of the Marxist Institute we were both attending at the Jefferson School of Social Sciences. There, in the hall, with comrades and sympathizers swarming up and down, we would confer hastily. Joel took it down in abbreviated notes and then destroyed my data sheet in my presence. He preferred to do it that way rather than have me come to his home.

He told me that he thought the F.B.I. was after him. He and
Dotty were taking extra precautions. He had his telephone
number changed to make it harder for comrades to call him.
My reports had started the investigation of Joel and I hoped
that the F.B.I. was finding out whether his chemical work was
vital to the national defense.

The entire program of the Party was absorbed into an enormous protest against "the trial of the twelve," whom the Party
press did not hesitate to liken to the Twelve Apostles. It was
explained that the fight at Foley Square was basic to everything else. If the Communists were outlawed, then the liberals
would be attacked. The Jews would be next. With no Party to
protest, the Negroes could be kept in bondage. Finally, everyone in the country would be threatened. It's an old Commie
trick to wrap everything up into one ball of dough.

Petitions and picketing were mobilized against public officials
"guilty" of bringing the indictment to trial. Front organizations jumped through the hoop and passed the prepared resolutions of alarm and concern. A great many earnest citizens
who wondered whether it was right to try a political party did
not realize that they were thinking in phrases supplied them
by the Communists.

The Civil Rights Congress changed signals on its long-
planned march on Washington for Negro rights and scheduled
a rousing attack there on the trial instead. It was the second
time that the Civil Rights Congress had shelved the Negro
problem for menaces closer to home. The march had once
been postponed so that the organization could throw its full
weight against the Mundt-Nixon Communist registration bill.

The F.B.I. was delighted to have me attend the January,
1949, convention as a delegate. I rode down to Washington in
a special train chartered for the Civil Rights Congress and
checked in, with comrades from my section, at a small, newly-
opened hotel the Party had chosen because it accepted both
Negro and white guests. We were, of course, strictly forbidden
to stop elsewhere.

The mimeographed agenda sheets we were given contained a warning note:

"Luncheon: Washington, D.C., is a Jim Crow town and the non-segregated restaurants are few. The nearest four are: Union Depot; National Gallery, Constitution Ave. and Sixth Street, N.W.; H.O.L.C. cafeteria, First Street and Indiana Ave.; and the General Accounting Office cafeteria at Fifth Street and F, N.W. Please limit yourself to a choice of one of these four."

When I arrived at the hotel, it looked as if I were going to have to share a room, which would have made it impossible for me to prepare notes for the F.B.I. in the evening. I had planned to plead some excuse to get a single, but when the clerk asked me to double up with a Negro girl, I knew that no excuse would protect me from the charge of "white chauvinism." My prospective roommate was freer to protest. She apparently had reasons of her own for wanting to be alone.

At the convention hall next day, speaker after speaker bemoaned the "political witch hunt" which was destroying American civil liberties. Like Hitler, the war makers were stifling the Communist Party so that they could turn the national economy to their own ends. Vito Marcantonio pledged that he would make his opposition to the trial known in the halls of Congress. "On the outcome of this trial hangs the issue of whether we will get housing or slums, price control or higher prices," he shouted. "I personally do not believe that the issue of the twelve Communist leaders will be settled in the courts. You just cannot get justice in a court which is stacked against you." He expressed the opinion that the jurors were being selected in such a way as to guarantee that their "interests lie with Wall Street."

In cloak room discussions, I became aware of the full audacity of the Communist strategy for the trial. If the Government was going to use the trial to spread its evidence against the Communists before the people, the Communists for their part were

going to pick up the challenge. They would read the Party's
entire political program into the record, and make the trial a
show case for Communism. "Just think of the free space we're
going to get in the bourgeois press," a comrade gloated.

"They've gone too far this time," another agreed. "The
liberals simply won't stand for a trial of books and schools and
political beliefs. All we have to do is to tell the people exactly
why the twelve are being indicted. Explain the relation of the
trial to war and peace and our other struggles."

The strategy was bold and simple: turn the tables. Try the
judge, the jury, the prosecutor, the Government. And to hear
the Communists talk, they expected to get away with it, too.
To some extent they did.

The hero of the convention was Leon Josephson, Communist
International operative who had been convicted of contempt of
Congress for refusing to answer the House Un-American Activities Committee. In a voice so small that the tense, dewy-eyed
audience had to strain to hear, he told us that the Federal
prison from which he had just been released was "the worst jail
I have ever been in." He certainly looked like the martyr his
wife said he was when Barbara and I had visited her in New
Jersey the summer before. The suit of clothes that had fitted
him before he went to the penitentiary flapped on his gaunt,
saint-like frame, dramatizing the privation he had supposedly
endured there.

According to his story, the dope peddlers and common criminals with whom he had been thrown shunned him at first, but
later came to adore him. Without humor or embarrassment, he
described how one charmed fellow inmate had told the prison
chaplain, "This Jesus you talk about must have been a man
like Leon Josephson." Communists make no bones of using
religious analogies where they serve the purpose. Judge Medina was likened to Pontius Pilate, Louis Budenz to Judas, and
during the trial Harry Sacher, one of the defense lawyers, said
in open court that Mr. McGohey, the prosecutor, would have
put Jesus Christ in the dock.

Later, at a more intimate convention meeting, Josephson denounced the indictment as a "frame-up" and talked like a prophet encouraging his persecuted followers. For the first time in my Party experience, I heard a leader flatly deny that the Party aimed at revolution. "If I ever hear one of you advocating the violent overthrow of the Government," he announced, all injured innocence, "I will personally see to it that you are expelled from the Party." This was the man who a year later was to cry, "Vengeance! Let those who wield the police power of the state tremble," when Carl Aldo Marzani, formerly of the Office of Strategic Services, went to jail for lying when he said he was not a Communist. Communists are wonderfully adept at playing both ends against the middle.

When I got back to New York, the longest criminal trial in our recent history had just begun with a record turnout of Communist protestors and a record cordon of police in Foley Square. Communists think of a picket line as a political rather than an economic weapon, even when a labor union pickets an employer. No one in the Party thought it strange that we were ordered to picket a court of law which could not properly yield to popular demand. To me, the picket lines before the court were proof that the comrades did not accept the very bases of our form of Government.

The Communist lawyers soon made it quite clear that they had no respect for the judicial processes of our country. They spent weeks attacking the jury system. They accused the court of conniving at the calling of a panel of "blue ribbon jurors" who would be prejudiced against the poor and oppressed. My comrades bombarded me with pleas to help organize the "continuous picket line," with every employed Communist picketing on his lunch hour, when the traffic was thickest. But all the time I was busy writing up my notes on the Civil Rights Convention, which I delivered a few pages at a time to an F.B.I. agent who met me at a subway station. The Bureau wanted a full report on the convention in a hurry.

The trial got off to a slow start. Selection of a jury dragged on through February. My conferences with Chick to review my old reports took more and more of my time. Meanwhile, I was living with the Communists on the other side of the battle line.

Barbara got a job as secretary to Harry Sacher, one of the defense attorneys whom I was to encounter in court. There was plenty of gossip in the Party concerning the defense headquarters at 401 Broadway—which lawyers worked and which ones shirked, which were employed for their "Anglo-Saxon names" and which for their legal talent; and the resentment between "defense workers" who were paid as Barbara was out of the Defense Fund we had collected, and those like Sue who volunteered their clerical services as their contribution to the cause. Sue was living on twenty dollars a week unemployment insurance at the time. Both girls were openly panning the leadership of the Party to me.

Barbara still regarded me as her only friend in the lower echelons of the Party. She begged me to help at defense headquarters by serving subpoenas on witnesses and investigating the panel of jurors which the Communist lawyers were attacking. The entire Party in Greater New York was mobilized to amass full dossiers on every name, I was in demand because I had a car. Through A.L.P. clubs and other front organizations, Party workers dug up each prospective juror's registration in a political party, his occupation and probable income, his national origins, his family ties and any other data which might help the defense attorneys decide whether or not to challenge him. At moments I thought it might be a great lark to investigate the jury before which I would testify, but the prosecution attorney with whom I met occasionally to help prepare the Government's case instructed me to ease out of these assignments and to refuse to have anything to do with defense counsel.

Barbara took me to a birthday party at the home of Leon and Lucy Josephson in honor of Barbara and of Lucy Josephson's mother. Leon Josephson dominated the conversation, which inevitably turned to the trial. "The Government is planning to put one hundred witnesses on the stand," Leon disclosed. "But the Party will have five hundred." I took a back seat in the discussion. The strain of the last month was getting too much for me and I feared I might make a slip.

Already I had begun to wonder what the courtroom I would appear in was like. Although comrades were urged to attend the sessions, and a faithful crew was always waiting hours before the court opened in order to preempt the seats open to the public, I decided against attending the trial to get the "lay of the land." But from all I heard and read in the newspapers, I knew that a Government witness would have no easy time on the stand.

Eugene Dennis was acting as his own defense attorney and reeling off Party propaganda at every turn. Dennis and Foster had announced publicly that they would not support the United States in the event of a war against Russia. It was obvious that they were not so much interested in winning their case as in putting up what they imagined to be a good show.

Communists inside and outside the courtroom worked together like a team with two objectives in mind: (1) to goad Judge Harold R. Medina into committing an error that would cause a mistrial; and (2) to drag the trial on so long that the press and the people of America would be bored with the whole matter. They succeeded in making it one of the strangest and longest trials in American history. It soon settled into an endurance contest in which the Communists pitted the harassing techniques learned in hundreds of similar struggles against the nerves of the judge and the prosecuting attorneys. Judge Medina, who is a man with a temper himself, exercised almost superhuman self-control to give the defendants a fair trial in spite of themselves. I followed the proceedings with the intense excitement of a football player on the bench waiting to be called into the game.

Six weeks after the Civil Rights Congress meeting in Washington, we were told to destroy our Party cards. No new ones were to be issued for 1949. As finance director of the branch,

I had to issue receipts without names. For the first time in my
Party membership, Communists were physically assaulted for
their membership in the Party. Rena Klein told our section
how a boys' club in Greenwich Village had scuttled a Communist street meeting, beat up the principals, followed them to
their Party headquarters, and smashed all the windows. I did
not know from one minute to the next, whether I was going to
be attacked for being a Communist or for being a "stoolie," but
violence seemed extremely likely. I thought longingly of the
day when I might live like any other citizen, but it seemed
remote. I got so I couldn't think beyond the day. The worst
thing about the future was its uncertainty.

At one time or another, the Party has committed every crime
in the book, up to the elaborately schemed murder which ended
Leon Trotzky's life. If murder could eliminate a hostile witness, there were willing hands to do it. And if I kept my secret
to the day of my appearance in court, the very least I could expect afterwards was a whispering campaign alleging immorality
with scurrilous details. I was very glad indeed that I had resisted all romantic entanglements with comrades. The Bureau
could protect me from sticks and stones, but it is very difficult
to defend yourself against words which can hurt you.

I had only one plan for rehabilitating myself afterwards: I
was going to continue to take pictures for a living. But where,
and for whom, I had not the slightest idea. At times I thought I
would have to leave New York and start over again. But there
are few opportunities for photographers outside the big cities
which breed active Communist machines. And I knew that I
couldn't ever work abroad in a world where Communist parties
are everywhere stronger than they are in the United States.
The Communist International has a long arm and a long
memory for counterrevolutionary spies. I would run into them
not only in Europe, but in China and South America. If I went
abroad under an assumed name, I would run afoul of the same
passport rules which had put so many American Communists in
jail.

Meanwhile, my sessions with the prosecution attorneys were getting more frequent and more involved. The plan of action and the briefs were constantly being changed. I was sure that other plants would be testifying too, for I realized that the Government lawyers would want to produce witnesses from all over the country. The sheer physical volume of the material the F.B.I. had on hand must have presented a difficult problem of selection. I'm sure that the Justice Department had been working on the case for years.

The Smith Act, under which the twelve leaders were charged, made it a crime to advocate or teach the overthrow of the Government by force or violence; to organize a group of people to advocate such overthrow, and finally to conspire to do any of these things. The indictment charged that William Z. Foster, Eugene Dennis, John B. Williamson, Jacob Stachel, Robert G. Thompson, Benjamin J. Davis, Jr., Henry Winston, John Gates, Irving Potash, Gilbert Green, Carl Winter and Gus Hall conspired in just this way when they reconstituted the Communist Party in 1945.

The Justice Department was anxious to secure a determination of the Smith Act. For almost a generation, G-men had been forced to resort to passport and immigration violations to curb the Communist conspiracy. The Smith Act attacked the real crime at its source. It did not require the Government to prove that the Communists intended to drop a bomb on the White House today in order to put them in jail. It established as a crime the teaching that such action was necessary and desirable. If the act was constitutional, Communists could no longer stand on their alleged civil rights while they were fomenting revolution.

My value as a witness was that the defendants had personally taught me the need to overthrow the Government. I could testify as to the curriculum of the Party schools I had attended before or after the Communist Political Association. Any one of them would have sufficed, in my mind, to clinch the crime, because they all taught the same thing. I could also testify to

personal contact with most of the defendants. Although I did
not know any of them intimately, I had attended meetings at
which nine of them had certainly taught the need to overthrow
the Government. I knew, as did every other comrade, that the
Politburo was responsible for everything that was taught, under
the Party theory of "democratic centralism."

It seemed to me that the lawyers were beating a long way
around the bush. My whole life was becoming progressively
more unreal. Conferences in moving automobiles were about
the last straw. In February, I broke down one day and told Mr.
Wallace that I didn't think I could concentrate in the car.
"Can't we get a blind office somewhere so that we can read a
document through to the end?"

Mr. Wallace hadn't realized my difficulties.

"What's the matter with my office?" he asked. Chick and I
looked at each other and we both thought he must be out of
his mind. The office of the United States Attorney for the
Southern District of New York is in the skyscraper Federal
courthouse at Foley Square, in which the trial was being held.
The F.B.I. offices are in the building too. For seven years I had
knocked myself out to avoid setting foot in the place. And now
that it was overrun with Communists milling and yelling all
day long, a Government attorney calmly suggested that I walk
right in!

"Well, why not?" he urged. He turned to Chick. "Please
arrange to get Miss Calomiris into the building," he said mildly.
"I'm sure we would all be more comfortable."

It was a challenge, and the F.B.I. agents worked it out like
a chess problem. They took me through the Communist pickets
by a ruse. They would pick me up at various locations in town.
I borrowed clothes from friends—without telling them why, of
course—things like a Persian lamb coat and a green hat. I don't
like fur coats and I never wear green. Sometimes I wore dark
glasses. When we got near Foley Square, I lay down in the
bottom of the car like a sack of potatoes and covered myself
with the daily newspaper. The agents drove through an under-

ground tunnel to the garage beneath the building. Then we made a quick dash for the elevator.

We rode a few floors up on the elevator, got off, walked down a flight, took another car up, went through several corridors, and eventually arrived at a private elevator leading to the nineteenth floor. An agent usually went ahead to see that the coast was clear. Sometimes he would leave me behind a pillar. Sometimes I'd carry a newspaper to hide my face. One Irish agent always carried a big clean handkerchief into which I could pretend to weep. Weeping women were a commonplace there.

Once in Attorney General Clark's New York office, I was safe. I could relax and smoke a cigarette. Then we would buckle down to work. The secretaries made the best coffee I ever tasted in my life and we drank cups and cups of it. From the office, I could look out and see the comrades marching up and down. The Party seemed very remote from the nineteenth floor, but I could see some of the banners. "FREE THE TWELVE AND STRIKE A BLOW FOR DEMOCRACY." "THE COMMUNISTS NOW: YOU'RE NEXT."

Everything I heard about the trial, from both sides of the fence, convinced me that I would be in for a thorough raking on the stand. With mounting fear, I listened to the stories the comrades proudly told me of the exploits of the Communist lawyers, from which I tried to judge how they would handle Government witnesses. The Communists boldly told the judge he was prejudiced, and unfit to sit in the case. They never stopped heckling him. Judge Medina announced from the bench that he had received threatening letters. Toward the end of the trial he finally sentenced several of the defendants to jail for contempt of court. They had to be brought to the courthouse every day in handcuffs.

The trial crawled along, and there was no way of estimating when I would be called. I wasn't sleeping. Subconsciously, I was turning over the past trying to figure out how I ever got into a mess like this. I felt like a fly entangled in a spider's web. Who was I to figure in a historic case of national and

international importance? I was too shaky to hold a camera
straight and I didn't dare to take picture assignments very far
in advance because I never knew whether I should be able to
carry them through. I paid up all my small debts so that I
would have a clear record on the stand. I decided to get out
of my apartment for a while. I told Barbara I was hard up—it
wasn't far from the truth—and would have to sublet my apartment for a while.

Barbara had a splendid idea. "Why don't you sublet to one
of the two defense lawyes we're trying to locate in town for the
trial? We're having a hard time finding a place for one of the
Negroes. Better yet, why not share your apartment with Yetta
Land?"

I suppose I must have been a little mad even to consider it,
but the thought of marching into court as a Government witness one morning after breakfasting with a defense attorney
struck me as a logical climax to my double identity. I phoned
Chick and told him it might be a cute trick. He phoned back
in an hour with instructions to keep out of any such entangle-
ment. I told Barbara that I didn't think Miss Land would be
very comfortable with me, which was no more than the truth.
I couldn't help imagining what the lady lawyer's reaction would
have been had she discovered that she was living with a "stoolpigeon."

In the tension of waiting, almost any kind of action appealed.
Barbara, who thought I was worried about Rena's charges, suggested one day that we do some picketing of our own. We
bought fruit, candy and magazines, and told Paul Crosbie's
secretary that we intended to sit outside his door until he
answered my letter demanding an investigation of the charge
that I was anti-Party. Paul Crosbie was very much amused at
the two girl pickets. We barraged him with protests in true
Communist fashion as he went in and out of his office.

There was something divinely ridiculous about the two of
us that day, but the joke would have been far better if we
could have told each other exactly what we were worrying

about. I wished I could tell Barbara about Ralph, the secret courier who had visited me, but I was afraid to disobey his orders against mentioning his visit to any other Party member, especially since I suspected that Barbara had been a courier herself, as Elizabeth Bentley later charged. I had sense enough, despite the mild hysteria of my mood, to keep quiet and so missed my only real chance to find out anything about Ralph, because he never came again.

Barbara seemed to have something on her mind too. Toward afternoon we both began to feel a little silly. Although the members of the Politburo were in the dock, the business of the Party at headquarters ticked on as usual. Visitors came and went. *The Daily Worker* got itself out with the usual noise and bustle. It was hard to imagine that I was in the storm center of an international conspiracy answering for itself in court.

We told Paul Crosbie that we were prepared to stay all night, but our hearts weren't in it. He promised at last that I would have word about my case the next day if we would go away. We went, of course. And of course there was no word.

Next Barbara and I decided that we ought to paint her apartment. We scheduled the job for night, since neither of us was sleeping anyway. When I arrived at her place she had been pouring herself drinks and she kept the bottle handy as we got to work. This was no time to trust the effects of alcohol. I poured so many of my drinks into the paint that it peeled off the next day, much to Barbara's surprise, for I had insisted on buying good paint.

After a few hours of painting and drinking, Barbara blurted her news: Lynn, her beau, and his sister Louise's husband had been disclosed as Communists and had lost their jobs within the week. The coincidence was too much for Barbara. She wanted to know if I thought their misfortune had anything to do with her. She was beginning to feel that everyone she touched got into trouble. I suppose she wanted me to tell her that she had nothing to do with the dismissals, but she couldn't have chosen a worse person to reassure her on that point. I know I should have experienced some kind of tragic emotion, but I felt drained of all feeling.

Once again, I had come face to face with the Government's application of my information. I longed to tell Barbara how sorry I was to see her mixed up with the Commie gang, but I couldn't really feel pity because I knew what Barbara and her friends would do if they got the chance. I was silent, though, a little too long.

"Angie, do you know you're an enigma?" Barbara burst out after looking at me curiously. "You make me laugh one minute and then the next minute you make me feel that you know all the answers. I know you're much smarter than you make out. Why, Angela?" She was very drunk, thank heavens.

It was the closest Barbara had ever come to doubting me, but it was close enough. I pulled myself together and told her the Board of Health would be after me if I didn't go home and do my laundry.

Time dragged on. Judge Medina allowed the defense to attack the jury system until March 4. After that, it took over two weeks to empanel a jury. The jurors should have pleased the Communists: several Negroes and several unemployed persons were included. But they were not pleased. Si Gerson, C.P. public relations aide to the defendants, and the defense attorneys had already written off the Negro members of the jury as hopeless "Uncle Toms" chosen to make the trial look fair when it was not.

The prosecution put Louis Budenz, ex-editor of *The Daily Worker,* on the stand to testify to the revolutionary purposes of the Party as seen from the Politburo, many sessions of which he had attended by reason of his membership on the National Committee and as Editor-in-Chief of *The Daily Worker.* Three other reformed Communists followed. Herbert A. Philbrick, a Boston advertising man, was the first F.B.I. plant to take the stand. He testified to Party plans for infiltrating trade unions in industries vital to national defense. The Party read him out the same day he testified.

Now that my turn was coming soon, I found I had plenty else to do. I turned down picture assignments and had to disappoint the Advertising Women's Spring Ball for the first time in five years. I was busy—and just like a woman, I was busy assembling a wardrobe. I was going to be publicly spotlighted for the first time in my life and I intended to look my best come hell or high water. The activity did a lot for my morale.

I experimented with brush and comb and mirror on novel hair arrangements but went back to the old comfortable slightly waved bob that is really the best hairdo for a long face on a little person. I shopped at high speed and in some frenzy for clothes to wear on the stand, but everything I tried on had the vague fit of a Mother Hubbard. I'm just too small for ready-made clothes. In desperation I called up Hilda, a girlhood friend who had gone through school with me. Hilda could sew.

"See here," I said, "I'm not being married or buried and don't waste time asking questions, but I've got to get some clothes that will fit. I've got a black gabardine dressmaker suit that swims on me and some Oxford gray all wool sharkskin for a suit with an all round pleated skirt and a brief mess jacket. Can you do something?" Hilda caught the excitement, but she knew me too well to probe.

"Sure thing," she said cheerfully. "I'll be right over."

Hilda came through at a rapid pace and with all the responsive warmth of long-established friendship, although I'm afraid she neglected her family to get me fitted out. She turned out the gray suit from my description of what I wanted, without a pattern.

I have little faith in any close association of my head with hats, but on this one occasion in my life a hat was going to be essential. Luckily, Hilda can make hats too. She took a small square of black velvet and in no time I was wearing a black velvet beret and nodding to the mirror that I liked it. I got hat fever. In a few days I owned an Oxford gray beret trimmed with a sheaf of wheat to wear with the gray suit, a natural

straw with a black velvet band and green Robin Hood feather
designed to bring something springlike into the courtroom. I
still didn't know what the courtroom would look like, but I
imagined it would be austere.

A white tailored blouse would look well with the gray suit,
I thought. . . . With the other, I can wear silver earrings and
the pin to match . . . or perhaps just the earrings and the
silver ring which everybody always admired . . . And then
there were shoes to get . . . a new gray covert cloth coat cut in
pseudo-princess lines which Hilda altered to fit . . . more new
blouses . . . several pairs of the short white gloves I like . . .
a new black calfskin purse with shoulderstrap. In short, I was a
very preoccupied spy.

On April 25, 1949, Chick smuggled me into the witness room
beside the courtroom, although we really didn't expect that I
would be called that day. It was terrifying to be so close to the
courtroom and not see it. I sat all the while court was in session
that day in a long bare room with office tables and chairs, a door
to the hall, and the door to the courtroom. Occasionally a court
attendant opened this last, and I instinctively shrank from the
line of vision that would have allowed anyone in court to get a
peek at me. It was a long day, and at the end of it I had to run
the gantlet getting out of the building, and then into it the next
morning.

My turn came shortly after eleven o'clock on the morning of
April 26. The marshal led me into the courtroom from the
judge's right. I paused for a moment, facing the National
Board of the Party, the defense attorneys ranged before them,
and the eager comrades on the front benches of the audience.
The room seemed smaller than I had imagined it, although it
was very impressive with its two-story ceiling, black walnut
panelling, and red velvet drapes at the high wide windows.
The raised witness box seemed to make me a giant. The court
reporter and attorneys came only up to my knees.

The defense attorneys went into a huddle as I was sworn in,
then separated to hear my first answers. In a low voice—so low

that Judge Medina and Mr. Wallace had continually to urge
me to speak up—I announced that I was born in New York,
raised in New York, had gone to school in New York, and lived
all my life to date in New York.

I won't soon forget the consternation on the faces of my
hitherto trusting comrades when I announced that I was at that
very moment financial secretary of the West Midtown Branch
of the Communist Party in New York City.

"Good Lord," I heard a comrade groan in anguish, "that
means she has the membership lists!"

Under questioning from Mr. Wallace, I told the court how I
became a Communist. Richard Gladstein of the defense objected like a stung bee when I pronounced the names of the
people who had recruited me to the Party. I knew what he was
worrying about: those comrades would be subject to investigation and expulsion for their innocent mistake. Judge Medina
interrupted when I came to the story of the mass rally at which
I was welcomed by Gilbert Green along with other new
members.

"Do you see Gil Green around here anywhere," he asked
quite conversationally.

"Yes, the gentleman with the brown suit and the curly black
hair," I answered. Mr. Wallace asked Mr. Green to stand up.

"I think it's better if the witness goes around and points him
out," Judge Medina suggested.

Mr. Gladstein was on his feet and objecting. "We are not
dealing with people who have robbed a bank, Your Honor."
The judge replied that we were in fact dealing with a criminal
charge.

I stepped down from the witness box, walked over to the
defendants and tapped Gil Green on the shoulder. He shrank
away and brushed his shoulder as if I had contaminated it.

The objections and gestures were repeated when I was asked
to identify the other defendants I knew, but I never touched a
comrade again. I simply stood in front of my man and rudely
pointed.

The courtroom rustled when I announced that I was a student at the Marxist Institute. "In fact," I added, "I have a class tonight, but I don't think I'll go."

I was very glad to be able to say that I had reported to the F.B.I. from the very day I joined the Communist Party.

After court was dismissed, my agents spirited me away to the St. George Hotel in Brooklyn Heights and registered me under the assumed name of Anita Zitos. I hate hotels, but I obviously couldn't go on living in my apartment while I was on the stand. The St. George was a good place for me because a number of G-men were planted in the vicinity. Chick and his fellow agent had gone ahead and searched my room.

We were all feeling very gleeful about the effect of my appearance in court as we read the afternoon papers. I heard that at noon recess, Harry Sacher had borrowed a nickel from Harry Raymond, *Daily Worker* reporter, and run for the telephone booth to phone his secretary. I would have cheerfully refunded him the nickel for a report on what Barbara said when he told her that I was one of the Government's witnesses. But I was never to know. The next day several members of my branch came to court to heckle me.

I spent a sleepless night, and the next morning I asked the boys if I couldn't have someone to stay in the room with me thereafter. Through Mr. McGohey, my policewoman friend who had stood by during Ralph's visitation was assigned to guard me for the duration of the trial and for two months after it.

The next morning, Mr. Sacher protested in court against a citation of me for patriotic assistance to the Government which the F.B.I. had released to the newspapers. His argument was that two of his clients had served in the armed forces and had been decorated for it. Their patriotic service, he claimed, was more valuable than that of a "lowly spy and stoolpigeon." *The Daily Worker* accused Mr. McGohey of "fishing in a cesspool for stool pigeons" and bringing up "the vilest kind of slime." The name calling was on.

Rena Klein was in the audience on the second day. From the stand, I saw her raise herself up from the bench to catch my attention and rattle me. She sneered and leered. I resisted an impish temptation to stick out my tongue. Sue came in for a short while. According to the policewoman guarding me, Sue was close to tears. After a few moments she slipped out of the courtroom murmuring, "I can't stand this any more." Barbara never came. Perhaps she was afraid to.

It was long, grueling work on the stand. I had to testify to the teaching I had received in the long succession of Party training schools I had attended. Defense lawyers objected at every turn. Once Judge Medina leaned over the bench to say, "Now don't let Mr. Sacher upset you. Speak up." Every time I got comfortable in the chair and leaned back, my voice sank so low that the defense attorneys claimed they couldn't hear it. It was one of the shocks of the trial to me. A person doesn't realize what kind of a voice he has until it's put to the test. Every once in a while I would shout, and Judge Medina would say, "There, that's fine."

On cross-examination, the defense lawyers tried to make it look as if I had been spying on labor unions and political parties when actually I had been sent into them by the Communist Party for its own purposes. And always, by niggling questions about chapter numbers and dates, they tried to make it appear that my memory was unreliable.

I knew that the worst would be at the end. Every afternoon, Harry Raymond, of *The Daily Worker,* promised his colleagues of the capitalist press some "startling disclosures" about the "Calomiris woman." I found out that Party workers were systematically interviewing everyone I had ever worked with. One of my friends was offered a bribe if she could produce any discreditable information about my moral character.

My agents and my policewoman friend did their best to keep to cheerful subjects, but they never left me for a minute. When I had to go to the ladies' room in the courthouse, an agent went with me and stood outside the door. We lunched together

every day on ham sandwiches and coffee sent into the Federal
Building. One evening my two agents patiently waited outside
the beauty parlor near Jane Street for two hours while I had
my hair done. My operator was thrilled and excited to see me
come in, and she lowered the shades and locked the door. No
other customer was admitted that evening. Here I got the first
real public reaction to my testimony: "Gee, how did you ever
do it? Weren't you afraid?"

I hadn't anticipated being on the stand for more than a day
or two, and I had to send an F.B.I. agent back to the apartment
for more clothes. Over the weekend the agents, my bodyguard
and I had a good time. On Saturday, we went to a baseball
game. It was wonderful to sit in a crowded ball park and not
be noticed. On Sunday, we all went on a picnic at Pound
Ridge.

The Communists had redoubled their efforts to uncover
material which would smear me, but in the end they were
forced to desperate, open insinuations which disgusted the
judge and won me a great deal of sympathy in the newspapers.
Mr. McCabe tried to question me about my home and family,
if any—questions to which Mr. Wallace objected successfully.
Then, suddenly, Mr. McCabe said softly, "Do you have a
child?"

The question startled me into an immediate and automatic
no.

"What is that last question?" Judge Medina asked sharply.
"I certainly would never have asked a question like that when
I was a lawyer!"

Mr. Wallace insisted that I be allowed to answer the question
for the record. Judge Medina agreed that it was the only fair
thing to do. The colloquy gave me a chance to pull myself
together. I was furious. When the question was put again, I
leaned forward and looked at Mr. McCabe steadily.

"I have no children," I said emphatically.

The attempted smear was a boomerang.

In the evenings my policewoman friend and I made drinks

in our hotel room and speculated on the next trick the Commies would pull. Despite all our fear and imaginings, I came through very well. The worst thing the Party scouts dug up about me was that I had paid a fifty dollar fine in Rockland County. When that line of questioning was ruled out, defense lawyer Richard Gladstein took another tack:

"Miss Calomiris, didn't you bill the F.B.I. for contributions, dues, fines and so forth?" He emphasized the word fines. The judge told him he couldn't bring up fines again; he had already sustained the Government's objections. Gladstein lamely explained that as an old labor union worker, he automatically used the word "fines" along with dues and contributions.

Of course, I did not bill the F.B.I. for "fines." The real story of the Rockland County incident is rather funny and I'm sorry the judge didn't let me tell it. One weekend I'd entertained three friends along with their pets—four cats and a wire-haired fox terrier—at my cabin near Haverstraw. We fed them catfish we had caught in a near-by lake. We tried to bury the fish heads, but the animals kept digging them up. Finally, I wrapped the bones in a newspaper and put the whole thing in a carton which happened to have my name on it. The animals still tore at the carton, so I drove the box several miles down the road and deposited it in some long grass. Unfortunately, the Spring Valley police saw me do it. They were out to make an example of garbage-dumping offenders from New York City and they stopped my car and summoned me to court for the misdemeanor. I pleaded guilty to the crime and paid a fifty dollar fine.

I spent five court days on the stand. By May 2, exactly one week after I had climbed into the witness chair, I was so tired and tense that I had to brace my hand when I reached for the glass of water the court attendant set before me. Richard Gladstein, Barbara's boss, kept showing me pamphlets and asking me for details about the occasions on which I had distributed them. It was obviously impossible to remember every one of the hundreds of occasions of the same kind, although I recalled the pamphlets themselves easily enough. Judge Medina stepped in to protest the long and fruitless attempt to prove my memory was unreliable. I was irritated, too, because the defense lawyers used these pamphlets, as they had all during the trial, to emphasize the Party's championing of the downtrodden. One of the pamphlets which Gladstein waved before me was a diatribe against lynchings.

As soon as the court dismissed me, in the middle of the afternoon, I went out to the Bierlys' on Long Island and slept myself out. When I got a chance to look over my clippings, I was amazed to discover that I had been billed as a "cool, quick-witted and poised witness."

12. THE MASQUERADE IS OVER

I WAS THOROUGHLY exhausted when I got off the stand and anxious to get out of town. The first Saturday morning after the trial I gathered up some of my friends and drove them up to the cabin.

As I turned Gazelle, my Pontiac, into the double rut that leads to the cabin, I saw one of the Roberts boys working in the field and I stopped to ask about his father who was very ill with cancer. Rich smiled shyly at me. Leaning on his hoe and looking down at his feet he said, with considerable embarrassment, "We read about you in the papers, Angie. We were all mighty proud."

It was wonderful to be in the country. We practiced rifle shooting, and I got a kick out of making a better score than my policewoman guard. We climbed High Tor, the mountain about which Maxwell Anderson wrote, and talked with Gus, the old man who lives on the top and takes care of the airplane beacon. I didn't mind the walk to get water from the spring or the business of balancing on moss-slippery rocks to draw up pails of water from the brook by the house. I didn't even mind the grimy job of cleaning all the kerosene lamps. My bodyguard amused herself by building an arbor of young saplings around the rosebushes at the kitchen door.

Next morning we carried our breakfast out to the back lawn

and I attacked the fan mail. Some of the letters were short notes of congratulations from friends and business associates. Others were longer and almost impossible to answer. The Party wrote me a letter addressed to "Judas." The New York Board of Education wanted to talk to me, presumably about Communist infiltration in the school system. An old Russian emigré who had picketed the Communist pickets at Foley Square warned me that the comrades would never let me alone. They had followed and annoyed him for fourteen years, he said. A woman wrote a long letter thanking me for helping to make America safe for her grandchildren.

I read with interest but without astonishment the accounts of me in the Communist press. In *The Daily Worker* I was "Angela Calomiris, a lady snooper for the F.B.I. who also dabbles in photography and other less popular pursuits." The phrase allowed the reader to draw on his imagination for scandalous details without violating the law of libel. Feature articles described my intimacy with workers for the defendants. I suppose they meant Sue and Barbara. Elizabeth Gurley Flynn, the only member of the Communist high command free to agitate, rushed into print with a pamphlet entitled "Stoolpigeon" in which she flayed the incredible duplicity of anyone who joined the Communist Party for the purpose of reporting its activities to the Government. An editorial in *Masses and Mainstream* referred to the prosecution witnesses, including myself, as "disease-bearing vermin" employed by the F.B.I. in its "germ warfare."

In the weeks that followed, I tried to get some perspective on my new role as a free citizen. For seven years I had been unable to discuss the broader aspects of my work in the Party except in hurried secret meetings with F.B.I. agents. I was almost stunned by the wide range of opinion on what I had done.

I was not particularly interested in the reactions of my former "comrades." I knew only too well what they would say and think, and I was delighted to enjoy their absence after so many years of enforced intimacy. But I did pick up, indirectly, an exceedingly interesting left-handed smear. According to some Party members, I had been a sincere Communist in the beginning. Later, when the going got tough, I turned state's evidence.

I also heard that the Photo League held a special meeting to discuss what should be done about Angela Calomiris. I've never been back there to see if I'm still a member, but I think it should be clear that my reports on the League were concerned with the use the Communists made of the organization. I certainly never incriminated non-Communists who happened to belong to the Photo League as innocently as I did before the F.B.I. enlisted me.

I knew that the Party would have to pin the blame for me on some one of my comrades. Theoretically, the culprit should have been Leona Saron, who failed to discover I was a spy when she recruited me. There was no news of Barbara or Rena or Sue. Paul Crosbie should have detected me when I appealed Rena's accusations, but when he died *The Daily Worker* wrote him up as a hero of the Party. For a long time I heard no word. I knew from my own experience that Communist "justice" is sometimes very long in coming. The goat was not chosen until January 17, 1950.

On that day, John Lautner was expelled from the Communist Party. According to *The Daily Worker,* he had been "instrumental in preventing the expulsion of the spy Calomiris." The *Worker* hinted that he was responsible for allowing hostile elements to creep into the office of the defense lawyers. For good measure, the Party accused him of being an "enemy agent" himself. Evidence was promised at "the proper time."

While I was recuperating from the trial old friends of mine from New York came up for dinner in the cabin and long, lazy evenings around the fire. It was good to be able to talk freely to them. A few were piqued because I had kept my F.B.I. work from them. Some of them plied me with questions I knew everyone wanted to ask. "Why did you do it, really? How could you stand it? Weren't you afraid? What are the Communists really like? Are they really plotting to overthrow the Government?" I told them as best I could, although it was difficult at first to find words for things I had not been able to say out loud for years.

These discussions helped me to see the ground I had covered since I was drawn into the Communist movement. In 1942, I was a photographer who, like many artists, paid very little attention to political theory. Years of observing the Communist Party and attending its schools gave me a political education I would never have sought on my own. The Communists often took over causes that appealed to me as right. I would like to see our country freed of discrimination against minorities. I would like to see a strong labor movement. I believe in freedom of speech. If some loyal Americans want to advocate Communism as a political theory, I think they should have every right to do so, with these provisos: that they preach their doctrine openly, not in secret meetings; that they desire to achieve their ends by peaceful, not violent means; and that they are not organized or directed by foreign elements. But in my role as objective observer I was in a position to see that an *American* Communist Party is a contradiction in terms. A Communist cannot sincerely put the interests of his country ahead of the interests of world-wide revolution. The basic principles of Communism make it an international movement.

Our bull sessions always descended from the general to the personal. Eventually, some liberal friend was sure to say, "I don't see how you did it, Angela. Now *I* couldn't have done a thing like that to save my life, much less my country." Remarks like this disturbed me because they implied that I had done something wrong.

I always tried to pin it down.

"Tell me honestly, now," I would say. "Do you think the Communist trial was right?" They almost always agreed that it was a good thing to expose the Party's methods.

"All right then. Now that you know what those methods

were, how do you suppose the Government could have collected its evidence on the Communist conspiracy if they didn't go undercover? Conspirators don't broadcast their plans."

This line of reasoning usually brought my friends to the heart of their uneasiness about my work. "It may have been necessary," they admitted grudgingly, "but I don't like the idea of spying just the same. I'd hate to have the Government pry into my life."

At this point, I was often tempted to ask why they would mind being observed if they had nothing to hide. But I found that the most effective reply was a direct question: what would you have done if the F.B.I. had come to you instead of to me?

Most Americans don't like to admit it, but all established governments have always had to use spies. The blunt facts are that there will be undercover agents as long as there are conspirators who can be detected in no other way. If the Communist Party goes underground, the F.B.I. will go underground with them. A government which refused to watch a group of conspirators who publicly declare their intention of pulling that Government down would abdicate its basic right of self preservation.

This reasoning often sounded harsh to my friends, but I explained that it makes a great deal of difference how undercover agents are used. I told them that the F.B.I. never provokes crimes for the purpose of catching criminals. Information of a personal nature involving no violation of Federal laws is carefully guarded. The F.B.I. can't produce them except on a court order. All my reports to the F.B.I. are classified material. I could not see them again myself for the purpose of writing this book, although I have reconstructed several from my notes.

I knew I was morally right, but I often felt depressed. I sometimes wondered whether I would have agreed so readily when Bill South and Ken Bierly visited me back in 1942 if I had foreseen the years of drudgery and the double-edged publicity of the trial. Some days I was discouraged enough to think about changing my name and starting all over again somewhere else. But I did not know how to run away.

Almost everyone I knew was concerned about my plans for the future. I could not see any difficulty about them. Obviously I was going to become the full-time photographer I had always wanted to be. But when I got back to New York and started showing my portfolio, I discovered that everyone wanted to see Angela Calomiris, the girl who had spied on the Communists, instead of Angela Calomiris, photographer. One editor I visited was actually surprised after I appeared for what I thought was a professional visit, to see that I had a portfolio with me. "So you're really a photographer?" he exclaimed, looking over my pictures in surprise and interest. "I thought that business about your studio was just a front!" This happened several times.

I went to Cape Cod, toward the end of the summer, for a short vacation. In the fall, I decided to go right back to my apartment and pick up the pieces of my life on my own home ground. I got rid of my bodyguard, but I protected myself from unpleasant incidents by avoiding encounters with Communists and Communist sympathizers.

In the fall, I got a threatening letter. It was printed in an obviously disguised hand, signed with a name which on investigation proved to be fictitious, and crumpled as if it had been rescued from a wastepaper basket before mailing. My mysterious correspondent predicted that I would soon be dead, and by his hand. He was getting paid for the job, and he always did what he was paid for. The F.B.I. couldn't protect me all the time. Across the bottom, the writer had scrawled, "Death Notice!" For a month, I had to have a bodyguard again. The F.B.I. is still on the trail of the writer, but it is very difficult to track down a letter that may have come from any one of sixty thousand Communists in the United States or a million fellow travelers.

I waited eagerly for the verdict of the trial. My personal future seemed tied up with the outcome. If they were innocent, then I had spent seven years of my life in vain. If they were guilty, I had done a useful job. At long last, on October 13, 1949, a jury containing three Negroes and two unemployed persons declared the eleven defendants guilty of conspiring to advocate the overthrow of the United States Government by force. In a well-reasoned opinion, Judge Harold R. Medina drew the distinction between freedom of speech and license to preach the violent overthrow of our form of government.

The trial in which I testified set a new high in hours and dollars and pages consumed. It was the longest in United States Federal history—the record ran to five million words. It required the largest concentration of police ever assigned to a courthouse in New York City. It cost the Government one million dollars in lawyers, jury fees, clerical expenses and investigation fees over many years. It attracted international coverage and millions of words were written on the issues involved. For their money and attention, the people of the United States got a clear, authoritative and extremely fair exposition of the activities of the Communist Party. I think they got a bargain.

The Communists immediately filed an appeal. As this is written, the Supreme Court of the United States has not yet had a chance to pass on the knottiest problem of all: is the Smith Act, which punishes a conspiracy to teach the overthrow of the Government, a violation of the constitutional right to free speech?

I hope that the Smith Act is upheld, but the American people cannot protect themselves by laws alone. They will be safe from the inroads of a foreign-inspired Fifth Column only insofar as they understand its purposes and its methods. If my testimony helped to make some of these obscure matters clear, my masquerade was well worth the sacrifice of my own personal freedom which I had to make.

If the Smith Act is constitutional, the Party will be outlawed. It will lose members as it always does when denied freedom to operate openly. It will have to cope with a legal warning to all potential recruits that they are playing with an organization disloyal to the United States. It won't be so easy, if the Party is outlawed, for clever Communists to draw disappointed idealists into the international conspiracy against democracy.

But outlawing the Party has its practical disadvantages. The Party will go underground, giving the F.B.I. considerably more trouble in observing it. More important, persecution has always been a source of Communist strength. The comrades know how to play martyr. And there are many stubborn liberals who will disregard the evidence we presented at the trial and still believe that the Communists are a legitimate domestic political party entitled to the protection of our Constitution.

These liberals would be right if the Communist Party were really a domestic party—or an entity that could be separated from the mother Party in Russia. It is not.

The Communist Party in the United States is an integral part of the international Communist body. If I learned nothing else from my seven years as a Communist Party member I did learn that single, hard fact. And you'll have to admit that I was in a fairly good position to be "educated" to the truth about Communism!

APPENDIX

The following brief sampling of Communist literature in its more inflammatory aspects may be of interest to the reader and serve the salutary purpose of helping to demonstrate the points at issue in the trial of the eleven top American Communists before Judge Medina. All these books and pamphlets were entered in evidence by the Government, either in their entirety or in part. When the latter, the quotations given here are from portions selected as exhibits to support the prosecution's case. In toto these exhibits represent many thousands of words, often repetitive. Communists quote from each other endlessly. They believe in repetition and fear "deviationism" worse than death.

These were among the texts which formed the basis of Communist teachings at the various Party schools attended by the author. It was her part as a Government witness in the trial to identify the publications and explain their educational employment by the Party within the scope of her own experience. If some of the dates of original publication suggest that obsolescence may have set in, it should be remembered that the basic Communist philosophy does not change. The words of Marx, Lenin and Stalin constitute a dogma to which all Communists must adhere and conform. In the passages cited the use of italics *(to which Communist writers are much addicted) follows the original version.*

1

Peters, J.
The Communist Party: A Manual on Organization
July, 1935, New York, Workers Library Publishers

(The pledge below is the one recited to the author upon her
induction.)

*"I now take my place in the ranks of the Communist Party, the
Party of the working class. I take this solemn oath to give the best
that is in me to the service of my class. I pledge myself to spare
no effort in uniting the worker in militant struggle against fascism
and war. I pledge myself to work unsparingly in the unions, in the
shops, among the unemployed, to lead the struggles for the daily
needs of the masses. I solemnly pledge to take my place in the forefront of the struggle for Negro rights; against Jim-Crowism and
lynching, against the chauvinist lies of the ruling class. I pledge
myself to rally the masses to defend the Soviet Union, the land of
victorious Socialism. I pledge myself to remain at all times a vigilant and firm defender of the Leninist line of the Party, the only
line that insures the triumph of Soviet Power in the United States."*

"THE ROLE AND AIM OF THE COMMUNIST PARTY
    "As the leader and organizer of the proletariat, the Communist
Party of the U.S.A. leads the working class in the fight for the
revolutionary overthrow of capitalism, for the establishment of a
Socialist Soviet Republic in the United States, for the complete
abolition of classes, for the establishment of socialism, the first stage
of the classless Communist society.
    "Our Party realizes that certain conditions must exist before the
outworn capitalist system can be overthrown.
    "What are the conditions? Comrade Lenin, in his pamphlet,

'Left-Wing Communist: An Infantile Disorder,' answers this question.

"'. . . for revolution it is essential, first, that a majority of the workers (or at least a majority of the class-conscious, thinking, politically active workers) should fully understand the necessity for revolution and be ready to sacrifice their lives for it; secondly, that the ruling classes be in a state of governmental crisis which draws even the most backward masses into politics,—weakens the government and makes it possible for the revolutionaries to overthrow it rapidly.' (Little Lenin Library, Vol. 20, p. 65.)

"These two conditions alone are not sufficient for the successful struggle of the working class. Even if the masses know that socialism liberates the working class, even if the masses know that socialism can be won only through revolution, unless there is a strongly organized Communist Party which explains the aims and methods of the struggle to the workers, unless it itself organizes these struggles, and is itself in the forefront of them, the revolution cannot be victorious. Lenin wrote about the need for a strong Communist Party as the advance guard of the working class in the following words:

"'In order that the mass of a definite class may learn how to understand its own interests, its situation, may learn how to carry on its own policy, precisely for this an organization of the advanced elements of the class is immediately necessary at any cost though at the beginning these elements may form a negligible section of the class.'

"How will the Communist Party convince the majority of the working class that a revolution is necessary? The Communist Party can do this by becoming the trusted vanguard, the beloved organizer and leader of the struggle of the working class. Agitation and propaganda alone are insufficient. Something more is needed to convince the masses of the proletariat of the necessity for the overthrow of the old order."

"The Communist Party puts the interest of the working class and the Party above everything. The Party subordinates all forms of Party organization to these interests. From this it follows that one form of organization is suitable for legal existence of the Party, and another for the conditions of underground, illegal existence."

"The main strategic aim of the Communist Party is to win the majority of the working class for the proletarian revolution. In order to achieve this aim the Communist Party establishes closely knit organizations everywhere where workers work for their living (factory), where they live (neighborhood), where they are organized for the defense of their economic interests (unions and unemployment organizations) or organized for satisfying their cultural desires (clubs, sports and cultural organizations). These Party organizations which lead the masses in the struggle for their economic and political demands are the following: (1) Shop and Street Units. Both of these forms of organizations are full-fledged Party bodies. (2) Fractions. The Party leads the masses organized in unions and other mass organizations through the fractions which are instruments in the hands of the Party to carry the policy of the Party among the masses."

"Our Agitational and Propaganda Literature—Theory
to the masses

"In order to educate our Party membership and the masses with whom we come in contact in our work, to combat the lies of the bourgeois press, books, radio, movies, etc., to expose and defeat the theories of the counter-revolutionary Trotskyites, the Lovestoneite renegades, and all the social-fascist and fascist demagogues and other agents of the bourgeoisie, our Party membership should study and spread as widely as possible among the masses the teachings of the great leaders of the revolutionary movement, as well as our current theoretical publications, and our agitational pamphlets on the every-day issues and problems which confront the masses.

"The Party has made and is making available the most important works of Marx, Engels, Lenin and Stalin in low-priced editions. There can be no sound revolutionary movement built without the distribution of this literature. This is why the importance of literature distribution is stressed so much by the Party."

Who Are the Professional Revolutionists?
"Comrade Lenin in his writings always stressed the necessity of developing a core of comrades from among the best, tested mass

leaders, to such a point that they would be able to serve the proletariat as trained, skilled revolutionary leaders. There is a misconception in the ranks of the Party as to what a professional revolutionist, in the Leninist sense, is. Some are of the opinion that a professional revolutionist is a comrade whom the Party takes out of the factory and assigns as full-time functionary: in other words, that the Party organization (Section-District-Center) supports him while he spends all his time on Party work. This notion is wrong."

"A professional revolutionist is a highly developed comrade, trained in revolutionary theory and practice, tested in struggles, who gives his whole life to the fight for the interests of his own class. A professional revolutionist is ready to go whenever and wherever the Party sends him. Today he may be working in a mine, organizing the Party, the trade unions, leading struggles; tomorrow, if the Party so decides, he may be in a steel mill; the day after tomorrow, he may be a leader and organizer of the unemployed. Naturally, these professional revolutionists are supported by the Party organization if their assignment doesn't send them to work in shops or mines. From these comrades the Party demands everything. They accept Party assignments—the matter of family associations and other personal problems are considered, but are not decisive. If the class struggle demands it, he will leave his family for months, even years. The professional revolutionist cannot be demoralized; he is steeled, stable. Nothing can shake him. Our task is to make every Party member a professional revolutionist in this sense."

"Every Communist must become a leader of the workers. Every Communist must know that the Party has a historical mission to fulfill, that it has the mission of liberating the oppressed exploited masses from the yoke of capitalism, that it has the mission of organizing and leading the masses for the revolutionary overthrow of capitalism, and for the establishment of the new world, a Soviet America."

2

Dimitroff, Georgi
United Front Against Fascism
October, 1945, New York, New Century Publishers

"But real revolutionary theory is irreconcilably hostile to any emasculated theorizing, any futile toying with abstract definitions. *Our theory is not a dogma, but a guide to action,* Lenin used to say. It is *such* a theory that our cadres need, and they need it as badly as they need their daily bread, as they need air, water. Whoever really wishes to rid our work of deadening, stereotyped schemes, of pernicious scholasticism, must sear them out with a red-hot iron, both by real, *practical,* active struggle waged together with and at the head of the masses, and by *untiring effort* to grasp the mighty, fertile, all-powerful Bolshevik theory, the teachings of Marx, Engels, Lenin, Stalin.

"In this connection I consider it particularly necessary to draw your attention to the work of our *Party schools.* It is not pendants, moralizers or adepts at quoting that our schools must train. No! It is practical front-rank fighters in the cause of the working class that must leave their walls—people who are front-rank fighters not only because of their boldness and readiness for self-sacrifice, but also because they see further than rank-and-file workers and know better than they the path that leads to the emancipation of the toilers. All sections of the Communist International must without any dilly-dallying seriously take up the question of the proper organization of Party schools, in order to turn them into *smithies* where these fighting cadres are to be forged."

"Revolutionary theory is the generalized, *summarized experience* of the revolutionary movement. Communists must carefully utilize in their countries not only the experience of the past but also the experience of the present struggle of other detachments of the international labor movement. However, correct utilization of experience does not by any means denote *mechanical transposition* of ready-made forms and methods of struggle from one set of conditions to another set, from one country to another, as so often happens in our Parties. Bare imitation, simple copying of methods and forms of work, even of the Communist Party of the Soviet Union, in countries where capitalism is still supreme, may with the best of intentions result in harm rather than good, as has so often actually been the case. It is precisely from the experience of the Russian Bolsheviks that we must learn to apply effectually, to the specific conditions of life in each country, the *single international line;* in the struggle against capitalism we must learn pitilessly to cast aside, pillory and hold up to general ridicule all *phrase-mongering, use of hackneyed formulas, pedantry and doctrinairism.*

"It is necessary to learn, comrades, to learn always, at every step, in the course of the struggle, at liberty and in jail. To learn and to fight, to fight and to learn. We must be able to combine the great teaching of Marx, Engels, Lenin and Stalin *with Stalin's firmness* at work and in struggle, *with Stalin's irreconcilability, on matters of principle,* toward the class enemy and deviators from the Bolshevik line, *with Stalin's fearlessness in face of difficulties, with Stalin's revolutionary realism."*

3

Stalin, Joseph
Foundations of Leninism
1939, New York, International Publishers Co., Inc.

"The question of the proletarian dictatorship is above all a question of the main content of the proletarian revolution. The proletarian revolution, its movement, its scope and its achievements acquire flesh and blood only through the dictatorship of the proletariat. The dictatorship of the proletariat is the instrument of the proletarian revolution, its organ, its most important mainstay, brought into being for the purpose of, firstly, crushing the resistance of the overthrown exploiters and consolidating the achievements of the proletarian revolution, and, secondly, carrying the proletarian revolution to its completion, carrying the revolution to the complete victory of socialism. The revolution can vanquish the bourgeoisie, can overthrow its power, without the dictatorship of the proletariat. But the revolution will be unable to crush the resistance of the bourgeoisie, to maintain its victory and to push forward to the final victory of socialism unless, at a certain stage in its development, it creates a special organ in the form of the dictatorship of the proletariat as its principal mainstay.

" 'The fundamental question of revolution is the question of power.' (Lenin) Does this mean that all that is required is to assume power, to seize it? No, it does not mean that. The seizure of power is only the beginning. For many reasons the bourgeoisie that is overthrown in one country remains for a long time stronger than the proletariat which has overthrown it. Therefore, the whole point is to retain power, to consolidate it, to make it invincible. What is needed to attain this? To attain this it is necessary to carry out at least the three main tasks that confront the dictatorship of the proletariat 'on the morrow' of victory:

(a) to break the resistance of the landlords and capitalists, who

have been overthrown and expropriated by the revolution, to liqui-
date every attempt on their part to restore the power of capital;

(b) to organize construction in such a way as to rally all the
labouring people around the proletariat, and to carry on this work
along the lines of preparing for the liquidation, the abolition of
classes;

(c) to arm the revolution, to organize the army of the revolution
for the struggle against foreign enemies, for the struggle against
imperialism.

"The dictatorship of the proletariat is needed to carry out, to
fulfil these tasks."

"The dictatorship of the proletariat is a revolutionary power
based on the use of force against the bourgeoisie."

4

Foster, William Z.
Toward Soviet America
1932, New York, Coward-McCann, Inc.

"By the term 'abolition' of capitalism we mean its overthrow in open struggle by the toiling masses, led by the proletariat. Although the world capitalist system constantly plunges deeper into crisis we cannot therefore conclude that it will collapse of its own weight. On the contrary, as Lenin has stated, no matter how difficult the capitalist crisis becomes, 'there is no complete absence of a way out' for the bourgeoisie until it faces the revolutionary proletariat in arms.

"For the capitalists the way out of the crisis is by forcing great masses of unemployed into semi-starvation, driving down the wage levels of the employed, waging desperate imperialist war, and instituting a regime of Fascist terrorism. This is the way the whole capitalist world development goes. For the workers, the capitalist way out means deeper enslavement and poverty than ever.

"The capitalists will never voluntarily give up control of society and abdicate their system of exploiting the masses. Regardless of the devastating effects of their decaying capitalism; let there be famine, war, pestilence, terrorism, they will hang on to their wealth and power until it is snatched from their hands by the revolutionary proletariat.

"The capitalists will not give up of their own accord; nor can they be talked, bought or voted out of power. To believe otherwise would be a deadly fatalism, disarming and paralyzing the workers in their struggle. No ruling class ever surrendered to a rising subject class without a last ditch open fight. To put an end to the capitalist system will require a consciously revolutionary act by the great toiling masses, led by the Communist party; that is, the conquest of the State power, the destruction of the State machine created by

the ruling class, and the organization of the proletarian dictatorship.
The lessons of history allow of no other conclusion."

"The American revolution, when the workers have finally seized
power, will develop even more swiftly in all its phases than has the
Russian revolution. This is because in the United States objective
conditions are more ripe for revolution than they were in old
Russia."

"Besides this more favorable industrial base, American workers,
once in control, will have other advantages which will greatly speed
the tempo of revolutionary development. These are, first, the vast
experience accumulated in the Russian revolution, and, second, the
practical assistance of the Soviet governments existing at the time
of the American revolution. These are enormous advantages. As
for the Russian workers, they were pioneers blazing the revolutionary trail. They had to work out for themselves a maze of unique
problems and to struggle against a whole hostile capitalist world.
The sum of all which is that the period of transition from capitalism
to Socialism in the United Soviet States will be much shorter and
easier than in the U.S.S.R."

"When the American working class actively enters the revolutionary path of abolishing capitalism it will orientate upon the
building of Soviets, not upon the adaptation of the existing capitalist government. Capitalist governments have nothing in common
with proletarian governments. They are especially constructed
throughout to maintain the rulership of the bourgeoisie. In the
revolutionary struggle they are smashed and Soviet governments
established, built according to the requirements of the toiling
masses.

"The building of Soviets is begun not after the revolution but before. When the eventual revolutionary crisis becomes acute the
workers begin the establishment of Soviets. The Soviets are not
only the foundation of the future Workers' State, but also the main
instruments to mobilize the masses for revolutionary struggle. The
decisions of the Soviets are enforced by the armed Red Guard of
the workers and peasants and by the direct seizure of the industry
through factory committees. A revolutionary American working

class will follow this general course, which is the way of proletarian revolution."

"The Soviet court system will be simple, speedy and direct. The judges, chosen by the corresponding Soviets, will be responsible to them. The Supreme Court, instead of being dictatorial and virtually legislative, as in the United States, will be purely juridical and entirely under the control of the C.E.C. The civil and criminal codes will be simplified, the aim being to proceed directly and quickly to a correct decision. In the acute stages of the revolutionary struggle special courts to fight the counter-revolution will probably be necessary. The pest of lawyers will be abolished. The courts will be class-courts, definitely warring against the class enemies of the toilers. They will make no hypocrisy like capitalist courts, which, while pretending to deal out equal justice to all classes, in reality are instruments of the capitalist State for the repression and exploitation of the toiling masses.

"In order to defeat the class enemies of the revolution, the counter-revolutionary intrigues within the United States and the attacks of foreign capitalist countries from without, the proletarian dictatorship must be supported by the organized armed might of the workers, soldiers, local militia, etc. In the early stages of the revolution, even before the seizure of power, the workers will organize the Red Guard. Later on this loosely constructed body becomes developed into a firmly-knit, well-disciplined Red Army.

"The leader of the revolution in all its stages is the Communist party. With its main base among the industrial workers, the Party makes a bloc with the revolutionary farmers and impoverished city petty bourgeoisie, drawing under its general leadership such revolutionary groups and organizations as these classes may have. Under the dictatorship all the capitalist parties—Republican, Democratic, Progressive, Socialist, etc.—will be liquidated, the Communist party functioning alone as the Party of the toiling masses. Likewise, will be dissolved all other organizations that are political props of the bourgeois rule, including chambers of commerce, employers' associations, rotary clubs, American Legion, Y.M.C.A., and such fraternal orders as the Masons, Odd Fellows, Elks, Knights of Columbus, etc."

"The actual strength of the Communist movement in the United States is not something that can be accurately stated in just so many figures . . . the influence of the Party stretches far and wide beyond the limits of its actual membership."

5

Marx, Karl and Engels, Friedrich
"Manifesto of the Communist Party"

"The Communists disdain to conceal their views and aims. They openly declare that their ends can be attained only by the forcible overthrow of all existing social conditions. Let the ruling classes tremble at a Communist revolution. The proletarians have nothing to lose but their chains. They have a world to win.

"Workingmen of all countries, unite!"

6

Stalin, Joseph
Problems of Leninism
1934, New York, International Publishers Co., Inc.

"Can such a radical transformation of the old bourgeois system
of society be achieved without a violent revolution, without the dictatorship of the proletariat?

"Obviously not. To think that such a revolution can be carried
out peacefully within the framework of bourgeois democracy, which
is adapted to the domination of the bourgeoisie, means one of two
things. It means either madness, and the loss of normal human
understanding, or else an open and gross repudiation of the proletarian revolution.

"It is necessary to insist on this all the more strongly, all the more
categorically, since we are dealing with the proletarian revolution
which has for the time being triumphed in only one country, a
country surrounded by hostile capitalist countries, a country the
bourgeoisie of which cannot fail to receive the support of international capital.

"That is why Lenin states that '. . . the liberation of the oppressed
class is impossible not only without a violent revolution, but *also
without the destruction* of the apparatus of state power, which was
created by the ruling class. . . .' "

(*Collected Works,* Vol. XXI, Book II, p. 155. Also *State and Revolution,* Little Lenin Library, p. 9.)

" 'In order to win the majority of the population to its side,'
Lenin continues, 'the proletariat must first of all overthrow the
bourgeoisie and seize state power and, secondly, it must introduce
Soviet rule, smash to pieces the old state apparatus, and thus at one
blow undermine the rule, authority and influence of the bourgeoisie
and of the petty-bourgeois compromisers in the ranks of the non-

proletarian toiling masses. Thirdly, the proletariat must *completely and finally destroy* the influence of the bourgeoisie and of the petty-bourgeoisie compromisers among the *majority* of the non-proletarian toiling masses by the *revolutionary* satisfaction of *their* economic needs *at the expense of the exploiters.*'" *Collected Works,* Vol. XXIV, Russian edition, p. 641.